THE SECRET LANGUAGE OF
ASTROLOGY

THE SECRET LANGUAGE OF
ASTROLOGY

The illustrated key to unlocking the secrets of the stars

ROY GILLETT

WATKINS PUBLISHING
LONDON

The Secret Language of Astrology
Roy Gillett

Distributed in the USA and Canada by
Sterling Publishing Co., Inc., 387 Park Avenue South
New York, NY 10016-8810

This edition first published in the UK and USA in 2011 by
Watkins Publishing, an imprint of Duncan Baird Publishers Ltd
Sixth Floor, Castle House, 75–76 Wells Street, London W1T 3QH

Managing Editor: Sandra Rigby
Senior Editor: Fiona Robertson
Editor: Peter Bently
Managing Designer: Lloyd Tilbury, cobalt id
Picture Research: Julia Brown and Emma Copestake
Commissioned Artwork: Grahame Baker Smith

Library of Congress Cataloging-in-Publication Data

Gillett, Roy.
 The secret language of astrology : the illustrated key to unlocking the secrets
of the stars / Roy Gillett.
    p. cm.
 Includes bibliographical references (p.   ) and index.
 ISBN 978-1-78028-027-1
1. Astrology. I. Title.
 BF1708.1.G55 2011
 133.5--dc22
                                    2011015227

ISBN: 978-1-78028-027-1

10 9 8 7 6 5 4 3 2 1

Typeset in Nexus Serif and Univers 57 Condensed
Color reproduction by Imagewrite
Printed in Singapore by Imago

For information about custom editions, special sales, premium and
corporate purchases, please contact Sterling Special Sales Department at
800-805-5489 or specialsales@sterlingpub.com.

Note on abbreviations used in this book:
CE Common Era (the equivalent of AD)
BCE Before the Common Era (the equivalent of BC)
CET Central European Time
EST Eastern Standard Time
LMT Local Mean Time (based on local longitude)
PST Pacific Standard Time
UT Universal Time (0 hours from Greenwich)

contents

WHAT IS THE SECRET LANGUAGE OF ASTROLOGY?

NOTHING COULD BE MORE VISIBLE than the Sun in the sky and, on a clear night, the Moon and stars in the heavens. In the days long before electric light and television, the changing patterns of the night sky would have been a source of interest to our ancestors. Inevitably, as they reflected on recent events in their lives, they would have begun to notice connections, to mark the seasons and the tides, and the best times to sow and harvest. Almanacs that combined astronomical and meteorological data with horoscopes were popular from medieval times and, even today, most people have at some time read their "star sign" prediction in the newspaper. What, then, can be secret about the language of astrology?

From the beginning, there has always been much more to astrology than the popular contemporary view. Thousands of years ago, in Babylon and Egypt, the knowledge was kept secret, because it was the powerbase of priests who ministered to the lives and deaths of their rulers. Even when astrology became better known and accepted in Classical and medieval times, its deeper truths remained the province of experts. Church leaders resisted its use

A WORLD IN THE SKY

For as long as we have observed the stars, we have told ourselves stories about them. This dramatic image shows Orion's Horsehead Nebula, named for the shape its whirling streams of dust and gas assume when viewed by our earthly instruments, some 1,340 light years away.

claiming that, by anticipating the movement of the heavens, humankind sought to replace God. For the last 300 years, the proponents of reductionist science have dismissed astrology as out of date, unproven and misleading. It is not taught in schools or in most Western universities. The media is not usually interested in serious discussion about astrology, offering only "star signs" and a platform to those making simplistic statements condemning popular astrology. So, in the 21st century, the language of astrology remains "secret", rejected by both sides on the science versus religion divide.

The first step in learning the language of astrology is to suspend disbelief and look beyond popular misconceptions. To answer one recent criticism, astrologers *do* know that the Earth orbits the Sun and that, owing to the Earth's tilt on its axis, the positions of the zodiac signs *appear* to be moving backward (see page 166). In fact, it is the observer's *view* that changes – like looking from the spinning "cup" in a fairground cup-and-saucer ride.

Astrologers study the cycles of the sky to orientate themselves to the experience of living on Earth. They then use the language developed by our forebears, who were much closer to the world's natural rhythms. This approach is not an alternative to the modern scientific view of reality. Astrology is entirely compatible with Darwinism, Big Bang Theory, the dynamics of space travel and everything that drives modern societies. Far from challenging other interpretations, astrology extends and gives them purpose. Better still, it offers an ancient language that can guide us as to how, and by whom, the great modern discoveries should be used. Maybe it is this potential, considered presumptuous by some, that frightens some contemporary scientists and their supporters.

HOW TO USE THIS BOOK

As well as offering many opportunities to experienced astrologers to enrich their understanding, this book is structured to guide a beginner through the process of acquiring the knowledge and skills necessary to interpret a birth chart – a chart that shows the astrological position of the skies at the time of an individual's birth. An introduction to the history of astrology is followed by

"The Elements of Astrology", which looks in detail at the planets (pages 26–47), signs (pages 48–131), houses (pages 132–45) and aspects (pages 146–9). These combine rather like the nouns, adjectives, verbs and adverbs of astrology. As with any other language, an understanding of astrology is built up from its grammar. Much more than in other languages, however, in astrology each word is rich in interdependent symbolism and association. At first sight its abundance overwhelms. Yet, as with conventional languages, as we begin to use it we see that it works. The third part of the book, "Putting the Pieces Together", shows step by step how to combine the different elements in a full birth-chart interpretation.

WORDS OF WARNING

Before you start to speak and use this language in your own life, bear in mind a few words of warning:

• Although you will observe many apparent connections between astro-cycles, human character and events, it has not been proven that the planets and signs directly cause anything to happen. They may be no more than reference points for a third factor yet to be discovered – markers for the integrated effect of all the elements of the solar system, perhaps.

• Knowing this, the wise astrologer takes account of the current range of astro-event variables, but always honours free will. Explore astrology's meanings to be better informed, but then make your own decisions. Do not allow the "stars" to dictate your life and never use them to dictate the lives of others.

BIRTH-CHART WEBSITE

www.secretlanguageofastrology.com is the website set up to accompany this book and give readers access to the Astrolabe™ birth-chart technology, free of charge. All you have to do to create a professional birth chart is supply the subject's name, time and date of birth, and the nearest large town and country (or US state) of birth. The website accesses the planetary movement and Earth rotation algorithms, and allows for latitude and longitude, time zone and summer time changes all over the world.

ASTROLOGY FROM THE EARLIEST TIMES

THE WILL TO LIVE IS THE FIRST INSTINCT of all animate beings. As humanity began to develop an understanding of its environment, people started to observe, assess and measure those things that seemed responsible for their sustenance, their comforts and the threats to their survival. The rising Sun brought warmth; the shape of the Moon affected the tides and women's menstrual cycles. The position of the Sun and the patterns of the stars were observed to change with the seasons, and so marked the times of plenty and hardship.

Fragments of this ancient celestial knowledge have survived. In the first chapter of his highly recommended two-volume *A History of Western Astrology*, Dr Nicholas Campion reports that remains of early *Homo sapiens* (c. 350,000–250,000 BCE) have been found buried with animal bones that bear what appear to be 28 notches. These may have been used for marking off the days of a lunar month. Clearer evidence of prehistoric time-keeping can be seen in a 29-notch baboon bone dated to c. 35,000 BCE, and an increasing number of these bone "calendars" occur as we approach the time of the cave paintings. The carving of a woman known as the Venus of Laussel (c. 20,000 BCE) in the Museum of Aquitaine, Bordeaux, France, shows her holding a horn shaped like a crescent Moon with 13 notches, one for each lunar month of the year. The Lascaux cave paintings (c. 15,000 BCE) are claimed to feature representations of the night sky that include the Pleiades, depicting the constellation's relationship to the seasons of the year.

There is evidence of a very ancient common culture of the heavens. Remarkably similar stories and myths of the Pleiades, involving sisters (or sometimes brothers) being chased through the sky by stars recognizable as Orion, exist in cultures as far apart

THE VENUS OF LAUSSEL
This 22,000-year-old carving discovered in the Dordogne region of southwestern France depicts a woman looking at the crescent moon she holds aloft in one hand. Clearly visible are the 13 notches on the moon: one for each month of the lunar year.

as Classical Greece and the Australian Aborigines, whose migration to Australia dates back at least to 40,000 BCE.

In Göbekli Tepe, Turkey, four stone circles have recently been excavated, each measuring up to 100ft (30m) across and bearing carved reliefs of animals. They date back to the ninth millennium BCE. Numerous other stone tombs and circles, including Stonehenge in southern England, have been found throughout Europe and in the Middle East, their construction apparently reaching a peak between 5,000 and 2,000 BCE. Many were evidently laid out to mark the solstices and the equinoxes, while other stone circles seem to have aided the calculation of the lunar calendar and eclipses.

The great effort that went into these megalithic constructions indicates that prehistoric peoples believed their lives to be a reflection of the cycles of the heavens, or at least to be closely linked to them. However, because their knowledge of the heavenly cycles may have been passed on orally, we have no written records to indicate what the builders of Stonehenge and the other stone monuments understood. There is greater evidence from later times. For example, the Nebra Sky Disc, dated *c.* 1600 BCE, found in Eastern Germany, depicts stars and their yearly cycle.

CHINESE ASTROLOGY

Traditional Chinese astrology may date back to the third millennium BCE or earlier. The earliest written references to Chinese astrology, and the earliest Chinese writing, are found on divination objects called oracle bones, dating from the early Shang Dynasty (*c.* 1500–1050 BCE). Discovered in their thousands, these are usually made from tortoise shells and ox shoulderblades. When the Shang king asked a question of the ancestors, the diviner would apply a hot iron to the bone, causing it to crack. The diviner then inscribed both the question and the meanings of the cracks on the bones. Since that time, the Chinese have developed many methods of understanding

MARKING THE MONTHS
The Sun bursts through Callanish standing stones on the island of Lewis, Outer Hebrides. Constructed *c.* 2600–2900 BCE, the site has been identified as a lunar calender, with the stones tracking the position of the Moon.

humanity's relationship with the world. Most people know about the cycle of 12 animals that rule each year. Behind this lies a complex system of astrological calculations and interpretation. The Chinese astrological archetypes are very different to those of Western astrology, but are still calculated from time, date and place of birth.

CENTRAL AND SOUTH AMERICA

From the Inca city of Machu Picchu in Peru to the Precolumbian pyramids of Central America, many examples have been found of the rich astrological traditions of the New World. As well as the 365-day year, the Maya used a 260-day sacred year, devised by the combination of two special numbers: 13 (the number of lunar months in the year) and 20 (close to the number of years in the Sun/Moon nodal cycle that is used to predict eclipses – see page 165). From this the Maya also devised their "Long Count", built from a cycle based on the numbers 18 and 20, and running from the beginning of the present world-era – believed to have begun in 3114 BCE – until the end of 13th b'ak'tun (a b'ak'tun is equivalent to 144,000 days), on 20 December 2012 (Gregorian calendar).

BABYLONIAN AND EGYPTIAN ASTROLOGY

BABYLON, ASSYRIA AND PERSIA

The recorded history of the astrology we use today began in the two great river valleys of the Middle East, the Tigris–Euphrates in Mesopotamia and the Nile in Egypt. Some claim that Babylonian astrology dates from the fifth millennium BCE. The earliest clay tablets found show that by the third millennium BCE, the Babylonians understood the movements of the Sun, the Moon and the five planets and interpreted them to guide their decision-making. They devised sacred calendars revealing that Venus was Ishtar, the goddess associated with love, Mars was Nergal, the god of the underworld, and Mercury was Mabu, the scribe of the gods.

The actual physical movements of the planets were seen as the way in which the presiding deity communicated with the Earth. By understanding these communications, it was possible to make predictions and to guide decisions regarding weather, harvest, drought, famine, war, peace and the fate of kings.

A priestly caste gave this guidance to society. Its knowledge was based on interactive empirical observation of the movement of

A PATH TO THE NEXT WORLD

The Great Pyramid of Giza was built over 4,500 years ago as a tomb for the pharaoh Khufu. A shaft in the King's Chamber is aligned with Orion, home of the death god Osiris, perhaps to give the pharaoh a passage to the afterlife.

the heavens relative to events on Earth. This knowledge was the heart of an enduring civilization that built pyramid temples called ziggurats as spiritual and administrative centres. One major city, Ur, was known as Kasdim ("light of the astrologers") when Mesopotamia was ruled by astrologer-kings.

Clay tablets from *c.* 1800 BCE show that an intricate understanding of the movements of the planets was passed down as natural law – as "rules and regulations laid down by gods", as Nicholas Campion aptly puts it. Astrological diaries were kept for around 700 years from 700 BCE, passing on knowledge from father to son.

The Persian occupation of Babylon in 539 BCE (which brought with it the liberation from captivity of the Judaeans, as described in the Old Testament), exposed not so much the shortcomings of astrology itself, as the shortcomings of the Babylonian astrologers of the time. Their encounter with the Zoroastrian Persian state was to lead to major advances in astrology. Clay tablets dated to 419 BCE reveal a systematic understanding of the 12-sign zodiac and give interpretations of the planets moving through signs – in other words, the technical foundation of the Western astrological language that we know today. The Magi or "wise men from the East" mentioned in St Matthew's account of the Nativity were Persian priestly astrologers. There are various suggestions for the identity of the Star of Bethlehem: Halley's Comet, which appeared in 10 BCE; Mars, Jupiter and Saturn together in Pisces (December 7 BCE); or a glorious occultation (passing over) of Jupiter by Venus in June, 2 BCE. Any of these would certainly have been of overwhelming astrological interest at the time.

EGYPT

From before the Old Kingdom in the third millennium BCE, the Egyptians believed that creation emanated from the union of Nut

THE NILE IN THE SKY
To the Egyptians, the stars of the Milky Way were islands in a great river that ran through the heavens, navigated by the gods of Sun and Moon.

(the heavens) and Geb (the Earth). This brought forth the gods Isis, Osiris, Nephthys and Seth. Until the New Kingdom in the second millennium, it was believed that the interplay of these deities marked the cycles of each day and the seasons of the year. As Nicholas Campion puts it, the Egyptians saw "the entire Universe as a single cosmic state. Mortals were confined to the physical surface of the Earth and the immortals, whether the gods or souls of the dead, occupied the heavens, represented by the Sun, Moon and stars ... astronomy [was] absolutely integral to ritual management of state politics and religion."

The pyramids of the Old and Middle Kingdom, and the vast subterranean tombs of the New Kingdom, reveal the Egyptian obsession with ensuring a successful transition from life to afterlife. The bodies and accompanying earthly objects that were placed in the tomb were carefully prepared. There is evidence that tombs were astronomically aligned to a proper path from life on Earth to immortality in the heavens. A shaft from the King's Chamber of the Great Pyramid at Giza points directly to the place in the constellation of Orion where (in *c.* 2500 BCE) Osiris, the god of the dead, was to be found. The Great Pyramid is also aligned less than three minutes of arc from due north. Many Egyptian temples were aligned to key points in the solar cycle.

The Egyptians divided the sky into 36 subdivisions known as decans and may have been the first to measure a 12-hour night. However, their celestial measurements were designed to serve the certainty of the heavens, rather that to predict and adjust human behaviour, as was the case with the Babylonians. That style of astrology came relatively late to Egypt, in the 1st millennium BCE, probably through direct links with the Assyrians, and the Persians who ruled Egypt during 525–402 and 343–332 BCE.

GRECO-ROMAN AND INDIAN ASTROLOGY

RECORDS OF THE GREEK USE OF ASTROLOGY prior to *c.* 500 BCE are fragmentary and point to Babylonian influence. In the middle of the fifth century BCE, the physician and astrologer Hippocrates (see page 33) developed effective treatments and was among the first to describe many diseases and other medical conditions.

The philosopher Plato (428–348 BCE) founded an academy in Athens that survived until 529 CE, when the Byzantine emperor Justinian closed it in an attempt to put an end to pagan learning. Aware of Babylonian astrology, Plato accepted that astrological knowledge could help with favourable timings, but rejected what he saw as its fatalistic, manipulative uses. Astrology was part of Plato's total philosophical understanding of the cosmos – the "world soul". The planets, he claimed, were in the heavens to reveal the creator's unfolding ideas. In his *Republic* (VI.488.D), Plato described man as "the true pilot [who] must give his attention to the time of year, the seasons, the sky, the winds, the stars and all that pertains to the art, if he is to be a true ruler of the ship".

By the fourth century BCE Greek theories of the mechanics of the universe included the notion of the Earth spinning on its axis, with Earth, Venus and Mercury all orbiting the Sun. Through the conquest of Mesopotamia by Alexander the Great in 331 BCE, Greek astrologers acquired an intimate knowledge of Babylonian astrology. The establishment of the great library at Alexandria, the capital of Greek-ruled Egypt, brought together over the next hundred years a wide range of scholarship and teaching from all over the Hellenistic world, which at that time embraced the entire eastern Mediterranean region. In the third century BCE Eratosthenes, the library's second librarian, measured the circumference of the Earth precisely and showed clearly that it could not be flat.

Greek and Babylonian knowledge of astrology became inextricably intermingled. A clay tablet provides the first documentary evidence of a person with a Greek name using a birth chart: a baby born in the morning of 3 June 235 BCE. Many other birth charts have been found dating from the following two hundred years, some bearing traditional Egyptian symbols.

Numerous texts survive from that great period of astrological flowering in the first two centuries of the Christian era. The most influential of these is the *Tetrabiblos* by Ptolemy of Alexandria, written in 120 CE. The *Tetrabiblos* describes the movement of planets and stars without magical or religious overtones, and indicates their qualities along with rules for interpretation. Ptolemy's work was to be a foundational text for medieval European thinkers and astrologers, alongside Christian theology.

TOOL OF THE POWERFUL

This relief shows a Roman deity (possibly Mithras) surrounded by the 12 zodiac signs. Rejected at first as foolish and impious, astrology was later used by the elite to confirm auspicious dates and to predict – even attempt to determine – future events.

Between 150 and 175 CE, the astrologer Vettius Valens wrote his *Anthology*, which contains over a hundred Greek horoscopes. While publicizing astrology, it seeks to keep to the Egyptian traditions of initiation and secrecy. However, alongside the works of Ptolemy, the *Anthology* remains a profound influence on Western astrology to this day.

ROMAN ASTROLOGY

Astrology came to Rome along with the other fruits of its vast imperial conquests. The rational, materialistic and politically manipulative nature of Roman society explains the ways in which astrology was often seen and used during the pre-Christian period of the empire.

At first, astrology was dismissed as unworldly and foreign. Throughout the centuries that followed, it was rejected by numerous Roman intellectuals, on the grounds that it seemed to be seeking messages from the gods, foolishly or impiously. From Cicero onward, Roman satirists' simplistic misunderstandings of astrological concepts have a remarkably modern ring.

However, with strong developments in Greece, Egypt and Mesopotamia occurring from the first century BCE, astrology became popular in Rome itself. In spite of attempts by the authorities to repress it, astrology became widely used by ordinary people. At the same time, it became intertwined with political machinations. The Roman elite soon found that astrology was a very useful tool for confirming that the birth dates of emperors and other leaders were auspicious, as well as the times of their inaugurations. It was also employed to predict or explain key events in their lives.

Astrologers advising the rich and powerful often led a perilous existence. A negative prediction might not be acceptable, or the astrologer might be accused of complicity in a negative outcome. Around the time of the Emperor Nero, astrologers to the Roman elite became obsessively preoccupied not only with successfully predicting events, but also with *causing* positive events. Death was often the price of failure. Such extreme misuse of astrology did not bode well for its future. A time of destruction and ignorance was not far away.

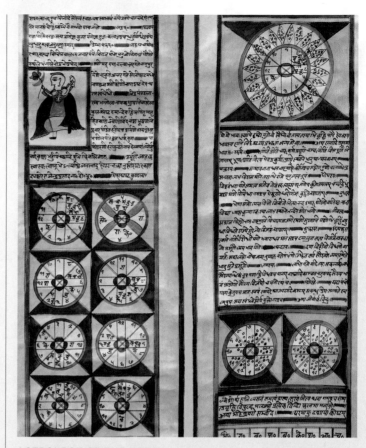

ASTROLOGY OF THE VEDAS

Astrologers have an importance in Indian society that far outweighs their standing in the West. They are traditionally consulted before taking a range of important decisions, from selecting a marriage partner and naming a child to choosing the site of a new home or business.

INDIAN ASTROLOGY

The various systems of astrology still flourishing today in India can trace an unbroken lineage that has been passed down for centuries, even millennia. Only in recent decades has the translation of various ancient Greek and Latin texts revealed how similar these Indian traditions are to techniques used by Greek, medieval and Renaissance astrologers in the West. It appears that the influence of Babylonian and Greek astrology reached India at the same time as it was flourishing in the Mediterranean. In India astrology acquired greater devotional respect than in the West, becoming the positive force in Indian society that it continues to be to this day.

THE REJECTION AND REVIVAL OF ASTROLOGY

ASTROLOGY UNDER FIRE

In the early centuries CE, Roman society became increasingly decadent and exposed to internal instability and threats from outside. While there were great advances in the recording and use of astrological cycles and methods in the first and second centuries CE, they tended to be applied with questionable motivation for simplistic everyday forecasting. This exposed astrology to challenges that it was ill equipped to answer.

Critics of astrology found a new ally in early Christianity. After three centuries of persecution, Christianity was declared a legal state religion in 312 CE by Constantine I. In 325 CE the emperor presided over the Council of Nicaea, where church leaders strove to develop orthodoxy in Church doctrine and worship. Christianity naturally sought to cleanse the Greco-Roman worldview of all that was deemed pagan. Astrology was one such target. By allowing itself to be used for simplistic prediction, astrology could be depicted by the Church as the demonic teaching of "fallen angels", seeking to deny free will and trap humanity in a false fatalism.

An edict of the emperor Theodosius I in 391 finally made paganism illegal in the Roman Empire, and all the temples to the old gods were closed down. Astrology came under a renewed attack by theologians, notably St. Augustine (354–430 CE), who asked how astrology could work "if twins lived different lives?" Furthermore, he asserted that the star followed by the wise men did not validate astrology, as Christian astrologers had argued, but on the contrary symbolized the practice's end. Augustine's criticism was to echo down the centuries and hold back the development of astrology.

HERETICAL ARTS
This 19th-century reworking of a medieval manuscript appears to show an astronomer accused of sorcery, holding a disc with magic figures. Merely studying the skies could lead to accusations of heresy.

In the third and fourth centuries CE many records of ancient astrological knowledge were lost. Some, held at the Library of Alexandria, had been burnt accidentally during Julius Caesar's 48 BCE battle at the port. The Library's remaining contents were lost in the third century during the emperor Aurelian's invasion, or taken to Constantinople (modern Istanbul) in the fourth century to adorn the new imperial capital.

ASTROLOGY AND ISLAM

Outside the Roman and Byzantine empires, astrology and other branches of Classical learning persisted among the Arabs. On 31 July 762 CE, following the advice of the most expert astrologers of the time, the first brick was laid in the city of Baghdad, founded by the Caliph al-Mansur as the new capital of the Islamic empire. Baghdad was to become one of the most magnificent cities the world had ever seen, a cosmopolitan centre of agriculture, trade, crafts, learning and art, with public fountains, parks, clean streets and running water. There was also a school of astrology. One of its principal scholars was Masha'allah ibn Athar (c. 740–815 CE), a Persian Jewish astrologer and astronomer, who wrote an astrological history of humankind, attempting to explain major changes based on conjunctions of Jupiter and Saturn, and eclipses. Omar Khayyam (1048–1131), better known in the West for his *Rubaiyat*, calculated the solar year to 365.24219858156 days.

As Islam expanded across North Africa into Spain, it brought scientific institutions and centres of learning. From the mid 10th century, Arab scholarly centres such as Cordoba and Toledo in Spain gave Western scholars further access to vast knowledge. Much of the learning of the Classical world, including Greco-Roman astronomy and astrology, had been translated from Greek into Arabic. This was then translated into Latin and passed back to the West along with new mathematical knowledge, including algebra and the Hindu–Arabic numerals with their all-important zero. Mathematics, poetry, philosophy and accurate astronomy flourished further for centuries in Persia and Mughal India.

A PRINCE IS BORN
In Islamic cultures, artistry combined with science to produce birth charts that were works of art. This chart of Iskandar, the grandson of the great Mongol emperor Tamerlane (or Timur), shows the position of the heavens at the moment of the prince's birth on 25 April 1384.

CHRISTIAN ASTROLOGY

HEN ABRAHAM, THE FIRST PATRIARCH of Judaism and Christianity, was born in Ur, the ancient city was known as the "light of the astrologers". Yet the Bible's relationship with astrology is ambivalent. On the one hand, Christian astrologers see parallels between the zodiac and the Bible's imagery. Humanity was given the Garden of Eden (Taurus), but tempted into sensuality by Satan (Scorpio, opposite sign of Taurus). To redeem humanity, the Virgin Mary (Virgo), gave birth to Jesus, a royal "Lion of Judah" (Leo) and "Fisher of Men" (Pisces) who would

sacrifice himself for our sins like the paschal Lamb and be resurrected (Aries, the start of the new cycle). And his birth was attended by three astrologers, who had followed an auspicious star.

On the other hand, the Old Testament expresses profound reservations about predicting and seeking to change the future, thereby usurping the prerogative and supremacy of God. Certainly, when its use in such a way has dominated, astrology has often lost its way, and faced attack and rejection.

The main explanation for the 12th-century restoration of astrology to prominence in the West was the old one of rulers seeking to gain an edge of power and to succeed in war. In the long term, these motivations were destined once more to cast a shadow on the future of astrology. However, for 500 years astrology was to experience a flowering, as it was increasingly used by monarchs, popes and their subjects alike.

In his *Summa Theologica*, St. Thomas Aquinas (1225–77) clearly laid out the new theological ground rules for astrologers. Astrology, he wrote, could influence humanity in potentially accurate and powerful ways, but it could not deny free will. Using astrology as a means of fortune-telling was opposed to Christianity.

Working within such justifications, it has been claimed that popes Sixtus IV, Julius II, Leo X and Paul III all used astrology, and the Vatican Library is said to possess a substantial astrological collection. Guido Bonatti, a 13th-century working astrologer, successfully used astrology in military strategy. The Medici family

TWO TRADITIONS
This painting from Sicily's Monreale Cathedral shows God placing the Sun and the Moon among the stars. Astrologers of this period were often able to reconcile their Christian faith with the practice of their craft.

and especially Catherine de' Medici, Queen of France, patronized astrologers.

Over the same period, astrology put down roots as a foundation for the practice of medicine. Through Latin translations of Arabic medical texts, Hippocrates' system of medicine was revived and treatments were based on how the parts of the body related to the signs, planets and the qualities of hot and cold, moist and dry. Astrology was also applied to explain epidemics such as the 1347–8 outbreak of Black Death, which was attributed to a lunar eclipse in Libra that took place in 1345 just as Mars, Jupiter and Saturn conjuncted in Aquarius.

Dr John Dee (1527–1608) used astrology to choose the most auspicious time for the coronation of Queen Elizabeth I, and gave her regular astrological advice. One of the most talented mathematicians of his day, he accepted the heliocentric solar system and became an expert cartographer. Shakespeare's plays abound with references to astrology, either favourable or unfavourable, depending upon the character. Mark Antony blames an eclipse for his final fall. It has been claimed parts of Shakespeare's texts relate to astronomical descriptions published in contemporary almanacs. This shows the maturity of astrological understanding in his day.

Astrology continued to flourish in the 17th century. Astrologers such as William Lilly answered myriad questions from the trivial to the most desperate. He used a range of techniques to determine individual natures and outcomes, many of which are outlined in his great work *Christian Astrology* (1647). Famously, Lilly used astrology to predict the Great Fire of London in 1666. Earlier, during the Civil War, his predictions of battle success were said to be worth many soldiers. The royalist astrologer Elias Ashmole gave precise astrological advice to Charles II.

Astrology continued to be used for medical diagnosis. A special chart, known as a decumbiture chart, drawn for the

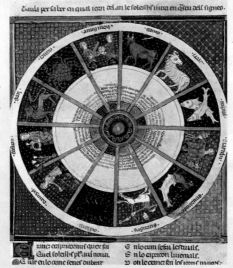

CHRISTIAN SCHOLARSHIP
This wheel showing the rotation of the 12 signs of the zodiac is taken from a late 13th- or early 14th-century edition of the *Breviary of Love*.

moment of an illness's onset, was used for prognosis and to suggest planetary treatments. Nicholas Culpeper's herbal guide to remedies, published in 1653, remains an invaluable reference work to this day, second only to the Bible as the English book in longest continuous publication.

Amid all this great success, the most advanced astronomer–astrologers – the two professions were not distinguished at the time – were questioning astrology's structural foundations. One of them, the brilliant German mathematician Johannes Kepler (1571–1630), was an early proponent of the sun-centred universe, a theory held back for 1,500 years by Christian orthodoxy, and the first to postulate that planetary orbits were not circular but elliptical. A highly successful military astrologer, Kepler wanted to use astrology to avert conflict, not to gain advantage. Although very critical of the contemporary superstitious and petty uses of astrology, he sought, with great love for the knowledge, to transform astrology and improve its application to social and political understanding.

It was the Italian Galileo (1564–1642) who proved by telescopic observations that the solar system was heliocentric. Galileo, too, was a devoted astrologer, and records survive of charts that he cast for himself, his daughters and even his patron Cosimo II de' Medici. Like Kepler, he sought to reform the astrology of his day, improving interpretation rather than rejecting astrology as outdated superstition.

While the discoveries of these great figures were adopted, their hopes for the future of astrology were not to be fulfilled. Perhaps because of a failure to heed the advice offered in the introduction to William Lilly's *Christian Astrology* – "the more holy thou art, and more near to God, the purer judgment thou shall give" – astrology was, by the end of the 17th century, again faced with challenge and decline.

ASTROLOGY'S DISMISSAL
AND REDISCOVERY

DISMISSAL

It is said that Isaac Newton (1642–1727) was motivated to devote himself to the study of celestial motion by the extreme dissatisfaction he felt when, at the age of 20, he purchased a book on the judicial astrology of his day (the forecasting of future events) and noted its essential emptiness. By the time of Newton's birth, increasing literacy, global exploration, the restoration of Classical knowledge and empirical scientific observation were undermining the Church's view of a divine geocentric universe. As the 17th century gave way to the 18th, the rational human being was replacing the Church as the central interpreter of what was and was not real in the universe. A new scientific force strove for rational idealism. The era known as the Enlightenment had dawned.

Astrology was one of the first of what seemed to be old ideas to be swept away in this rush to rationalism. It appeared to rest too easily upon the old geocentric world picture. Its interpretative methods, although based on thousands of years of empirical observation, lacked a clear mechanical chain of causal explanation. Many practitioners pandered to superstition and vulnerable individuals. While such criticisms could be applied equally to the established religions, these had always held astrology at an uneasy arm's length. So, lacking powerful Church-establishment support, astrology was easy to strike from university curricula.

The discovery of Uranus in 1781 symbolized a revolutionary awakening of human consciousness. Humanity was in the early

MEASURING THE HEAVENS FROM THE EARTH
The bands in this armillary sphere represent the lines of celestial longitude and latitude, plus the Sun's ecliptic (apparent diurnal cycle). These measure the planetary positions and the Earth's revolution on its axis.

stages of a long process of overthrowing old political orders, developing democracy and advancing scientific knowledge and industrialization. Astrology, as it was then, seemed irrelevant, except to the "ignorant" masses who continued to read popular almanacs.

By the early 18th century, undermining astrology had become a sport. Jonathan Swift merely needed to use a pseudonym to forecast and falsely confirm the death of astrologer John Partridge to discredit him. In this he seems to have prepared the ground for the facile methods of discrediting astrology that some otherwise conscientious scientists use to this day.

REDISCOVERY

Although now vulnerable to prosecution as vagrants, astrologers continued to practise in a low-key manner, and from the late 18th century astrology enjoyed the beginnings of a revival. The traumas of the Napoleonic Wars stirred interest in the subject. A growing reaction to Enlightenment rationalism can be seen in the work of visionaries such as William Blake. In the early decades of the 19th century there was an increase in astrological publishing – notably by Raphael (Robert Cross Smith, 1795–1832), whose annual is published to this day as *Raphael's Ephemeris*.

At the same time, the colonial powers' assumption of their divine right to instruct the entire world was beginning to experience an unexpected reversal. The wisdom of distant lands was coming to instruct the conquerors. As Nicholas Campion points out, the 19th-century French philosopher Eliphas Lévi was among the first to observe the common ground shared by ancient wisdom from all over the world: the old books on alchemy and western mysticism; the ancient writings from Nineveh, Thebes, Assyria and ancient Egypt; the Indian religious paintings and the pages of the Vedas. His insight touched a fundamental thread from Plato's concept of "world soul" via Masha'allah and Kepler: "[within all were] to be found indications of a doctrine which is everywhere the same and everywhere carefully concealed."

The 1846 discovery of Neptune represented this realization, as well as the adoption of incredible energies that are now the driving force of our world: gas, electricity and petroleum. The planet's discovery also symbolized the 19th century's emerging sensitivity to rights that we now take for granted, such as women's, children's, welfare, education and sexuality. At the same time, science fiction became a literary genre. Yet this century was to seed more than these radical developments in science, technology and social and sexual relationships.

In 1891–2, Neptune conjuncted Pluto (discovered in 1930) for the first time in 592 years. This conjunction symbolizes the birth of a unity of spiritual understanding that even today we are only just beginning to grasp. On 11 September 1893, the Parliament of World Religions opened in Chicago, marking the first formal gathering of representatives of Eastern and Western spiritual traditions. Taking a complementary approach in her 1888 book *The Secret Doctrine*, Madame Blavatsky (1831–91) tried to interpret the ancient knowledge at the core of all religions. These are just two of many indications that pointed to the start of a period when ancient wisdom and especially the full language of astrology was to become available to the general public.

Founded in New York in 1875, the Theosophical Society's stated aim was "to take the entire world into its next great historical phase, a time of promised enlightenment, equality, peace and justice". While the Theosophical Society was to flourish and then fade, its central idea, in whole or part, has been taken up by numerous individuals and movements ever since. Especially significant is the role its early members played in the renaissance of astrology during the 20th century.

MANY PERSPECTIVES

This 17th-century engraving depicts star constellations in the northern and southern latitudes, planetary models according to Tycho Brahe, Ptolemy and Copernicus, the lunar phases, the Earth's path around the Sun and the effect of the Moon on tides.

ASTROLOGY IN THE 20TH CENTURY

THE ASTROLOGY THAT WAS TO DEVELOP through the 20th century was radically different in method and intention to that rejected two centuries earlier. To Theosophists, such as Alan Leo, astrology was a tool of understanding and a preparation for a more enlightened age, not a series of intricate rules to find lost objects and predict mundane events. For, although astrology was infallible, human beings were not. By understanding astrology, humanity could change itself and the world for the better. In 1923 Alice Bailey founded the Arcane School to prepare people on a path of discipleship to world service in the "New Age".

Psychology was another new development to emerge from the era of the 1891–2 Neptune/Pluto conjunction. Freud's psychoanalysis, based on early life experience, fitted well with the 20th-century obsession with self. Much to Freud's disapproval, Carl Jung, an early friend and associate, was to take the obvious step of seeing the birth-moment chart as a basic diagnostic tool. Although this suggestion, and the theory of archetypes that evolved from it, was to keep him at the fringe of mainstream psychology, Jung and his daughter discretely used astrology in their practice, as do many Jungian analysts to this day. Jung's

EXPLORING THE INFINITE

Instruments such as this radio telescope, at Jodrell Bank in Cheshire (England), can reach ever further into distant space, providing invaluable precision in our understanding of the universe. Astrology uses these exact measurements to explore how our solar system impacts upon the experience of being born at, and living through, specific times on Earth.

courageous vision will place his importance far higher when psychology's history is written from a wiser, future perspective.

Before it was repressed by the rise of Nazism, German astrology seemed to rewrite astrology's rule book. Rudolf Steiner's Anthroposophy offered a complete system, from spiritual interpretation to mundane tools for use in agriculture. Reinhold Ebertin's Cosmobiology sought to systematize psychological and medical interpretation. Alfred Witte and his successors introduced a new range of hypothetical Uranian cycles and highly technical approaches to combining the planets. And for much of the century, Mark Edmund Jones and Dane Rudhyar gave an esoteric and psychological emphasis to astrology in the United States.

JUNG'S ARCHETYPES
Astrology's key concepts work like Jungian archetypes to indicate how we express free will by choosing from many alternatives within a clearly definable range; they mould behaviour but do not determine actual outcomes.

In the United Kingdom, Charles Carter, John Addey, Charles Harvey and Margaret Hone developed astrological institutions, methods and academic links.

From the 1970s, the study and use of astrology was to experience a massive resurgence, alongside the rapid expansion of interest in New Age ideas. Fledgling private schools of astrology founded from the late 1940s were to offer complete studies, with certificates and diplomas comparable to a Higher National Certificate or even a first degree.

REDISCOVERING THE TRADITION

In 1985, the publication of a facsimile of the 1647 edition of William Lilly's great *Christian Astrology* came as a clarion call to scholars to rediscover medieval and Renaissance astrology. Those with Latin, Greek and Hebrew linguistic ability quickly saw the need to translate texts, many of which had not before been accessible in English and other modern languages. At the time of writing, astrological scholarship is in the midst of rediscovering a

heritage that had, until very recently, hung by the thread of medieval contacts with Islamic culture. As more becomes known, similarities to the unbroken lineage of Indian astrology are remarkable; especially when allowing for 17 centuries of separation.

Although dismissed by "secular fundamentalists" for three centuries, astrology entered the 21st century with a broader scholarship of self-understanding than ever before. Unfortunately, there remained a vast gap of knowledge between that scholarship and a fascinated, yet incredulous general public.

"STAR SIGNS"

In 1930, R.H. Naylor published an astro-study in the British *Sunday Express* newspaper describing the newborn Princess Margaret. Using a progression technique (originally developed by Johannes Kepler) he projected that "events of tremendous importance to the Royal Family will come about near to her seventh year, and these events will indirectly affect her fortunes." In 1936, her Uncle Edward VIII abdicated and her father became King George VI. This was to cast a shadow over the rest of Margaret's life.

Because newspapers could not offer all their readers such detail, the recently devised "Sun's position at birth" system was used. Popularly known as "star signs", these columns have come to be a media phenomenon. In spite of their extremely generalized nature, Nicholas Campion reports that 25–75 percent of people read them and 50–70 percent of young people check the sign of an intended partner. The phenomenon is a mixed blessing to the proper understanding of astrology. While revealing and responding to a clear public appetite, its very superficiality seems to characterize astrology as simplistic, outdated naïvety. Whether that is so can only be decided by proper study; that is the path this book aims to start you upon.

THE FUTURE OF ASTROLOGY

ASTROLOGERS' FAILURE TO PREDICT World War II in the 1930s inspired the French astrologer André Barbault to focus on mundane astrology (the relationship between astro-cycles and political/social events). By 1990, Barbault's expertise was such that he forecast a major world economic upheaval building to 2010, owing to the Saturn/Uranus opposition as Pluto entered Capricorn. In 1967, his Ordinastral-Astroflash was the first service to offer in-depth astrology charts and readings to the masses. In the following decades American, European and Australian experts established calculation and interpretation software that radically advanced the capacity of modern astrology.

Astrologers now have immediate access to information that previously took days, even months, to prepare. They can look back over centuries, even millennia, to detect causes and consequences of events. For example, remarkable astrological connections can be shown between the Emperor Hadrian's destruction of the Jewish Temple in 70 CE, the foundation of modern Israel, the development of the oil industry and recent Middle East wars. At the click of a mouse, the most intricate subtleties of Indian, Classical, medieval and Renaissance astrology can be displayed and advanced over time.

Computers help astrologers to avoid errors of judgment that come from partial information. Astro-cycles repeat regularly, but at each moment combine uniquely. A person's decision at each moment is based upon his or her different life experience. In the 21st century, for the first time, everyone can use astrology properly; that is, grasp the facts fully and decide for themselves.

As the "secret" knowledge of the past is rediscovered and combined with the technology of the 21st century, open minds may be able to unravel the basis of ancient astrological systems, and relate and synthesize them with the astronomy of today. The time may well be approaching when it is possible for the vision of Plato, Masha'allah, Aquinas, Kepler, Lévi, Blavatsky, Jung, Bailey and so many of their ancient and modern associates to be realized. The cycle of the heavens, and of each individual consciousness within it, may be seen as a reflection of one unified world soul.

At the root of achieving this lies an Eastern word that sums up a universal concept: karma. Its meaning is rather like Newton's third law of mechanics applied to morality; to every action there is an equal and opposite reaction. Astronomers observe heavenly bodies tolerating and reacting to each other proportionately. They see severe consequences when explosions interfere with this flow. In the same way, human anger activates anger; and kindness, kindness. Greed expands need and hunger. Working intelligently within the limitations of each moment is the most effective path to tread; to be as if at sea sailing with the wind. Similarly, working with astro-cycles clarifies decisions and makes life smoother; as above so below, as within, so without.

Some contemporary scientists and academics find such claims for astrology preposterous and insist that modern scientific method should be the absolute arbiter. Others, however, suggest that science in a healthy society should be a broader, more evolving "church" than such "secular fundamentalism" allows. Modern science is essential in many ways, but to base every decision we make upon

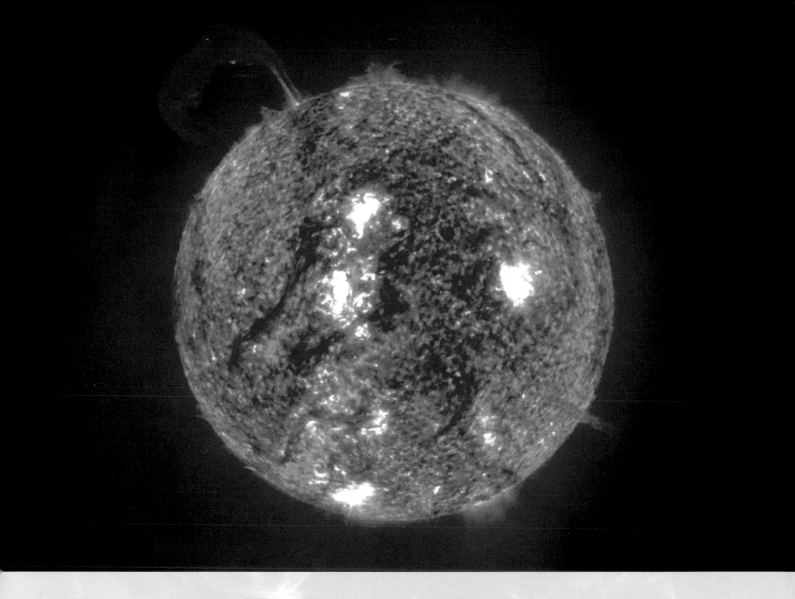

causal links, constantly subject to reassessment, is a recipe for disappointment and disaster. New discoveries pollute, while the research facts are being argued. Weapons destroy. The economist's worship of growth limits us to constant boom and bust, puts us on a treadmill of endless endeavour and emasculates human happiness. Lacking a value system, contemporary science leaves humanity on the edge of an abyss of amorality.

Should we accept, from a way of knowing that is less that 500 years old, the belief that the physical brain determines our functions and that human kindness and religious experience derive from nothing more than a "god spot"? With so much at stake, it is surely not unreasonable to also take into consideration a way of

SOURCE OF LIFE
All that we are and will be is reflected by the Earth's position in relation to the Sun, the position of the Moon and planets in our solar system and the way they moderate the Earth's movement.

understanding the world that has a history of at least 5,000 years. How the planets accommodate themselves to each other mirrors how we address our karmic challenges. If we work in accordance with the times, our decisions have much happier outcomes. By giving clear insight into human behaviour this way, astrology can fill a vital gap in modern culture.

This book is designed to help you to learn and use the basics of the secret language of astrology.

The first step in understanding our role in the infinite and beautiful universe is to know our relationship to the Sun, Moon and planets, which hold the Earth in place and keep us on our paths in life. The following pages explain an ancient language that interprets the Sun, Moon and planets in their zodiac signs (divisions of the celestial sphere) and their houses (areas of our lives), and shows how these affect each other and reflect our character and lives. Many find this language as valuable in the modern world as it has been to people from myriad cultures for thousands of years.

THE ELEMENTS OF ASTROLOGY

GETTING TO KNOW THE PLANETS

S CIENCE HAS TAUGHT US MUCH about the planets that our ancient ancestors never knew. We may remember the first time we looked at a diagram of the planets revolving around the Sun. Some of us may even have learned the details: distances, circumferences, times of heliocentric travel, rotations on axes, satellites and so on. Yet with all our scientific knowledge we also continue to view the heavens geocentrically, with the Earth as the focal point. This perception of the heavens is radically different from that of a sun-centred system viewed from space. Seen from Earth, the Sun appears to rise and set each day and to change height and strength through the year. The Moon appears to grow and to decrease, again and again. Beyond the Sun and Moon lies the vast encircling canopy of the stars, among which we can see five larger

THE "NEW" PLANETS ✳ URANUS, NEPTUNE AND PLUTO

A dramatic improvement in optics from the 18th century expanded our physical knowledge of the solar system by leading to the discovery of Uranus (1781), Neptune (1846) and Pluto (1930), described on pages 42–7. While these planets were not in the conscious minds of astrologers before their first sighting, discovering their cycles deepened the understanding developed in earlier centuries.

Pluto

bodies that the ancient Greeks called *planetes asteres* or "wandering stars": Venus, Mercury, Mars, Jupiter and Saturn. Seen from Earth, they move faster than all the other lights in the heavens, and even sometimes appear to move backward.

AS ABOVE, SO BELOW

If the geocentric experience of the heavens continues to exercise a powerful hold over the human imagination, it had even greater significance for our ancestors in the pre-scientific age. Without modern astronomical knowledge or instruments, and unhindered by pollution from artificial light, our forebears watched and recorded the changing patterns of the heavens as they appeared to the naked eye. Assuming our world to be the centre of creation, they saw what seemed to be obvious connections between these patterns and what happened here on Earth, in accordance with the ancient maxim "as above, so below". The seasons, tides, times to sow and reap, and even the lives and behaviour of people and animals seemed to respond to the cycles of the Sun, Moon and visible planets. The planetary cycles were regular, measurable and predictable, and by carefully observing the heavens our forebears

A SUN-CENTRED SYSTEM
An artist's impression of the solar system viewed from space. The planets' appearances are beautifully captured, but they are not to scale or correctly positioned on their orbits around the Sun.

grew accustomed to understanding and anticipating events and experiences on Earth. Modern astrology continues this tradition.

In ancient times, the visible planets were personified as deities. Over time they became associated with certain characteristics and personality types. In Act II, Scene VII of *As You Like It*, Shakespeare famously describes the "ages" of a person's life, from babyhood to old age. The following pages refer to descriptions of the ages that, in Shakespeare's day, were understood to be ruled and typified by the Moon and the five planets out to Saturn.

Emerging from the observed and precisely measured cycles of the heavens, and tested and adjusted over thousands of years, these planetary archetypes – the "heavenly beings" and their tales and characteristics – are deeply embedded in the human psyche. Even today we may describe someone as "mercurial", "jovial" (from Jove, another name for Jupiter) or "saturnine", while the words "lunatic",

ANCIENT ASTRONOMY

In this once-in-a-lifetime event, Jupiter shines brightly high above Stonehenge just after the Sun and Moon have set. The triangle of Mars, Venus and Saturn is also visible above a lintel stone, with Mercury fainter to the right.

"venereal" and "martial" also echo ancient perceptions of the Moon, Venus and Mars.

The planetary archetypes can also be applied to individual aspects of our personality: thus Mercury represents our thinking and intellect; Venus, our love and creativity; and so on. Likewise, they can also apply to aspects of society: Mercury represents education and communications; Venus, business and art; Mars, action, sport and war; and so on. The following pages are a guide to the characteristics of each planet. They explain each planet's cultural and historical associations, and describe its use and meaning in modern astrology.

THE SUN

GREAT CREATOR

THE RADIANT ENERGY OF SELF-EXPRESSION
* HOW WE CREATE

CENTRAL TO EVERYTHING, the Sun radiates light, life and hope. Rising in splendour at dawn, it builds to glorious noon-time power, only to fade and set at dusk. Even on cloudy days and in busy cities when its radiance seems distant, the solar day rules our routines and marks our creative power from birth to death.

Small wonder, then, that the Sun has been the centre of worship since ancient times, and that an all-powerful creator linked to the Sun lies at the heart of many religions. Ra, the Sun, was the supreme deity of the ancient Egyptians, and took several forms for the Sun's various aspects: Khepri, for the rising sun; Atum, the setting sun; and Ra, or Ra-Harakhte, at noon. Aten, the visible disc of the sun, was venerated as Egypt's supreme creator deity under Pharaoh Akhenaten (1353–36 BCE).

GEOCENTRIC * THE SEASONS OF THE YEAR

The ancients, ever dependent on the seasons of the year for food and shelter, knew only too well the importance of the coming and going of the Sun's heat. Each year, they watched and measured where the Sun rose and set on the horizon and noted how warmth depended upon its height above them at noon. The Sun was at its lowest at midwinter, an anxious time when rituals were devoted to ensuring that it would once more climb the sky, returning warmth and light to the barren land. Today we know that it is the relationship between the Earth's tilting axis and its path around the Sun that causes the seasons.

The Greco-Roman world depicted the Sun god Helios, or Sol, riding in a four-horse chariot, an image used by the early Christians to represent Christ, the Sun of Righteousness. The Sun's creativity was expressed in the god Apollo, the patron of light, truth, prophecy, medicine, healing, music, poetry and the arts, and the leader of the Muses. If not honoured, Apollo could bring ill-health and deadly plague, hinting at the Sun's more destructive side.

In Ayurveda, the Sun's gift of life and heat is called *prana*, meaning energy. The Maoris of New Zealand use the word Ra to name both the Sun and the day. From earliest times, kings and other absolute rulers have sought to be revered like the Sun as providers of all their peoples' needs.

EYE OF HORUS
The supreme Egyptian Sun god Ra was closely linked with the great sky god Horus, who flew in the form of a falcon that held the Sun in his right eye and the Moon in his left.

CHARACTERISTICS OF THE SUN

The Sun represents the core of our self-expression. Its position in the zodiac at the time of our birth is the first and, for many of us, the only astrological fact we consider. This position reveals how our light shines – how we seek to project ourselves upon, and influence, our family, friends and society. The Sun represents all those experiences that make us believe in ourselves. It determines how we create, not only artistically, but also in terms of having fun, of experiencing pleasure ourselves and bringing it to others. This planet also symbolizes the breathless, naïve joy of childhood and youth, those times when all seems possible, so long as we, like the Sun, just keep moving on.

THE LIGHT OF OUR LIVES

The Sun is the heavenly body that we know and love the best. Its rising and setting divides our lives into day and night and we greet with joy its nearer approach to Earth each spring, bringing warmth and light.

Yet such self-confidence has its shortcomings. The Sun may lead to egocentricity that can blind us to the interests and experience of others and, albeit unwittingly and for the best of reasons, we may ride roughshod over people and do harm. We may plough on counterproductively or, conversely, we may be blind to our own achievements and our own best interests and accept failure too easily. As art becomes great by being constantly reassessed, so we need some touchstone against which to measure what we do.

THE MOON
RULER OF NIGHT

THE ENERGY OF REFLECTION
⁎ HOW WE REACT

Numbers ⁎ 2 and 7
Day ⁎ Monday
Colour ⁎ Whitish
Parts of body ⁎ Breasts and alimentary system
Metal ⁎ Silver
Stones ⁎ Crystal, mother of pearl and moonstone
Herbs/Incense ⁎ Camphor and frankincense
Plants ⁎ Melons, broom tops and willow

WHILE THE SHEER FORCE of the Moon's physical cycle affects the essentials of life on Earth – tides, growth of plants, cycles of female fertility – its light exists only as a reflection of the Sun's. In its endless cycle of waxing and waning, the Moon represents change and potential, the myriad possibilities that we face in the course of our lives. From the brightness of the full Moon to the darkness of the new Moon, this planet represents the ambivalence in us all: alongside our potential for creativity, beauty, romance and kindness is the shadow side that lurks within our souls – the side that gives rise to fear and uncertainty, and sometimes unkindness and dishonesty.

The Moon is the planet of nurture and for our forebears it governed the period of birth and infancy, the first of the "seven ages of man" described by Shakespeare. In ancient times the Moon was associated with a range of powerful female deities. In Greece the lunar goddess, Artemis, was the twin sister of the solar god, Apollo. Artemis was

LIFE AND DEATH
The Mayan lunar deity was Ix Chel, an aged crone with the ears of a jaguar. Linked to birth and healing, she was also sometimes associated with war or appeared as a rain goddess, releasing floods to bring about the world's end.

represented as goddess of the hunt, wild animals, wilderness, childbirth, virginity and young girls, and she carried a bow and arrows. If offended her wrath could be fierce, as when the hunter Actaeon came across Artemis bathing among her nymphs. Artemis turned him into stag, to be torn to pieces by his own hounds. A special form of Artemis as a many-breasted fertility goddess was worshipped at Ephesus in Asia Minor. When Rome conquered Ephesus, the Greek Artemis became merged with Diana the huntress, the Roman lunar goddess.

A similar ambivalence is found in the Mayan lunar deity, Ix Chel. The goddess of midwifery and medicine, she also poured destructive floods and rainstorms on the Earth when she overturned the great jug that she carried.

The Moon is also linked with profound and hidden wisdom. Cerridwen was the Celtic keeper of the cauldron of knowledge, which was filled with lunar wisdom, inspiration and intuition. As a goddess of the underworld, she was seen as a crone, as well as a mother, to be honoured at the full Moon. In ancient Egypt, the Moon replaced the Sun at night and ruled the stars. Its phases were an image of cyclical renewal.

CHARACTERISTICS OF THE MOON

The Moon reveals our emotional disposition and our intuition: how we feel and how we react. It shows how we like to be treated, and how we in turn treat other people. With the Moon strongly placed in our chart we are likely to act protectively and defensively, until we feel safe. The issue is how to do this without seeming to reject the kind intentions of others.

When we consider the Moon in the zodiac sign in which it appears on our birth chart, our way of reassuring others will become clear, as will the way we wish them to reassure us. There are many right reactions: right touch, as well as right words, actions and gifts. Sometimes simply the chance to help and be understood will be welcome and enough. Tolerance not tightness is often the way. As the Moon reflects the sunlight, so it may be wise to see ourselves and our actions in the eyes of others, and be open to adjusting our behaviour accordingly. In this way, we can nurture each other, harnessing the energy of the Moon to nurse the infant within us.

THE MOON IN ISLAM

The Moon is an important symbol in Islam. Crescent moons are placed on the high points of mosques and the Moon appears next to a star on the flags of several Islamic countries. The Muslim month of Ramadan (the year's ninth) commences after the first sunset sighting of the new Moon.

GEOCENTRIC ✳ LUNAR PHASES AND ECLIPSES

For our forebears, who knew nothing of the interplay of the Moon's gravity with the Sun and Earth, it was the changing shape of the Moon that was responsible for the tides, the behaviour of sap in plants and the female menstrual cycle. It is not surprising that many religions use a lunar calendar to decide their festivals.

The different Moon shapes through each lunar month are owing to the Moon's changing position relative to us and to its solar light source. Twice most years, the Sun's plane lines up with that of the Moon and the Earth and these three bodies cast a total or partial shadow on each other. From some places on Earth, the Moon can be seen passing in front of the Sun. Two weeks later, the Earth's shadow obscures the Sun and so dims the Moon's reflected light. Ancient peoples looked upon eclipses with foreboding, especially solar eclipses when the daylight sky was briefly darkened. Even today, some astrologers have seen correspondences between eclipse paths and natural disasters.

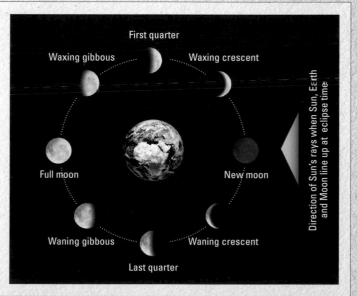

First quarter

Waxing gibbous   Waxing crescent

Full moon   New moon

Waning gibbous   Waning crescent

Last quarter

Direction of Sun's rays when Sun, Earth and Moon line up at eclipse time

MERCURY

MESSENGER OF THE GODS

THE ENERGY OF INTELLIGENCE * HOW WE THINK

Number * 5
Day * Wednesday
Colour * Orange
Parts of body * Respiratory system and brain
Metal * Platinum
Stone * Agate
Herbs/Incense * Clove and coriander
Plant * Hazel

APPARENTLY DARTING HITHER AND THITHER, bright Mercury brings us brilliant ideas, illuminating messages and amazing connections. Under its influence, flashes of insight blaze along our brain's neural pathways, seeking and, perhaps, attaining true wisdom and understanding.

The planet Mercury was identified by the Greeks with the god Hermes, the messenger of the gods, the guide of souls and the swift-footed deity of transitions, communication and exchange. Mercury was the name that the Romans gave to both god and planet. In Greco-Roman mythology, winged Hermes or Mercury functioned as an enabler of all kinds of activities that broke down barriers, be that for good or ill: he helped healers and robbers alike. He was also a god of trade and profit, and of travellers and merchants, for Mercury also rules over our material transactions – his name is related to both "market" (*mercatus*) and "commerce" (*commercium*).

In his left hand Hermes holds a staff known as the caduceus, around which curl two intertwined snakes. This shows that we find the middle way of truth by reconciling opposites. In his right hand, Hermes holds a scroll, symbolizing the true wisdom to which our cultivation of insight can lead; for this reason the Greeks identified Hermes with the

Egyptian Thoth, the begetter of all wisdom and esoteric knowledge. Thoth was the scribe of the gods, and recorded the weighing of the soul of the departed (represented by the heart) against the feather of truth. As Hermes Trismegistus ("Thrice-Great Hermes"), Thoth was the author of ancient magical lore.

Ancient Irish and Indian astrologers, living thousands of miles apart, used the word *budh* (to "awaken", "enlighten" in Sanskrit) for Mercury. This suggests that their craft came from a common Indo-European root. Earlier, in Babylon, Mercury was called Bebo or Nabu, "the proclaimer" and god of wisdom. His relationship to the dominant god Marduk was culturally entwined and even obscured, rather as the planet Mercury itself is so close to the Sun for three periods each year that it cannot be seen.

For our ancestors, Mercury governed the second of our "seven ages": childhood. This is the time when – often reluctantly, like Shakespeare's "whining schoolboy" creeping to school – we begin to acquire the knowledge and wisdom that can counterbalance our untamed energies.

SPREADING OUR WINGS
Both gods Hermes and Mercury wore winged shoes that enabled them to dart from place to place, as the planet Mercury itself follows a winding path. The word "mercurial" derives from this quality of restlessness.

Mercury's caduceus is the symbol of the medical profession. Hippocrates, the originator of the oath that is taken by doctors to this day, said: "A physician without knowledge of astrology has no right to call himself a physician."

CHARACTERISTICS OF MERCURY

Mercury rules our communication – our mind, thoughts and words. Its place in our birth chart reveals our way of thinking, writing and speaking and the other means by which we present ourselves to those about us: our bright smile or worried frown; our tidy or untidy writing style; our way of making contact; how we learn; our relationship with computers.

Mercury rules all places of learning, publishing, libraries and the media, as well as the marketing and spin that dominate the modern world. Mercury can be fickle: slick, exciting words that seem to resolve issues and bring news of success may just as easily stir up fresh difficulties. If we are not careful our interactions can go awry, with understanding turning to misunderstanding and success to failure. Intellectual genius, unless firmly grounded, can spin off into neurotic failure as the lines of communication overheat and burn out. Similarly, communication can sometimes be too quick and we may find change too rapid for comfort, as the word "mercurial" suggests. Mercury the quick-witted, insightful thinker can become Mercury the trickster and deceiver. The antidote to such dangers is to seek knowledge with a kind and caring heart. This alone can lead us to true wisdom and understanding.

GEOCENTRIC ✳ MERCURY'S WINDING PATH

Seen from Earth over a two-year period, the path of Mercury makes a series of loops, apparently moving backward against the stars behind it. Known as retrogression, this effect happens three times a year and occurs because the 88-day orbit of Mercury around the Sun is far shorter than the 365-day orbit of the Earth. As Mercury moves through its various retrograde stages, our ideas and decisions can change radically and become unreliable. Mercury's retrograde periods require extra attention to details. This can transform disadvantage into advantage.

Mercury's geocentric path

THE WEIGHING OF SOULS

Mercury is linked to the Egyptian god Thoth, who interrogated each dead person's heart (thought to be the seat of the soul) about its sins. The heart was weighed against a feather of truth in the scales of Ma'at, the goddess of justice (see page 99).

VENUS

GODDESS OF LOVE

THE ENERGY OF PLEASURE ⁎ HOW WE LOVE

Number ⁎ 6
Day ⁎ Friday
Colour ⁎ Green
Parts of body ⁎ Throat and kidneys
Metal ⁎ Copper
Stone ⁎ Emerald
Herbs/Incense ⁎ Strawberry and raspberry
Plant ⁎ Rose

VENUS SYMBOLIZES ALL that is beautiful, graceful, charming and tasteful. She enriches our senses with delightful flavours, smells, sights, sounds and sensations. Her creativity urges us to value and accumulate objects, ideas and experiences.

Yet the planet also has a darker side. Its irresistible charm can entice and seduce, and so poison our happiness. Our need to have, to possess, may become so intense that it is impossible for us to let go. When this happens, contentment is impossible. Only in letting go – in appreciating and knowing without grasping and needing to have – can we find true lasting happiness.

This ambiguity is reflected in the myths surrounding the goddess with whom the planet is identified. Known to the Greeks as Aphrodite ("born of foam"), the goddess of love and beauty was the oldest of the Olympian gods and emerged from the foaming blood and semen of the castrated god Uranus at the point where his severed genitals fell into the sea. She married Hephaistos (Vulcan), craftsman of the gods, but had many affairs with other gods – notably Ares (Mars) – as well as with mortals, such as Adonis, who was slain by the jealous Ares in the guise of a boar.

The mother of Eros (sexual love, the Roman Cupid) and Harmonia (harmony), but also of Deimus (fear) and Phobus (panic), Aphrodite personifies the mix of delight and destructiveness, of harmony and conflict, that can arise from beauty, love and desire. When Paris, a prince of Troy, was asked to name the fairest goddess, he chose Aphrodite after she promised him Helen of Sparta, the most beautiful woman in the world. Paris's choice

GEOCENTRIC ⁎ THE PATH OF BEAUTY

This diagram shows the path of Venus seen over exactly eight years, during which time it makes five loops caused by apparent retrograde motion owing to the different speed of its solar orbit (see page 51). Its symmetry, strikingly akin to that of a rose, shows how the planet's movement touches our consciousness with a subtle physical experience of beauty. Yet modern space exploration has discovered the crushingly heavy, poisonous atmosphere of Venus. Taken together, ancient and modern perspectives instruct us that beauty may best be experienced when we maintain a degree of detachment.

Venus's geocentric path   *Symmetry of a rose*

earned Troy the enmity of Athene and Artemis; and his kidnap of Helen from her husband led to the war that destroyed Troy.

Claiming descent from Venus and the Trojan Aeneas, Julius Caesar and his heir Augustus adopted the goddess as their family protector, acknowledging that she provided not only beauty of form, but also the material wealth that enabled successful enterprise. A similar tradition surrounds the Indian goddess Lakshmi.

Venus–Aphrodite was identified with the Egyptian goddess Isis, daughter of the Earth god Geb and the sky goddess Nut, and mother of the solar god, Horus. Mistress of nature and magic, Isis was revered by pharaohs and common folk alike. In Babylon, as the goddess Ishtar, who braved and survived the underworld, the planet controlled fertility, love, war, sex and sacred prostitution.

In contrast to the Old World, Central American civilizations traditionally saw Venus as male and often malign. Aztecs viewed Tlahuizcalpantecuhtli (the god of the planet Venus as a morning star) as a dangerous and malevolent deity, who shot self-destructive darts and arrows. Mayan astrologers tracked Venus's 584-day heliacal cycle from the moment when, as a morning star, it first became visible above the eastern horizon, just before sunrise. Mayan wars could be timed to coincide with the stages of this cycle.

BIRTH OF A GODDESS
Botticelli's famous depiction of Venus shows the goddess emerging beautiful and fully grown from the foaming sea, as did her Greek equivalent Aphrodite (whose names means "born of foam").

CHARACTERISTICS OF VENUS

Venus in our chart shows our passions – how intensely we are attracted toward experiences, possessions and people. Its position indicates how and when we fall in love and governs the third of our "seven ages", as described by Shakespeare: the age of the youthful lover, "Sighing like furnace, with a woeful ballad / Made to his mistress' eyebrow." This is also the planet of gardeners and every kind of artist, as well as of those who wish to succeed in business. The position of Venus in our birth chart reveals who and what we value, and how we express that appreciation. Loving intensely can make us strong, ready to take risks and to endure in the search for satisfaction. But it can also expose us to disappointment, jealousy and a broken heart. We need to learn to move beyond attachment. Accepting loss by welcoming change and still being loving, even in our darkest hours, is what truly endears us to others.

MARS

GOD OF WAR

THE ENERGY OF FORCE
✳ HOW WE ACT

THE UPWARD-THRUSTING ARROW OF MARS symbolizes raw power that instigates and keeps things moving: war with its courage and brutality; the unreasoning fury of a demanding two-year-old; the urgent elegance of a ballroom dancer; the coward fleeing to his hideaway; the idealist standing tall amid intolerance and abuse. These are only some of the ways in which we may be influenced by Mars in our birth chart.

Mars in its highest and most effective sense is much more about style than brute force. While delighting in pure adventure and the chase, Mars works best when we train its energies – when we focus the passion and aggressive desires that it engenders. The downhill ski racer secures the fastest time not merely through speed, but through the subtle adjustments that control the raw

GEOCENTRIC ✳ THE WAY OF THE WARRIOR

This diagram shows the path of Mars seen over exactly 16 years, during which time it makes seven loops caused by apparent retrograde motion. Unlike the Venus pattern (see page 34), the pattern of these loops is not the same. This is because Mars retrogresses only once in its two-year path around the zodiac and, whenever it does, the Earth is differently placed. Intuitively sensing this pattern, we are stirred to master the

underlying current of the planet's erratic unreliability. Being unable to rest upon any certainty can make us impatient, even furious. Yet, if we respond to new challenges with considered effectiveness, there is little that we cannot achieve.

Mars's geocentric path

force of gravity. To wait alert and ready to act can be more effective than the loudest roar.

The ancient Babylonian god of war and destruction, who corresponds to the planet Mars, was Nergal. He was passionately and faithfully devoted to the goddess Erishkigal, with whom he ruled the underworld. The Greek war god Ares, lover of Aphrodite, was a strong, even brutal, warrior who relished the violence and carnage of battle and was famously humiliated when Hephaistos,

ELEGANCE AND POWER
Mars achieves its highest expression when the raw power of this planet is tempered with skill and subtlety, as illustrated in the graceful technique and dynamism of a downhill skier.

CHARACTERISTICS OF MARS

The position of Mars in our birth chart indicates the nature and strength of the way we act: whether we address challenges or avoid them; whether we work with or around what confronts us in life; whether we display courage and confidence, or an inclination to dissemble; whether we respond quickly or slowly, with or without considering our options. Mars invites us to examine whether we are warriors or diplomats, and what kind of behaviour and (male) role models we follow. Mars may lead us to act, attack and even destroy for the joy of the adrenaline rush, or it may arouse in us the purposeful courage of the warrior, defending his country and keeping others safe from harm. This planet is often associated with those displaying excellence and courage in the fields of sport, dance and adventure.

In Shakespeare's day, Mars was held to rule the fourth age of man, or early adulthood. This is the time of the greatest masculine activity and vigour, as represented by a soldier: "Full of strange oaths, and bearded like the pard, / Jealous in honour, sudden and quick in quarrel, / Seeking the bubble reputation / Even in the cannon's mouth." As the Sun needs the Moon, so Mars needs a consort of substance to interact with, to transform his actions and make them excellent and positive. Mars is more effective, and far happier at heart, when working with Venus to chart a path through the world.

WEAPONS AND SHIELDS
The medieval figure of Mars, clad head to foot in armour, shows the self-protection necessary whenever a champion of good or evil sets forth in battle.

Aphrodite's jealous husband, trapped the lovers in a golden net. However, Ares gave his name to the higher qualities of action (*arete*, excellence), and his Roman equivalent, Mars, was an altogether nobler and more prominent figure. In origin a god of the land, Mars was revered as the fierce protector of Rome and second only to Jupiter.

Mars features prominently in the seminal work on "individuation" by the psychoanalyst Carl Jung. He used this term to describe the second half of our life, when we go through a process of psychological maturing and self-realization. By developing a strong and healthy Mars, our actions become confident and effective, and we truly become individuals.

HYMN TO ARES

Shine down upon our lives
Your gentle light and your warrior's power
So I may drive away bitter cowardice from my head
And subdue my soul's beguiling impulse,
So may I restrain the shrill rage in my heart
Which excites me to charge
Into the chilling din of battle.
Rather, blessed god, give me the courage
To stand my ground within the safe laws of peace,
Shunning hostility and hatred
And the fate of a violent death.

Homeric hymn, *c.* 7th–4th century BCE

JUPITER

KING OF THE GODS

THE ENERGY OF GENEROSITY
∗ HOW WE EXPAND

Number ∗ 3
Day ∗ Thursday
Colour ∗ Purple
Parts of body ∗ Liver and pituitary gland
Metal ∗ Tin
Stones ∗ Sapphire, amethyst and turquoise
Herbs/Incense ∗ Jasmine, nutmeg and sage
Plants ∗ Oak and poplar

THE LARGEST OF THE PLANETS, Jupiter is the lord of light, the emperor, judge and teacher of all that is. Jovian generosity makes just about anything possible, offering hope even in the greatest adversity. Yet this blessing can grow into a Faustian curse, in which we crave endless expansion in every direction and the continual consumption of all we desire. Without Jupiter there is little prospect of hope, but there is no hope at all when we are overwhelmed by limitless craving.

In ancient Babylon the planet was identified with the god Marduk, who in the first millennium BCE was elevated to supreme god of Mesopotamia. Ruler of water, vegetation, judgment and magic, he received the control of humanity when his father, Ea, recognized his superiority.

Zeus, king of the gods and ruler of life, light and the sky, was not all-powerful but, like all gods and mortals, was subject to the Moiræ (Fates). He often visited humankind in the form of a mortal or in various other disguises, and as the god of storms wielded his thunderbolt with awesome power.

MARDUK OF BABYLON
This ancient boundary stone shows the Babylonian king Marduk-apla-iddina II, who ruled in the 8th century BCE. Through his name, the king drew on the divine authority of the supreme god Marduk, whom the Babylonians also associated with the vast planet Jupiter.

GEOCENTRIC ∗ THE BRINGER OF OPPORTUNITY

The geocentric path of Jupiter over two cycles, or 24 years, makes loops caused by the planet's apparent annual five-month retrogression seen against the "fixed" pattern of the stars. As we pass through these months each year, the force of opportunity naturally slows, readjusts and then starts again, often in radically different ways.

As the god Jupiter had many lovers, so this planet also attracts a huge number of followers. Jupiter is so large that its gravity holds not only its moons, but numerous captured asteroids, called the Trojans, which orbit with the planet. In 1994 even the comet Shoemaker-Levy 9 could not resist crashing into the surface of Jupiter.

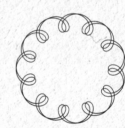

Jupiter's geocentric path

In Rome, as Jupiter, he was the supreme god of heaven. As such, he never appeared upon Earth and had absolute power over life and death. The temple of Jupiter Optimus Maximus ("best and greatest Jupiter") on the Capitoline Hill was the largest in Rome, and the god was revered there as the source of the city's imperial greatness, the bringer of military victories and economic prosperity.

Through his many love affairs, Jupiter fathered the deities of commerce, love, spring, the Sun, the Moon, wisdom and

THE STORM GODS

Indra, the Vedic supreme deity, is shown here being anointed with the divine drink *soma*, of which he was said to consume copious quantities. Like Zeus, who was also associated with Jupiter, Indra ruled the weather and a lightning bolt was his weapon of choice.

many more. When we swear "by almighty God" in a court of law we are following a tradition that goes back to the Roman practice of swearing "by Jove" (as Jupiter is also called). When our judges bang their gavels, they invoke the hammer with which, amid lightning and thunder, Jupiter passed judgment and corrected error.

In Vedic India, Jupiter was associated with Indra, the supreme ruler of the gods, and lord of war, thunder and storms. He was the greatest of warriors, wielding his celestial *vajra*, or lightning bolt. He defended gods and people against the forces of evil. Hindus call this planet Guru, or teacher; and they say the greatest lesson in life is to have an opportunity and then learn how to master it.

CHARACTERISTICS OF JUPITER

Jupiter in our chart offers us opportunities to overcome problems and barriers. Opportunity may come in the form of knowledge, reassurance, a helping hand or even funds. More than this, the position of Jupiter shows where we can be generous. A well-placed Jupiter can help us to advise and support others in liberating ways. Jupiter was said to govern the fifth age of man, the time of responsible maturity that Shakespeare characterizes as the well-fed justice dispensing wisdom: "In fair round belly with good capon lin'd, / With eyes severe and beard of formal cut, / Full of wise saws and modern instances."

Jupiter is a friend, but we should not follow him blindly. Too many ideas at once can confuse us and over-activity can lead to exhaustion or an accident. Excessive passion or kindness can expose us to hurt, while over-indulgence can dull discrimination.

SATURN

THE ENERGY OF STRUCTURE
* HOW WE CONTROL

Number * 8
Day * Saturday
Colour * Black
Parts of body * Gall bladder, skin and bones
Metal * Lead
Stones * jet, onyx and black diamond
Herbs/Incense * musk, camomile, poppy seeds and cinnamon
Plants * thistle, yew, ash, alder and cypress

BEING FURTHEST FROM THE SUN, Saturn has the longest cycle of all the visible planets. For this reason, Classical cultures represented Saturn as Father Time, an aged man who marked the natural seasons in our lives with his scythe. He was both lord of the harvest and of death. Riding the heavens in a chariot drawn by winged dragon-snakes coiled like spiralling DNA, Saturn structures our life, its ending and its transcendence to higher consciousness.

Saturn's dedication to structure and discipline suits order in business and politics, as well as the physical frames upon which our buildings and bodies depend. Yet too much control can calcify our actions and attitudes, freezing the juices of creativity and rendering us impotent. There must be a limit to limitation. If we keep this in mind, we can benefit from the positive aspects of Saturn's control and strength.

In ancient Babylon, Saturn was identified with the god Ninurta, whose name means "lord of the earth". Ninurta was a god of rain and storms, fertility and (like Saturn) agriculture, as well as war, wells, canals, floods and the plough. He also released humans from sickness and the power of demons.

The Roman Saturn was an ancient agriculture god (hence the scythe) who came to be identified with the Greek Kronos (or Cronus), the ruler of heaven who was overthrown by his son Zeus. His role as Father Time arose from association with the Greek for "time", *chronos*. The Romans looked back to a mythical Golden Age when Saturn ruled and brought abundance and peace. They celebrated this each year around the winter solstice by a week of

HARVESTER OF LIVES
This 1559 painting depicts Saturn–Kronos, who consumed five of his children before being overthrown by the sixth, Zeus (Jupiter). He carries the scythe with which he reaps both the harvest and our lives.

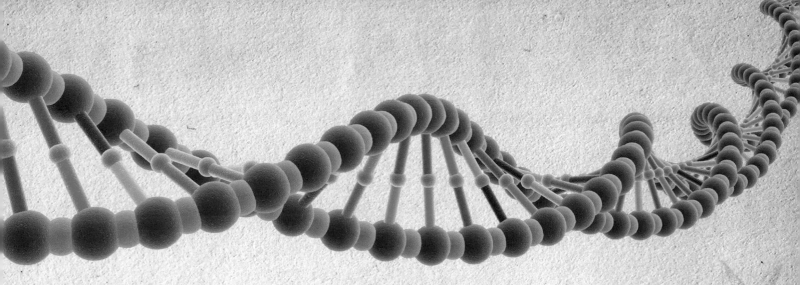

STRUCTURE OF OUR LIVES

Saturn reveals the meaning of life's framework, from the cellular structure of DNA to the architecture of our houses. Structure can give us freedom; it does not have to limit us.

feasting called Saturnalia. During this time, normal social rules were turned upside down. The roles of master and slave were reversed, moral restrictions loosened and etiquette ignored.

In contrast, in medieval times Saturn was associated with the temperament of melancholy, hence "saturnine", meaning morose or gloomy. Physicians, scholars, philosophers, scientists, writers and musicians were all said to have a strong Saturn placement in their charts, inclining them toward melancholy, but also imparting serenity and the wisdom of the Earth itself. Saturn presided over the sixth age of man, old age, caricatured by Shakespeare as a shuffling, shrunken, squeaky-voiced "pantaloon" (an elderly buffoon in pantomime), prefacing the last age of all, "second childishness and mere oblivion".

CHARACTERISTICS OF SATURN

In Indian astrology Saturn, or Shani, has a similar ambivalence to that found in the West: the planet presides over career and longevity, but can also bring bad luck and hardship. However, these aspects are complementary, and a strong Saturn in our chart should not make us downhearted. Saturn indicates where problems, restrictions and barriers are likely in our lives and confronts us with the reality of impermanence. But Saturn

presides over much more than failure and endings: as the planet of firm foundations, it can show us how to strengthen our endeavours and make them more sustainable. In understanding Saturn, we make a friend who will never give false hope and will always be there to support us, providing a framework for our progress through life, just as it also presides over the skeletons that our bodies need to stand tall, and the foundations that hold up buildings. With Saturn as our guide, we become more powerful by working with and mastering problems. The strength of Saturn will sustain us, whatever happens.

GEOCENTRIC ✳ A COSMIC STRUGGLE

This diagram shows that Saturn's 29-year transit of the zodiac is two and half times longer than Jupiter's, which means that the planets are conjunct and opposed on alternate ten years. This explains the ongoing struggle in our lives between expansion (Jupiter) and contraction (Saturn), between opportunity and consolidation. Every year is also fine-tuned by the disparate timing of the two planets' retrograde motions.

This struggle may explain the Classical myth of Rhea, the earth

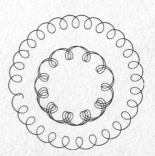

goddess who hid her sixth child, Zeus (Jupiter), lest her husband Kronos (Saturn) should eat him, as he had his other five children. When he ate the substitute stone wrapped in swaddling clothes, he was forced to disgorge the other children and Zeus–Jupiter became supreme ruler of the cosmos (see page 43).

Jupiter's cycles inside Saturn's geocentric path

URANUS

GOD OF THE SKY

THE ENERGY OF AWAKENING AND SUDDEN CHANGE * HOW WE INVENT

Colour * Electric blue
Parts of body * Pineal gland and circulatory system
Metal * Copper
Stones * Turquoise and malachite
Modern * Revolutionary inventiveness

WHEN SIR WILLIAM HERSCHEL discovered Uranus in 1781, the world was on the move in myriad dramatic ways that included new methods of scientific investigation; advances in industrial technology; migration from the countryside to the towns; colonial expansion; and the political upheavals that climaxed in the French Revolution and the birth of the United States, with its insistence on "The Rights of Man". Such typically radical Uranian developments gave birth to the modern world and ultimately to today's globally integrated society with all its benefits, possibilities and problems.

The planet was named after Uranus because he was the father of Saturn, just as Saturn was the father of Jupiter. In astrological terms the name was an apt one. The planet's key phrase is "drastic change", and Uranus (Ouranos), god of the sky, son and consort of Gaia, the Earth, himself fell victim to just such a drastic change when he was castrated and overthrown by his son, Kronos (Saturn).

SHAPER OF WORLDS

Uranus symbolizes both creation and destruction. Since the planet's discovery in the 18th century, mankind's inventiveness has led to ambivalent outcomes. Industrialization brought immense benefits, yet also ripped societies apart and damaged the natural world. This picture of the 1900 Paris Exposition Universelle shows both the power of change, and how this can dominate lives.

Today this planet has come to represent the creative power of the human will: new inventions, theories, discoveries and relationships that may seem startling at first.

The dynamic possibilities of Uranus are sudden, exciting, earth-shattering – and dangerous. Such energy must be harnessed with care, but its very nature makes that difficult. Although Uranian inventiveness can be highly beneficial, its impetus may bring suffering in its wake, as seen in the brutality meted out to perceived opponents of the French Revolution, and the appalling conditions of workers during industrialization. The Uranian archetype, associated with Promethean inventiveness, can also be tyrannical and restrictive.

Uranus was the essential creative force behind love, vengeance and the growth of vegetation. He fathered extraordinary offspring – Titans, giants and Cyclopes – only to imprison them deep within the Earth. His pained wife Gaia made a great flint-bladed sickle and instructed their youngest son Kronos (Saturn) to castrate his father. Fearing a similar fate Kronos ate his own children after birth, but the sixth child Zeus (Jupiter) tricked him, escaped and eventually overthrew his father and released the Titans. This myth is an allegory of the relationships between the planets Jupiter, Saturn and Uranus, which track the drama of loss and new awakening in Earth's societies.

CHARACTERISTICS OF URANUS

Uranus rules our inventive side through which we excite and surprise even ourselves. Its placing in our chart reveals the ease of our relationship with innovation, such as new technology, and whether we tend to accept or question conventional attitudes. A well-placed Uranus may indicate that we have innovative talent, but we should recognize that personal brilliance alone can have its limitations. We should avoid being didactic about "scientific truth" and "vital" social causes. Uranian arrogance can impose change on others "for their own good", whether or not they want or need it.

Uranus has an 84-year orbit, passing through each zodiac sign for seven years and influencing assumptions about technology and society during that period. This explains various crazes and the rise and fall of gadgets and media. When printing was first demonstrated in the 1440s, Uranus was in Gemini. It was in the same sign in the 1940s, when the electronic computer was invented.

GEOCENTRIC ✶ A CREATIVE PULSE

This diagram illustrates Uranus's entire 84-year cycle as seen from the Earth. The detail, of three years, shows that, unlike the planets nearer to the Sun, Uranus's annual retrograde loops actually touch each other.

Now we are aware of the planet, we respond more consciously to this annual pulse of seeking out the familiar, then moving on. Changes associated with Uranus's journey through each sign are explained in the zodiac chapter, at the end of each sign.

Five months retrograde each year

Uranus's geocentric path

NEPTUNE

GOD OF THE SEA

Colours * Dull grey to black * Parts of body * Nervous systems * Metal * Silver * Stones * Rock crystal and opal * Modern * Emergence of hidden powers and processes

THE ENERGY OF THE MYSTERIOUS * HOW WE INSPIRE

NEPTUNE WAS DISCOVERED IN 1846 and named, in keeping with the other planets, after a Classical deity, in this case the god of the sea. This proved appropriate in visual terms (Neptune, like Uranus, is blue in appearance) and also in astrological terms, because Neptune rules the seas of our subconscious selves. Neptune (Poseidon) is the ruler of the oceans, drawing us with his trident toward the captivating images of our inner realm. Such visions can inspire our spirit to ideals and dreams, to great kindness and sacrifice for the greater good. Neptune can also inspire us to produce art, music and literature, and to other forms of creativity.

GEOCENTRIC * CONFUSION AND WONDER

This diagram shows Neptune's 164-year cycle around the zodiac as seen from Earth. The detail shows three years, with each year's retrograding months highlighted in blue. Note how the annual loops go back further than those of Uranus and actually cross. Each year, Neptune returns to a position before the zodiac position of its previous year's retrograde station (the point at which it appears to stop before appearing to move backward). Constantly having to reassess, we move between being lost in confusion and in magical wonder.

Five months retrograde each year

Neptune's geocentric path

However, Neptune can also lead us adrift in the deep, as what seemed to be solid proves to be fluid and insubstantial, leaving us sinking, deceived and lost, neurotic and self-pitying, not knowing where to turn. We can move beyond this danger by identifying with others, perhaps by developing empathy through a meditation practice that constantly broadens awareness. Then, we may gain a real understanding of ourselves.

Neptune symbolizes uncertainty about assumptions, the undermining and remoulding of beliefs. Scientific breakthroughs and radical new social, political, spiritual and artistic outlooks

RIDER OF THE WHITE-CAPPED WAVES

The Greek god Poseidon and his Roman equivalent, Neptune, both ride chariots drawn by sea-horses. In Roman times, Neptune was associated with horse-racing and worshipped in the form of Neptune Equester.

were evident at the time of the planet's discovery in 1846. Around this time Michael Faraday was making major advances in electricity, William Morton used anaesthetic for the first time and Carl Gustav Carus published a pioneer work on the subconscious. The USA, inspired by the new vision of its "Manifest Destiny" to unite North America "from sea to shining sea", went to war with Mexico and occupied Texas, New Mexico and California. The seething political currents of the time also erupted in the 1848 "Year of Revolutions" and the publication of Karl Marx's *Communist Manifesto*. The year 1848 also saw the founding of the Pre-Raphaelite Brotherhood.

The first children born with Neptune now known to be in their birth charts were to live through the time of the US Civil War, the advance of socialism and the late 19th-century spiritual revival. They were to pioneer the use of gas, electricity, petroleum and the motor car.

In mythology, Neptune is the Roman equivalent of the Greek Poseidon, god of the sea and brother of Zeus (Jupiter) and Hades (Pluto). Riding the white-topped waves on a sea-horse, Poseidon was a god of awesome powers, manifested in tempests and earthquakes. He was married to the sea nymph Amphitrite but, like his brothers, had many affairs. His adultery with Medusa led to her transformation into the snake-haired monster.

CHARACTERISTICS OF NEPTUNE

Neptune's cycle is not completed during a single human lifespan, hence it is associated with experiences that may be new and uncertain. To help us cope where we might otherwise feel adrift in a sea of impermanence, some of us may turn to religion or to political or social idealism, others to the creative arts; or we may latch on to hero-worship, fashion, drugs or alcohol. If we have Neptune in our birth chart, it is vital to avoid the attachment and dependence that come from putting ourselves first. To offset disappointment, (self-) deception and destructive addiction, we must care for others and their interests. In this way we remain grounded in reality. Likewise, when things are going well and we are enjoying all the glory that Neptune offers, we should remember not to keep it all to ourselves.

Neptune's 14-year transit through a particular zodiac sign determines the fashions, assumptions and beliefs of that generation. Taking account of these changes can be an invaluable aid in all kinds of social planning.

LORD OF THE MYSTERIOUS OCEANS
Neptune commands the mighty seas of our subconscious self. In these sometimes dangerous, unfathomable depths dwells our intuition as well as our inspiration and imagination.

PLUTO
GOD OF THE UNDERWORLD

THE ENERGY OF DEATH AND REBIRTH
* HOW WE TRANSFORM

Colours * Brown and maroon
Parts of body * Gonads, cells and reproductive system
Metal * Iron
Stones * Diamond, bloodstone topaz and agate
Modern * Atomic power

PLUTO'S REALM CONTAINS ALL that we most fear and seek to avoid. Yet its cycle teaches that we are not lost, whatever happens. The phoenix rising from its own ashes symbolizes the freedom that Pluto offers: the planet shows us that we can embrace radical change when we realize that even losing everything is an opportunity to start again, purified and in better shape. This is the natural way of the seasons of the year, when new life appears out of decay and death in an eternal cycle. Insecurity is born from a fear of what will happen next, of the unseen future. We cease to be the slave of the future (and also of the past) by living mindfully with insecurity from moment to moment.

Thinking in this way takes courage. What we hold most dear may seem to be on the line, yet by facing all life's "little deaths" and learning how to regenerate, we become more confident and free. In this sense, we come to understand why Hades, "the unseen", was also known as Pluto, the lord of wealth.

A body so small and far away is unlikely on its own to have much direct effect on Earth. Indeed, in 2006 the International Astronomical Union (IAU) downgraded Pluto's status to that of "dwarf planet". However, when used as a focus for reference, its cycle does appear to reflect patterns of major social upheaval (see the information about the influence of the planets, including Pluto, given in this book for each zodiac sign).

Events either side of Pluto's discovery by Clyde Tombaugh in 1930 suggest that the planet was appropriately named, especially the 1929 Wall Street Crash and the rule of dictators in the 1930s that culminated in World War II. This war ended with the nuclear devastation of Hiroshima and Nagasaki in 1945, which was set in train by the first splitting of the atom in 1932.

This event changed our relationship with the Earth for ever by giving us, for the first time, the power to destroy it if we so choose. The splitting of the atom led to the nuclear arms race and

YUM CIMIL
As Pluto ruled over the underworld (Hades), so the realm of Yum Cimil, the Mayan Lord of Death, was Xibalba. Souls could only reach this underworld by making a tortuous journey through oozing blood, bats and spiders.

The circular diagram (right) shows Pluto's 246-year cycle, seen from Earth. The length of time Pluto stays in each sign varies erratically from 14 to 30 years. The heliocentric diagram (below) shows the cause: Pluto's path moves in and out of Neptune's, so its annual apparent retrograde loops are also erratic. When fully inside Neptune's path, Pluto's loops just touch. When furthest out, the loops cross before the previous year's retrograde station, more so than Neptune's do. As a result, Pluto's cycle feels traumatic and unnerving.

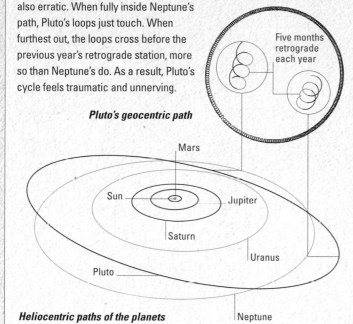

Five months retrograde each year

Pluto's geocentric path

Mars

Sun

Jupiter

Saturn

Uranus

Pluto

Neptune

Heliocentric paths of the planets

CHARACTERISTICS OF PLUTO

Pluto helps us to face our subconscious fears. Many of us still prefer to stay distant from anxiety and other negative aspects of our lives, either denying them or putting off dealing with them, even when we are aware that they exist. Or we may turn to simplistic doctrines or plain self-indulgence. But Pluto makes the problems we face difficult to avoid and deny. Its cycle constantly tempts, fuels and then undermines our obsessions.

With Pluto in each zodiac sign for a generation, we surrender to that period's excesses as though Pluto will stay there for ever. So, when its sign changes, we are left with major problems to sort out. It moved from Sagittarius to Capricorn during the 2008 start of the world economic crisis. Other Pluto sign changes marked two major wars and periods of social transformation. As well as describing the characteristics of our generation, Pluto's birth-chart position shows our individual vulnerabilities. It tests whether our fears are valid and how long the dangers we face may last. This in turn may reveal ways in which we can be courageous and successful. As the French scientist Louis Pasteur put it, "chance favours the prepared mind". Accepting missions that heal our lives is the happiest and safest way. Then Pluto cannot undermine us. It is on our side.

the intensely scientific world we live in today. More recently, in 1990, André Barbault's projection of a 2010 economic crisis (see page 22) depended upon Pluto's cycle.

The planet Pluto was so named because, like the Classical underworld, it is a distant, dark and cold world. Hades was the god of the underworld in Greek myth, and his name was also applied to his dark realm, the land of the dead. Perhaps because precious metals and minerals come from below the ground, the Greeks also called him Ploutos, from *plouton*, "wealth", hence his Roman name, Pluto. The lord of death and winter, Pluto was a gloomy and forbidding god but not an evil one, because death is inevitable and winter always brings the promise of spring. Few who entered his dark realm ever returned from it, exceptions being heroic figures such as Hercules, Persephone, Orpheus and Aeneas, who faced and mastered painful and unnatural horrors.

CYCLE OF LIFE
Contained within the bleakness of winter is the promise of spring. Pluto encourages us to embrace the ending of each stage of life, for the sake of the new beginning that is inevitably to follow.

UNDERSTANDING THE ZODIAC SIGNS

OUR FOREBEARS TRACKED THE PATHS of the Sun, the Moon and the visible planets against the background of other lights in the night sky, which moved so slowly they called them "fixed stars". To ancient eyes gazing on the sumptuous starlit nights of the pre-industrial age, many of these stars seemed to form patterns and even pictures. In their attempts to make sense of the cosmos, observers came to the conclusion that the heavens mirrored the Earth – which was assumed to be the centre of the universe – and that the skies were home to the gods and other creatures whose shapes could be discerned in the stars. Over many centuries and then millennia of heaven-watching, people accumulated and passed on a huge body of lore that encompassed precise measurements of stellar movements and planetary cycles, as well as myths and legends surrounding individual planets, stars and star patterns (constellations). Because the astronomical cycles that our forebears measured were seen from Earth to repeat in predictable patterns, it was considered that the heavenly bodies were also directly related to what went on here ("as above, so below"). In effect, the stories of the stars and planets became the stories of our ancestors' lives.

The heavens were understood as a great sphere with the Earth as its centre and the ecliptic – the Sun's apparent path around the Earth – as the celestial equator. The key constellations were those that touched the ecliptic, for within these celestial latitudes the Moon and the visible planets also moved. There were 12 such constellations, which gave their names to the signs of the zodiac (the word zodiac itself comes from the Greek *zodiakos kuklos*, "circle of animals", as most of the constellations are represented by creatures). However, the constellations and signs are not exactly the same. We may give a local name to a world time zone (for example, Greenwich), but that zone is much more than the place it is named after. The zodiac is not simply the constellations, but a reference framework that divides the celestial sphere into 12 equal segments, or signs, of 30° each.

A WORLD OF CORRESPONDENCES
This 16th-century ceiling fresco depicts the constellations in terms of the astrological creatures whose characteristics, over time, have become associated with different aspects of the human pysche.

In fact, the constellations vary in size and sometimes overlap. In many constellations, some of the stars that make up the apparent patterns of the zodiac are in reality light years apart and have no astronomical coherence.

Understanding of the meaning of the 12 signs, explained in the following pages, has been gained by relating thousands of years of earthly experience to the patterns in the movements of the Earth, Sun, Moon and planets as they pass through the signs. This knowledge is expressed through a remarkably rich, poetic language that is used to interpret precise astronomical observations.

KEY CONCEPTS

For each zodiac sign, a list of "key concepts" is given. These concepts are simple and easy to understand. Each sign is described according to its polarity (positive or negative), quality (cardinal, fixed or mutable) and associated element (fire, earth, air or water). Thus Cancer is "negative cardinal water" and Capricorn "negative cardinal earth". The significance of polarity, quality and element is explained on pages 52–9. However, even without knowing more we can see that "positive mutable fire" is likely to lead to a markedly different interpretation than "negative fixed earth".

These concepts lend colour and expression to the planets as they pass from one sign to another. Mercury represents our thoughts: in a fire sign, these turn to action; in an earth sign, to possessing; in an air sign, to words and new ideas; and when Mercury is passing through a water sign, our emotions tend to rule our decisions.

Another of the key concepts given for each sign is its planetary ruler. Sometimes the influence of a planet resonates so well with that of a particular sign that the planet is said to "rule" that sign.

For example, Mars rules Aries, because both reflect fiery and positive qualities. This is not the only way of judging how well a planet goes with a particular sign. Because the Sun is fiery, it is said to be "exalted" in Aries. On the other hand, the more sensitive and discriminating qualities of Venus can easily be diminished, "burned up", even dangerously infatuated in a fire sign. Venus is therefore said to be "in detriment" there. The discipline and structure associated with Saturn sits uneasily with Aries' sometimes fiercely turbulent energy, and hence Saturn is said to be "in fall" here. (Page 159 has a symbol table showing the planets that rule or are exalted, in detriment or in fall for each sign.)

The last key concepts are "beneficial" and "unbeneficial" ways of using the sign's potential for happy or unhappy outcomes.

DESCRIBED BY ALL THE SIGNS

Every chart contains all the zodiac signs; not just the Sun sign used for media "star signs". Every person and event needs to be described with reference to *all* the zodiac signs. Depending upon the positions of the planets, some signs are more emphasized in a birth chart than others. The astrologer's skill is to juxtapose the various elements and meanings to give an integrated understanding.

ASSOCIATIONS

Also given for each sign is a list of "associations", which add further depth and colour to an astrological reading. First comes the keyword, which synthesizes the beneficial and unbeneficial effects of the planets in a sign (see "Planets in Signs", opposite).

Another important association is favourite phrase. Bizarre though it may seem, those born under a particular sign are prone to repeating a particular significant phrase. Aquarians tend to say "I know", Scorpios "I want" and Taureans "I have".

There is deep, helpful meaning in the next association – aspiration – because it points to the quality that the sign finds hardest to master. With Aries, for instance, the aspiration is control, as Arians tend to be out of control. Aquarians tend to be distant and objective, so their aspiration is love. Achieving our sign's aspiration is a key stage in the process of personal evolution. The fully evolved person will attain all 12 aspirations and so come closer to the Divine.

A sign's associated colour, metal, stone, plant and herb can help to inform our understanding of zodiac or planetary meaning. Red, iron, bloodstone and pine, for example, make the raw and active energy of Aries live in our minds, while green, copper,

THE BODY'S VULNERABILITIES
This page from an astronomical calendar dating to *c.* 1424 shows the relation of the zodiac signs to the health of different parts of the body. For example, Leo was associated with heart attacks, Cancer with illnesses of the chest and stomach and Virgo with problems relating to the joints and nervous systems.

emerald and apple lend Taurus a softer, earthier and more creative feel.

As well as informing astrological meanings, these associations are often used together with ingestion and aroma in complementary therapies and even attempts at magical operation. For example, if Venus is afflicted in our birth chart or at a particular stage in our lives, some claim that it is helpful to wear an emerald, to dress in green, or to burn incense of rose or strawberry. If we are feeling in need of an energy boost, a bowl of Mars's nettle soup is full of nutritious iron. However we should be careful before placing too much reliance on these therapies, which involve much detail and embrace different systems.

The final associations are parts of the body and related vulnerabilities. These associations are based on ancient traditional ideas that allocated planets and signs to parts of the body. Because our forebears did not possess our astonishing medical expertise this does not mean that they knew nothing, and many of these associations remain remarkably valid. Thus an afflicted Mercury in Taurus may indicate throat strain, while Capricorn under stress may suggest problems to the bones and knees. Such assumptions are not set in stone, of course: an in-depth expert study of the birth chart is needed. Comparing planetary transits to birth charts may also indicate the timing of an illness and its treatment. For lay beginners, fully expert in neither astrology nor medicine, it is important to do no more than observe and take notes. Any genuine medical concerns that arise from a reading must be referred to a doctor who is qualified in modern medicine. And if he or she has a knowledge of astrology, then so much the better.

BRINGING OUT THE BEST IN OURSELVES: THE LABOURS OF HERCULES

Associated with each of the zodiac signs is one the 12 labours of the Ancient Greek hero Hercules. Apollodorus of Athens (born *c.* 180 BCE) wrote down this oral tradition, but neither his narratives, nor the order he gave to the labours, is universally accepted. In her book *The Labours of Hercules*, Alice A. Bailey altered Apollodorus's order when she interpreted the 12 labours as zodiac-based allegories to show how astrological understanding can liberate us from self-destructive patterns. This book follows Bailey's storylines and her order for the labours, except assigns the capture of the red cattle of Geryon to Capricorn and the overcoming of Cerberus to Pisces.

PLANETS IN SIGNS

We use the key concepts and associations to build a picture of how each planet is expressed in a particular sign (your planets' zodiac positions are shown in your birth chart). If you refer to this book's "planet-in-sign" pages that conclude each zodiac sign, you'll see that the explanation of each planet starts with a phrase that summarizes its beneficial and unbeneficial expression in that sign. For example, Mercury in Aries "communicates quickly [beneficial] and thoughtlessly [unbeneficial]". These extremes are then developed into fuller explanations.

It is important to allow for the length of the planetary cycle. The Moon takes just 29 days to pass through all 12 signs of the zodiac. The Sun, of course, takes exactly one year. With apparent retrograde motion, Mercury and Venus take around the same time. Mars's cycle is two years, Jupiter's 12 and Saturn's more than 29. Uranus, Neptune and Pluto, with cycles of 84, 165 and 256 years respectively, spend 7, 14 and 13–30 years in each zodiac sign. So, the inner planets describe individuals, while the outer planets describe whole generations and periods of history. Generational examples are therefore given in the "planet-in-sign" explanations for Uranus, Neptune and Pluto.

When assessing the strength of each planet, you should also allow for its pattern of retrogression (see page 33). This can suggest when individuals may hold back and/or be confident.

DIVISION BY 12

The great rose window in Seville's cathedral has 12 petals, symbolizing the 12 disciples of Christ. The number 12 has had an important cultural and spiritual significance throughout history. There are 12 hours, 12 months, 12 jury members and 12 times tables to learn by rote at school. Israel had 12 tribes, Christ had 12 disciples and Shia Islam has 12 imams. Buddhism has 12 links in the chain of causality enslaving us in the cycle of rebirth, as well as 12 Buddha deeds of liberation. To measure the movements of the bodies in the heavens, we project a frame of 12 zodiac signs, and for each day we construct 12 astrological houses to describe how the planets work in our lives.

THE POLARITIES
POSITIVE AND NEGATIVE

EACH OF THE 12 ZODIAC SIGNS is described as being either "positive" or "negative" in quality. Characteristics that are associated with these qualities are suggested opposite. It would be a mistake to assume that either quality is better than the other, or to see one as wrong and the other right. Duality – dividing the cosmos into opposing pairs – is the first and most fundamental distinction that our minds make in everything we do. Yes or no, happy or sad, full or empty, giving or taking – the list of polar opposites goes on and on. It is important to remember that all opposing pairs must be interdependent. Neither positive nor negative can exist alone because these terms are relative, just as there can be no light without dark, no silence without sound, and no male without female.

In Taoism this interdependence is expressed in the idea of yin and yang, the two opposing but complementary forces that interact eternally throughout the universe. Broadly, yin is passive, female and nocturnal, while yang is active, male and bright. The *taiji*, also known as the yin–yang symbol, is a powerful representation of interwoven opposites that symbolizes the cosmos as a dynamic balance of constant movement and change. Owing to our natural human insecurity,

ETERNAL DUALITY
The yin–yang symbol is a powerful visual representation of the duality that structures our universe. Within the yin (dark area) there is always the seed of yang (the light spot), while within the yang the seed of yin is always present.

our temptation is to seek absolute answers, but Taosim teaches that in doing so we close the door to real answers.

In "Putting the Pieces Together" (pages 150–67) we will learn how to assess, combine and synthesize the many elements of a birth chart, to make a coherent whole. We will see that all people and events are combinations of many interdependent "negative" and "positive" elements. Everyone's attitudes and reactions are different in different situations. Sometimes we may naturally take charge; at others times we prefer to be led. This is normal. Everyone is a mass of contradictions. The most hardened professional footballer can break down into tears in victory or throw a temper tantrum on the pitch when facing defeat. The kindest mother will fight like a tigress to defend her offspring.

Honouring the contradictory polarities that exist within all of us clarifies and pacifies any anxieties about sexual identity. Some men can be feminine some or all of the time; some women are masculine in nature. Most of us are characterized by both qualities. This need not be a crisis to struggle with, but rather an experience of variety that makes our life richer and wiser and sets us free to be all that we are.

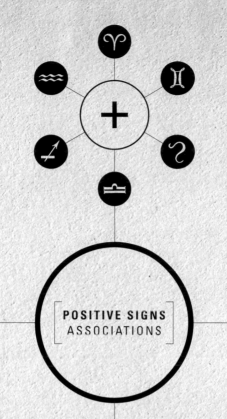

Signs: There are six positive signs of the zodiac: Aries, Gemini, Leo, Libra, Sagittarius and Aquarius.

Objects: The plug, the bolt, the match that lights the fire, the ignition that starts the engine, the car, plane or ship that cuts through air or water

Actions: Running, dancing, thinking, embracing, celebrating, exalting, challenging, fighting, pushing and pulling, taking up space

POSITIVE SIGNS
ASSOCIATIONS

Attitudes: The Sun shines for us, we view all as potentially bright and abundant. We thrust out with creative endeavour, without regard for barriers or reactions. We are certain that smiles, happiness and opportunity will not cease. Unstoppable and determined to succeed, we seek to further agendas by means of actions and intimidation, words and ideas. Not caring a jot for the consequences, we express raw archetypal male pride that brooks no resistance.

Signs: There are six negative signs: Taurus, Cancer, Virgo, Scorpio, Capricorn and Pisces.

Objects: The socket, the steel nut, the kindling, the engine sparked by the ignition, the space that air or water yield to the car, plane or ship

Actions: Experiencing, resting, absorbing, tempting, adorning the celebration, avoiding, being pushed and pulled, being the space taken up

NEGATIVE SIGNS
ASSOCIATIONS

Attitudes: Open, insatiable, deliciously receptive, needing and accepting, we absorb and embrace, offering reassurance to encourage more and more giving. We are always full of anticipation and ready for completion, but unlikely to feel we have achieved it. Reflective, critical and monitoring, we react seductively to encourage improvement in quality and experience, but rarely seem satisfied. Ever ready for more, this is the raw expression of archetypal female nurturing and need.

THE TRIPLICITIES

SIGNS OF EARTH, AIR, FIRE AND WATER

THE PERIODIC TABLE lists an ever-increasing number of elements – some 118 in eleven categories at the present time. However, for thousands of years various cultures have explained physical manifestation with reference to just four or five basic elements or principles. In ancient Western traditions, including astrology, there are said to be four elements: earth, air, fire and water. Indian Ayurveda includes a fifth element – ether – that is the source of the other four. The Chinese tradition also posits five elements: air, earth, fire, metal and wood.

The four elements are very different to the elements of the Periodic Table. They are not substances but archetypal concepts that cannot exist separately from one another. "Earth", "air", "fire" and "water" are the names given to interdependent principles or forces that combine to form everything that exists; and everything that exists contains all elements in various proportions. It is the dominance of an element that gives each phenomenon its unique character. These phenomena include the 12 zodiac signs. On the following pages, the dominant element is given for each sign. Although it is a key factor in the sign's character, the dominant element must be considered in combination with other factors, such as the sign's polarity and quality: a negative cardinal earth sign differs markedly from a negative mutable earth sign.

FIRE

Fire can ignite instantly, then spread and consume all in its path. The essence of the element of fire is action and movement; saying "yes", often without a thought for the consequences. But fire is the initiating spark of *all* that is created, and that means also gentler possibilities. The character of fire can be revealed in many subtle ways: when we walk, run or dance; when we pick something up and put it down; and when we engage in all kinds of sport. These minor actions are all part of embracing life. Action can be expressed in many different ways: it may be constructive, creative, joyous, loving or triumphant; or it may be destructive, angry, brutal or violent.

Fire is an element that builds up and breaks down, and it also intimidates others into action, even if it is just by reminding them "don't get too close to the fire". Fire also brings light and life-giving warmth. In pre-modern Western physiology, the fire element is represented in the human body by choler or yellow bile, and a preponderance of it was manifested in a "choleric" temperament that was quick to anger, hasty and prone to pride.

In the I Ching, the ancient Chinese divinatory text, fire's gentle positive power is beautifully described as "clinging fire" and the "light-giver" that is the "second daughter" of heaven and Earth. Fire is thus linked with insight and enlightenment, with seeing what is and what needs to be done.

EARTH

The element of earth represents the material world. In nature, earth is the raw resources from which much of our material existence is derived – from food to metals – and the place that subsumes life forms after death. The element earth is also linked to wealth and possessions, and hence rules all business activity. To succeed in business, we need to be able to manipulate a range of resources and systems. Then we can generate riches, as well as products and services that can be used by others.

FIRE AND EARTH

The fire element stands for action: fire's violence that prepares the ground for new growth or the more subtle energy of our movements. Earth is reflected in the world that nurtures us, in our appetites and possessions.

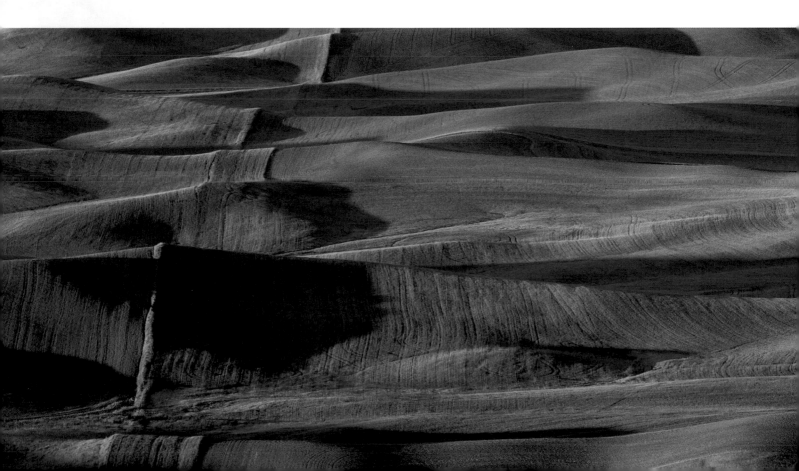

An excessive appetite for the riches of the earth can seduce us into acquisitiveness and indulgence. We may become bloated in body, our houses cluttered with unnecessary things. Consumption can be a deceptive path that leads to exhaustion and ultimately even self-destruction.

In pre-modern Western physiology, the earth element was represented by melancholia, literally "black bile". An excess of melancholia was manifested as a melancholic temperament – gloomy, despondent or depressed. In Ayurveda, the solidity of the earth suggests stability, permanence and rigidity. So, the earth element relates to the more stable parts of the body, such as bones and teeth. Traditional Chinese thought makes clear distinctions between the soil itself, what lies within it and what grows from it, distinguishing the elements of earth, metal and wood.

AIR

The air we breathe appears to have no substance or form, and nor do our thoughts and anxieties. Hence the element air is related to these mental processes and, like the winged god Hermes or Mercury, to all forms of communication. Air describes our ideas and the words we find to express them, the stories we tell, the letters and emails we send, the books and articles we write, the news we relate. Air also signifies the reassurance that leads to understanding and forgiveness, and the explanations and arguments we urge upon others. On the other hand, air can also relate to mental anxiety and neurosis. Misused, it can generate the lies, "spin" and manipulation that draw us onto the rocks of disappointed hopes.

In pre-modern Western physiology, the air element is represented by blood (*sanguis* in Latin). A predominance of air was manifested in a sanguine temperament that was cheerful, energetic, courageous – and perhaps, like the wind, even unruly. The I Ching described the contrasting characteristics of the air element, from the "arousing thunder" to the "gentle, penetrating breeze". In Ayurveda, because air is gaseous, mobile and dynamic, it is seen as enabling the body's transfer of energy. It brings oxygen from the lungs to the bloodstream and then to the brain, so that we can think and control our actions.

WATER

The waters of the Earth, from the tiniest trickling mountain stream to the largest raging river, all eventually flow into the oceans or evaporate back into the air to fall as rain and flow again. In this way water connects and unifies all that lives. It is also the source of life, since all life originated from the sea. Water is our very being, making up a high percentage of our bodies.

Water buoys up, relaxes, heals and nurtures. Like a caring mother, it finds a way around any obstacle and, however slowly, wears down anything hard or harsh standing in its path. Just as water can clear the most resistant blockages in nature, the element of water is the force that helps us to find clarity and a way through emotional blockages, so that we may move forward with our lives. Like the waters of the womb, water as the force of nurture allows us to answer the needs of ourselves and others. Water is the element that draws us together.

As the ruler of our emotions, water is a powerful force that can also cause us to accumulate anxiety and resentment when we feel manipulated, used or abused. As flood waters build up behind a dam and eventually overwhelm it, our emotional pressure can burst out uncontrollably, leaving hurt that is hard to heal. With awareness, we can use the positive energy of water to make cracks in the dam of pent-up emotions and relieve the pressure.

In pre-modern Western physiology, the water element is represented by phlegm, and those with a predominance of phlegm were said to have a "phlegmatic" temperament that was rational, calm, considered and slow to anger. This was believed to arise from a healthy relationship between the brain and the lungs. The I Ching understood the potential extremes of the water element as the "abysmal dangerous water" and "the joyous lake". In Ayurveda, water plays a key role in blood and other internal bodily fluids. It brings energy, carries away waste, regulates temperature and helps in the fight against disease.

AIR AND WATER

Air cannot be seen or grasped, and so our thoughts and words move like the wind and change as do clouds in the sky. Water rules emotions that understand, unify, nurture and heal or, equally, accumulate to overwhelm us, as a powerful river carries away all that lies in its path.

THE QUADRUPLICITIES
SIGNS OF CARDINAL, FIXED AND MUTABLE

EACH ZODIAC SIGN IS SAID to be predominantly "cardinal", "fixed" or "mutable". These complementary qualities, or "quadruplicities", may be compared to the spoon, bowl and ingredients that are all needed to prepare a cake for the oven. The various ingredients (mutable) – flour, butter, sugar, eggs, dried fruit and so on – are of little use without a mixing bowl to hold them in (fixed) or a spoon (cardinal) to stir them up. Similarly, the bowl is of no use without the ingredients and the spoon. Whichever quality dominates a sign, for any action – or life – to be fully effective, all three are needed.

CARDINAL ACTIVATION
The spark that lights the fire, the touch that strengthens confidence, the idea that opens the door, the endurance that enables success: cardinal force can make anything possible.

CARDINAL: THE SPOON

The word cardinal comes from Latin *cardo* ("hinge"), hence cardinal signs are those that mark the turning of the year and the start of the seasons: Aries, Cancer, Libra and Capricorn. For this reason cardinal signs (formerly also called "moveable") are said to possess the vital force that "gets the show on the road", initiating and leading, providing the first spark of an idea that makes us think and plan, or the reassurance or encouragement that confirms that we have the support of others. Cardinal activation is often physical, like the spoon that stirs things up, the encouraging hand that restrains our hastiness or the shove that helps the parachutist out of the plane.

In the abstract form of pure loving-kindness, cardinal force can energize us to move mountains, but we must beware of emotional manipulation that inculcates a sense of fear, guilt or obligation. While the hope for material reward or the fear of loss are powerful common motivations, we would be deluded to believe that permanent security is possible. All we can do is control our own systems of management, to be the cardinal point of our own world.

If taken to excess, cardinal force can agitate and overwhelm. To be told too often that all is well can convince us that it is not, and so create insecurity. To be pushing hither and thither and never be allowed to rest; to be continually reminded of our responsibilities, even guilt; to be constantly told what to do – all these are counterproductive.

FIXED: THE BOWL

The four "fixed" signs are Taurus, Leo, Scorpio and Aquarius, and as the term suggests they are associated with deep-rooted firmness, stability and perseverance. These signs are the holders, the ones that provide the essential focus, form and structure that enable the world to function. They are the bowl that contains the ingredients for mixing, then the cake tin that holds the mixture for baking; they are the wood that retains the screw; they are the coach that keeps the team together; they are the CEO who puts in place an overarching plan. Being born under a fixed sign often means feeling compelled to acquire the knowledge to solve all problems and to master everything that can possibly be discovered.

Of course, having the inclination, flair and will to be the fixed centre of things brings with it the risk that we may become intransigent, rigid and inflexible: convinced of our own rightness, deaf to the views of others and closed to approaches other than our own. Being too fixed leads to sterility and inactivity. If other signs do not hand over all power to their fixed fellows, perspective will be retained and the presence of the fixed sign will remain a beneficial one.

MUTABLE: THE INGREDIENTS

Gemini, Virgo, Sagittarius and Pisces are the "mutable" signs, occupying positions in the year when the seasons are beginning to change. It is sometimes said that these signs are less stable than the others and possess neither the single-minded will of the fixed signs nor the powerful initiative of the cardinals. On the other hand, the strength of these signs lies in their very mutability. Those born under them often have the flexibility and resilience to accept and withstand the storms of life.

As ice, when heated, turns to water and steam, so mutability creates the variety of our lives. An enemy can become a friend; a stranger, our lover. Many ideas come together to create a book, a body of knowledge. Dissolving sugar sweetens our cup of tea; medicine eases pain and heals. If we listen to each other, we can address all our needs.

However, this does not mean that all change is for the best, to be accepted without question. Those born under mutable signs should not accept every adverse eventuality as inevitable, nor yield to pressure without complaint. Change cannot be avoided, but sometimes we can determine the nature of changes within our own sphere. If we feel a persistent pain, we can ask a doctor to

check us over. If our boat is heading for rapids and we have a chance to grab an overhanging branch, we would be foolish not to attempt that bold leap. By drawing upon the stability and energy of the cardinal and fixed signs, mutable people can acquire a rounded strength that is second to none. By providing the resources in return, they bring riches to what would otherwise be a barren world.

MUTABLE RESOURCES
Ice softening into water, minds melting into understanding, the accommodating response that gives us control, the clay yielding the form of a pot – all are the mutable materials from which our lives are made.

ARIES

Polarity * Positive
Quality * Cardinal
Element * Fire
Ruler * Mars

Beneficial * Confidence *
Courage * Pioneer spirit

Unbeneficial * Impulsiveness *
Impatience * Unreliability

ARIES – THE FIRST SIGN OF THE ZODIAC

ARIES SYMBOLIZES THE VERY FIRST SPARK of creation. It rushes to activate, as if the coming into being of everything else depends upon it. This is hardly surprising, with all four of its key concepts expressing positivity.

The sign of the early Northern spring, Aries is like the seed bursting out from its pod, oblivious to danger and not knowing whether it can be sustained by the unfamiliar, alien environment in which it finds itself. Its great courage has the force of a bulldozer to break new ground, or of a machete-wielding pioneer cutting through virgin jungle. Not that the energy of Aries is always so brutal or lacking in forethought. As the embodiment of renewal, Aries can also express the gentle, powerful promise of an innocent newborn lamb, taking its awkward first steps.

Aries is at its strongest when casing back and focused, when tempering its actions with intelligence. Unfortunately, it is often easier for headstrong Aries to express its immature and reckless side, leaving behind a trail of faded enthusiasms. Uncomfortable

CREATIVE SPARK
An early 18th-century Persian image of Aries the ram. Headstrong when fired up with excitement about a new project, Aries needs that initial impetus to get going as a prerequisite to achieving anything of substance.

with making considered emotional judgments, Mars-ruled Aries can go to war on the slightest provocation, justifying its hasty actions on the grounds that there is no time to ask questions.

Aries is heroic, at one with the cutting edge of danger and the entrepreneurial side of business. Arian confidence empowers everyone with whom it comes into contact. All but the most timid will be encouraged to follow Aries – initially, at least. For unlike Scorpio, the fixed water sign also ruled by Mars, Aries works in bursts that can leave others unsatisfied. Aries can push people into decisions that may not ultimately be in their best interest, and the Arian urge to press ahead into pastures new may leave them in the lurch. Action needs to be followed through in order to create the strong base from which pioneering efforts are to be sustained. This is where the next sign, Taurus, comes in.

ASSOCIATIONS

Keyword * Urgently
Favourite phrase * I am
Aspiration * Control
Colour * Red
Metal * Iron
Stones * Sardonyx and bloodstone

Parts of body * Head and face
Vulnerabilities * Headaches and anger
Plants * Pine and cypress
Herbs * Geranium and nettles

THE RAM

ARIES DECODED

THE ESSENCE OF INITIATION

The Arian motto could easily be "nothing ventured, nothing gained" – whether for good or ill. Life never seems dull for Arians and those who follow them. Assertive, independent, courageous and adventurous, these freedom-loving natural leaders are always caught up in new experiences. They enjoy initiating enterprises and rising to challenges, and will face any obstacles head-on.

Of course, life is not always that simple. However hard Arians assume the right to push ahead, this may not lead immediately to a preferred or expected outcome. That may require far more effort

RISING TO THE CHALLENGE

The vibrant energy of Aries is most effective when this sign has something to work for, a challenge to rise to or a sudden crisis – like a race to run, a tree to fell or a team to marshal and encourage.

than Arians are typically willing to give. Venus is in detriment in Aries, its influence weak and hence easy to ignore: this often leads Arians into not consulting the opinions of others, although these may be vital for the success of a project. By rushing headlong into things, they may overlook far easier ways of accomplishing them. With Saturn also ill-placed (in fall), Aries has little time for the persistence and solid structure that are needed for truly sustainable success. As their initial flush of enthusiasm wanes, Arians easily become bored or impatient and end up either leaving schemes unfinished or rushing to complete them hastily and carelessly.

However, when things go wrong or not as planned, Aries quickly returns to the positive. Whatever Arians' flaws, their courage, raw energy and natural confidence have a value that cannot be overestimated. With their "give it a go" attitude Arians respond readily to any dare or challenge, when most other signs would spend far too long anxiously dithering.

HERCULES CAPTURES THE MARES OF DIOMEDES

The first labour of the hero Hercules was simple, but required great power and courage: to capture the fierce man-eating mares belonging to King Diomedes and so make safe the land that was being terrorized by these ferocious beasts.

To accomplish the task, Hercules called for his dear friend Abderis. They followed the mares and quickly cornered, caught and tethered them. Hercules yelled with joy, but soon tired of the task of driving them toward the gate of Diomedes' palace. Impatient pride made him prefer to lead the way, leaving Abderis to drive the mares and follow the path set out by Hercules. But on his own Abderis was too weak and fearful. In no time the mares had escaped, trampling Hercules' old friend and leaving him mortally wounded.

Humbled and grief-stricken, Hercules returned to the task. He again caught the horses and this time drove them through the gate. But by this time his friend lay dead.

An incisive parable, this story clearly shows the Arian predicament of power and weakness. Everything appears easy at the beginning, but initial success is so seductive that we tend to "take our eye off the ball"; or, like a mountaineer who has reached a narrow summit, we take one careless step back and fall to disaster. By seriously and clearly assessing the risks of failure, we will remember to consolidate and so make every success permanent.

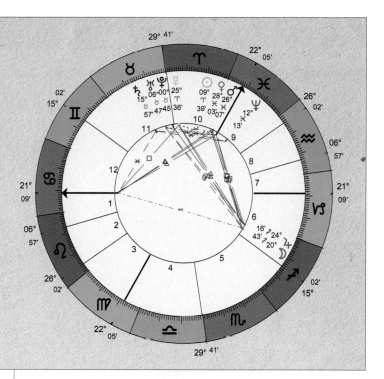

BIRTH CHART ⋆ VINCENT VAN GOGH

Born at 1100 LMT on 30 March 1853 at Zundert, Netherlands, Vincent van Gogh expressed his Aries Sun through ruling Mars close to Venus in Pisces by the chart's Midheaven. This explains his fame and notoriety as a deeply passionate but self-destructive genius (and supports French astro-researcher Michel Gauquelin's claim that Mars

near here indicates success through striving for recognition). The shape of the head in van Gogh's self-portrait reflects the Aries symbol, while the red colour of the beard and intensity of the brush strokes express the urgent sensitivity of Aries' ruling Mars in Pisces squared by a Sagittarian Moon. The closeness of Venus to all this explains the hurt and angry disappointment in the artist's eyes.

SUSTAINING THE POWER

Freedom on its own is too intangible to satisfy Arians for long. Sparks of excitement will soon set them going again. It is also crucial for them to plan what to do when their initial enthusiasm flags, as it surely will. This has to come from themselves. Well-meaning attempts to lecture Arians about responsibility fall on deaf ears. At best an Arian will grudgingly accept our counsel, but more likely it will lead to an argument and the Arian walking away.

There are two ways for Arians to prevent this happening. One is to take up projects that offer constant new challenges, such as working in sales or playing competitive sports.

Alternatively, Arians can try letting the need for sustained effort itself become the

THE RAM WITH THE GOLDEN FLEECE
This 19th-century illustration shows Phrixos at Colchis, sacrificing to Zeus the magic ram that had saved him. Later, his cousin Jason sailed on a quest to retrieve its golden fleece.

enterprise. Before starting any project, they could accept the necessity of switching off impatience and boredom. Developing this capacity can awaken the deepest Arian potential. An Aries operating at this level has the power to accomplish almost anything.

HEROIC ENTERPRISE

In the Neo-Babylonian zodiac, the first point of Aries came to represent the vernal equinox. Ever since, the Ram's constellation has played a key initiating role. In Classical mythology, Aries was associated with heroic enterprise. It was the magic flying ram with fleece of gold that Zeus sent to save Helle and Phrixos (King Boeotia's children) from their murderous stepmother. As they crossed between Europe and Asia, Helle fell off the ram's back and perished in the sea, in the waters we know as the Hellespont. The ram then took Phrixos safely to the land of Colchis at the eastern end of the Black Sea.

The Sun creates confidently and impulsively. With the Sun strong in this sign, Arians reassure people with an air of attractive optimism. It is a pleasure to follow them. They are fun to be with and will face and bravely overcome any difficulties. However, Arians can easily be distracted into something different and leave people and projects in the lurch. If constantly motivated to maintain interest in their missions in life, they become a source of fresh hope wherever they go.

The Moon reacts quickly and impatiently. Those with the Moon in their sign have a tendency to agree right away. They are happy to give a positive push to most things, providing this does not threaten their freedom of action or take away personal control over their own destiny. The sensitive Moon does not find it easy to express itself in fiery, cardinal Aries, so inappropriate reactions and irritation are likely, often leading to misunderstandings.

[THE SUN]

[THE MOON]

PLANETS IN
ARIES

[MERCURY]

[MARS]

[VENUS]

Mercury communicates quickly and thoughtlessly. Quicksilver agreement that hurries agendas along and bypasses alternatives can open doors to amazing possibilities. This is a good way to get things started – but it can leave ends untied. With Mercury in Aries, plans can be too individualistic and undisciplined to stand up on their own. Also, Mercury here can lead us to speak or make decisions without thinking, which can potentially upset the apple cart.

Venus loves innocently and impulsively. Venus's main need is to experience and express appreciation, to satisfy and feel satisfied, to comfort and be comforted. It is in detriment in Mars-ruled Aries, for while Mars will excite with seductive possibilities, it can also overwhelm and threaten all that is most beautiful. Venus here is prone to infatuation and the temptation to follow too readily. At the other extreme, it can feel ignored or even brutalized.

Mars acts bravely and aggressively. Here in its fiery home Mars rules supreme, acting on impulse and pushing all before it. Such is its confidence that barriers are not considered. If they do arise, Mars's naturally aggressive reaction breaks them down with little thought for the consequences. Such a courageous, if headstrong, disposition is ideally suited to action sports and adventure – anything that requires supreme confidence and unquestioning bursts of energy.

Jupiter expands spontaneously and irresponsibly. In Aries, Jupiter's natural optimism can be supremely glorious, if not always realistic. It is driven by the simple idealistic belief that freedom of action leads to truth and so carries all before it – given the opportunity and the chance to grow in their own way, people and situations will turn out for the best. While wasteful, uncompleted projects are very possible, this approach can often lead to remarkable advances.

Saturn controls strongly and with difficulty. In Aries Saturn is in fall, and people with the planet here find that everything they do seems to begin with problems. Nothing comes easily and they constantly feel held back. They are often the first to set up structures and establish guidelines, which can be a burdensome and lonely responsibility but also a rewarding one. Avoiding resentment and being patient in adversity leads to the satisfaction that comes from steady progress.

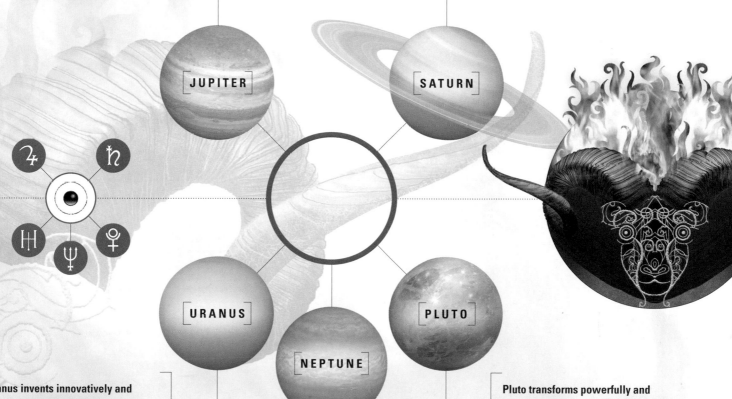

JUPITER

SATURN

URANUS

NEPTUNE

PLUTO

Uranus invents innovatively and destructively. When Uranus moves through Aries, revolutionary social changes make radical alterations to previously held assumptions. But many changes are ill-considered and indiscriminate, and lead to unfortunate results. The history of Uranus's last two transits through Aries (1845–52 and 1928–35) shows this clearly – periods, respectively, of social unrest and revolution, and of totalitarianism and economic woes.

Neptune inspires optimistically and over-idealistically. With Neptune here we enthuse over beliefs. 1533–48 brought fanatical religious struggles and the dissolution of the English monasteries, while 1697–1712 seeded the Enlightenment. In 1861–75 there was extremism over slavery and new colonial and industrial "utopias", and the Theosophical Society was founded. Seeing deeply rather than believing fanatically is the key to genuine understanding.

Pluto transforms powerfully and frighteningly. Pluto's transit through Aries can upset past social assumptions. Society's courageous agents of change can use such times to seed new futures. During the 1577–1608 transit, the Bourbon dynasty began in France, while England's defeat of the Spanish Armada sowed the seeds of its imperial power. During 1822–53 world financial upheaval and radical movements helped to shape the relative racial and social liberation we enjoy today.

TAURUS

Polarity ∗ Negative	**Beneficial** ∗ Strong
Quality ∗ Fixed	∗ Nourishing ∗ Creative
Element ∗ Earth	**Unbeneficial** ∗ Possessive
Ruler ∗ Venus	∗ Stubborn ∗ Self-indulgent

✝AURUS – THE SECOND SIGN OF THE ZODIAC

TAURUS EPITOMIZES THE RICH BEAUTY, fullness and strength of the material world. The key concepts of this sign – negative fixed earth – are a necessary antidote to those of trailblazing Arians. In Taurus we stop, take stock, consolidate and create something of real and lasting beauty.

The way of Taurus is essentially that of soft, well-watered and fertile ground that embraces and nurtures a seedling's roots, which in turn sustain the plant through its life above ground. An approach involving nurture and firmness of purpose applies not only to horticultural activity: Taureans are often adept at cookery, pottery and other handicrafts, the practicalities of business and the study of history – especially the history of how societies hold together and develop. They take joy in the ownership of beautiful things such as paintings, sculpture, furniture and clothing.

Taurus rules the consumption as well as the creation of food. It enjoys not only the rich tastes and aromas, but also the experience of having a satisfying and nourishing meal within the body.

TAURUS THE BULL
The power, determination and artistry of a typical Taurean are captured in this image from an Islamic manuscript of 1498.

However, consumption of one kind or another can become addictive for Taureans. They can find it difficult to relinquish material possessions and also control. Concerns for security can dominate their life and intrude on the lives of others. As taking risks could lead to loss, Taurean decision-making can be inflexible and bound up in familiar, established traditions.

For Taureans, beauty can be both a blessing and a curse. It is a blessing when Taurus is not enslaved to the idea of possessing it. For the superficial beauty of the material world is impermanent; a more lasting beauty lies deeper, in eternal truths, as Keats wrote: "Truth is beauty, beauty truth, – that is all / Ye know on earth, and all ye need to know."

ASSOCIATIONS

Keyword ∗ Realistically	**Stone** ∗ Emerald
Favourite phrase ∗ I have	**Parts of body** ∗ Throat and neck
Aspiration ∗ Obedience	**Vulnerabilities** ∗ Colds and obesity
Colour ∗ Green	**Plants** ∗ Roots of all plants; ash tree
Metal ∗ Copper	**Herbs** ∗ Apple and beans

THE BULL
TAURUS DECODED

THE ESSENCE OF INGESTION

Two of the central Taurean characteristics are strength and intransigence. At best Taurean solidity is a fount of goodness: receiving, absorbing into itself, transforming and then giving back nourishment for the benefit of all. Taurus is realistic and businesslike, but also materially creative and artistic. Taureans prize their possessions, because they represent what they value most.

An earth sign ruled by Venus, Taurus shares the fruits of reliable relationships and business success, both for pleasure and to ensure security. The more we interact creatively with the environment, the more beautiful and sustainable the world we create will be.

Taurus will "stick to its guns" in any argument. With Mars in detriment, Taurus will firmly define and defend boundaries. Even when in the wrong, a Taurean may argue for the indefensible, standing tenaciously against any use of force and refusing to submit to emotional intimidation.

EGYPT'S BULL GOD
The stout heart, power and fertility of a bull made Apis an appropriate symbol of the pharaoh. The ruler's protector after death, Apis was the only Egyptian deity depicted as a complete animal and never shown with a human head.

HERCULES CAPTURES THE CRETAN BULL

Still saddened and chastened by the death of Abderis (see page 62), Hercules embarked upon his second labour: to save a sacred bull from being sacrificed by Minos, King of Crete, and to deliver it to the safekeeping of the Cyclopes. Avoiding the lure of the king's maze (the Labyrinth), Hercules instead followed the light of the star on the bull's forehead. He captured the bull, mounted it and rode it across the sea to the holy place of the Cyclopes. Watching Hercules singing on his way, the Cyclopes remarked on the hero's strength, light and speed.

Alice A. Bailey emphasizes the two great lessons of this task that express the essence of Taurus at its very best. First is the need for proportion: just the right amount of strength and effort to complete the task. Second is the importance of light (the light of spiritual insight, or enlightenment) if we are to find our path out of the trap of materialistic indulgence. "Within the light shall you see light; walk in that light and there see light. Your light must brighter shine."

GIVING AND RECEIVING

With the Moon exalted in their sign, Taureans respond positively to glamour and charm. Restaurant meetings over a good meal should go well. Taureans enjoy both giving and receiving rich gifts; they give without obligation and receive with the joy of mere possession. In business, however, they will drive a hard bargain, seeking to gain the advantage over others and then ensuring that they stick firmly to what is agreed.

Problems in relationships with Taureans often emerge from their excessive need to acquire for the sake of it. At their worst, they can become stuck in patterns of material self-indulgence that include overeating and obesity, and ride roughshod over the feelings of others in order to satisfy their appetites. Victims of their own possessiveness and trapped in their personal viewpoints, such Taureans need a true friend to guide them to see beyond personal gratification.

FERTILITY AND STRENGTH

In Babylonian times Taurus was the start of the new zodiac year, the sun's presence in the sign coinciding with the spring equinox. This may have reinforced the bull's role in many cultures as a symbol of fertility, growth and power. Ancient Egyptians worshipped Apis, the bull god associated with the virility and strength of the pharaoh.

Ancient Greek mythology associated Taurus with the Cretan bull captured by Hercules from King Minos. This bull was the father of the famous Minotaur. Taurus has also been linked to another bull myth involving Crete and Minos – that of Zeus and Europa. Disguised as a friendly bull, Zeus permitted the beautiful princess Europa to climb upon his back. He strolled to the

ABDUCTION OF EUROPA
Titian was one of several artists to depict this story. Europa was playing with her attendants on the beach when Zeus appeared to her in the guise of a gentle, snow-white bull, with hoofs of mother-of-pearl.

seashore, then suddenly charged into the waves and carried the princess across the sea to Crete, where Zeus returned to his normal form and seduced her. King Minos was one of their offspring. Zeus later placed a bull among the stars as the constellation of Taurus.

In India, the cow is revered as a maternal care-giver. As well as providing dairy products and tilling the fields, the cow produces dung that is a source of fuel and fertilizer. Furthermore, the burning of cow dung as fuel creates an insect-repellent smoke and leaves ash for the fields.

BIRTH CHART ✳ LEONARDO DA VINCI

The great artist and polymath was born at 2140 LMT on 23 April 1452 (Gregorian calendar) at Vinci, Italy. Leonardo's exceptionally exalted birth chart draws its strength from his Taurean Sun in the creative Fifth House in a positive sextile to ruling Jupiter and Moon in Pisces. The enduring fame of his creative genius is indicated by ruling Venus in Sixth House Taurus, harmoniously trined to Tenth House Neptune. With the Aquarian Mars sextiled to Mercury in Aries, Leonardo is also celebrated as a scientist; he was a pioneer in anatomy and a designer of flying machines and many other extraordinarily prescient devices.

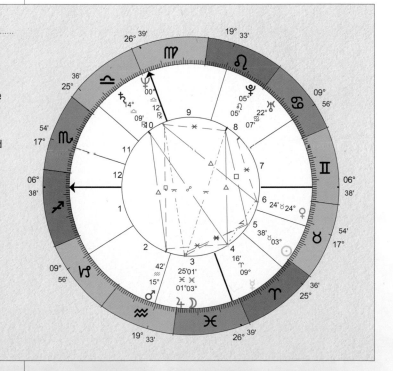

The Sun creates practically and greedily. Loving to immerse themselves in rich, beautiful things, Taureans need to feel they are in control of resources and systems. Because they discipline their world to be reliable and methodical, others come to depend upon them. However, the power this brings must be used for the right reasons. Possessive, self-indulgent attitudes may not bring Taureans security, but merely bloat and clutter their life.

The Moon reacts charmingly and needily. We are drawn to people with a Taurean Moon by the reassuring way they appreciate us. They love to provide and share the pleasures of life, especially cultural outings, and to compare notes over a meal afterwards. Although a support in times of need, their apparent dependability may be a projection of their own need for the comfort of reliable routines. This could lead to uncertainty over who is supporting whom.

[THE SUN]

[THE MOON]

PLANETS IN
TAURUS

[MERCURY]

[MARS]

[VENUS]

Mercury communicates firmly and insistently. Slaves to tradition, people with Mercury in Taurus stick to what they believe, preferring judgments that have stood the test of time. Only reliable alternatives based on carefully structured and presented arguments might change their minds. Until such alternatives are available, they will argue determinedly for existing approaches – even when they themselves are beginning to doubt their validity.

Venus loves beautifully and self-indulgently. Venus rules Taurus. When the planet is placed here it comfortably enriches love and devotion for all the beautiful people and things that fill our hearts with joy. We feel that our world is reliable and secure. Affection and creative power provide the resources, strength and time for projects to grow into splendid completion. However, with so much readily available, it is important to temper temptation. Satisfying appetites is fine, but beware of excess.

Mars acts firmly and truculently. Mars's martial force struggles with, and gains power from, the fixed aspect of Taurus. It symbolizes a valuable ally: strong and passionately determined, brave and sure in defence, capable of moving mountains when attacking. Being in detriment here, it tends to indicate obsession with, even ravishing of, Venusian beauty. People with an excessive Martian tenacity can tend to ride roughshod over gentle solutions, and to fail to see the obvious truth.

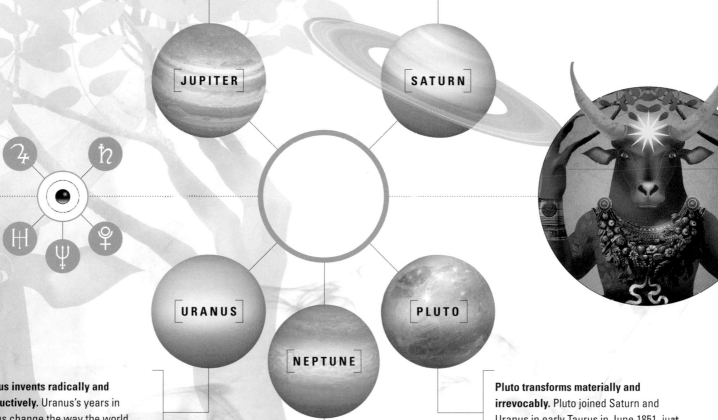

Jupiter expands physically and indulgently. Jupiter in Taurus searches for the certainty of solid principles, seeking a system of permanent truth that will never let anyone down. Such idealism encourages a following and enables empire-building in business and politics. It promises to expand opportunities and justice, but can also be irresponsible. By going too far, offering too much and forcing too hard, it can lead to excess that overwhelms its perpetrators – and everything else.

Saturn controls methodically and intransigently. Methods of control dominate the world when Saturn is in this sign, with radically different, even conflicting attempts at laying firm foundations on offer. During 1939–42, 1969–72 and 1998–2000, varying visions of Saturnian "common sense" sought to contain the excesses of other planetary cycles. Restriction, while tempering excess, can also prevent creative innovation and make solutions harder to find.

JUPITER

SATURN

URANUS

NEPTUNE

PLUTO

Uranus invents radically and destructively. Uranus's years in Taurus change the way the world works. New machines are invented. Citizens rebel. Social values are turned upside down. We are still dealing with the change brought about by the last two transits of Uranus in Taurus. In the period 1851–9, as the USA expanded west and struggled to deal with slavery, the first drilling for oil took place. During the transit of 1934–42, the world erupted into war.

Neptune inspires profoundly and indulgently. With Neptune in Taurus, society seeks spiritual experience in material ways. When expressed through ruling Venus, as was the art of the late Renaissance and the Pre-Raphaelites, it creates glorious beauty. With Venus ignored, beliefs become dogmatic, as under England's Protestant King Edward VI and his Catholic sister, Mary I. The last Neptune transit in Taurus (1874–89) saw the beginning of a revival in esoteric spirituality and increased acceptance of Darwinism.

Pluto transforms materially and irrevocably. Pluto joined Saturn and Uranus in early Taurus in June 1851, just after the opening of London's Great Exhibition. This marked the start of a period, lasting until 1884, of rapid invention, social change and expansion throughout Europe and America that challenged the status quo and made past assumptions unsustainable. This created the space for the new discoveries and political upheavals that were to shape our current world.

GEMINI

Polarity ∗ Positive
Quality ∗ Mutable
Element ∗ Air
Ruler ∗ Mercury

Beneficial ∗ Intelligent
∗ Communicating ∗ Curious

Unbeneficial ∗ Restless
∗ Gossiping ∗ Neurotic

GEMINI – THE THIRD SIGN OF THE ZODIAC

GEMINI'S FLEXIBLE INTELLIGENCE is naturally inclined to say yes. The excited spontaneity of this sign can make almost anything seem possible. Intensely curious, Geminis read avidly, exchange information and engage in conversations to explore and play with ideas. This sign asks questions, fits together the answers and communicates with as many people as possible. There is also a readiness to consider opposites, turn the "truth" upside down and change minds. This can seem no more than restless flitting from one idea or person to another, idle gossip or obsession with the media-driven celebrity culture. Exactly what do Geminis believe or wish to do? Where does their loyalty lie? Is all their pleasant reassurance no more than easy-sounding words?

While it is important to avoid such pitfalls, to see the sign as no more than this misunderstands and devalues its vital role in our lives. Its insatiable curiosity gathers information that connects people and ideas, and brings alternatives that can change lives for

THE SICKLE AND THE LYRE
In this medieval illustration, the twins exchange practicality (the sickle) with art (the lyre). A salutary lesson in our own times that the mind and the heart cannot be explained by each other; rather, by bringing them together, we make ourselves whole.

the better. New knowledge and ways of doing things offer hope in our darkest days and the courage to carry on, and can turn anger to laughter and sadness to acceptance. No matter how bad a situation may seem, understanding it is the vital first step to turning it around. Questioning only harms assumptions that were mistaken in the first place. Truth that liberates stands any amount of questioning. Coming face to face with our opposite can answer all questions and make us feel whole.

ASSOCIATIONS

Keyword ∗ Intelligently	**Parts of body** ∗ Nerves, shoulders, arms and lungs
Favourite phrase ∗ I think	
Aspiration ∗ Wisdom	**Vulnerabilities** ∗ Asthma and nervous disorders
Colour ∗ Yellow	
Metal ∗ Mercury	**Plants** ∗ Flowers of all plants; nut-bearing trees
Stone ∗ Agate	
	Herbs ∗ Lavender and carrot

THE TWINS
GEMINI DECODED

THE ESSENCE OF COMMUNICATION

Gemini's airy mutability suggests taking things as they come and easily adding an intelligent slant to almost any idea or possibility. Eager for social interaction, Geminis connect with everyone as with a brother or sister. However, with Jupiter in detriment here, Gemini's encouraging words can be unreliable, even unnerving, and others may feel let down when yet another fascinating alternative comes along. For Geminis, the conflicts and contradictions in so many "irresistible" interests can be overwhelming. Their minds can become overstretched into neurotic anxiety. They, and everyone around them, just do not know what to believe.

LIGHT IN THE DARKNESS
Having knowledge of both the dark and light sides of life, Gemini of all the signs is best able to shine a beacon of understanding and hope into the troubled depths of another's soul.

THE SEARCH FOR A TWIN

Just as there are two sides to every question, so there are two sides to human nature. Gemini's urge for information and communication is based on a lonely need for completion – the search for a twin, the other part of ourselves symbolized in this sign. Without someone to share ideas and experiences, life can be dark and uninteresting. Yet constant attraction to easy answers and to new ideas and experiences can scatter Geminis' focus. They lose their bearings and neglect, even forget, their best interests.

True friends will not just offer more distractions. We will encourage our Gemini friend to search within, to realize that lasting happiness lies in accepting both the difficult and the easy, the sad and the happy, the darkness and the light. When things go wrong, the answer is not to look for a new distraction to "take their mind off things", but rather to accept and transcend the duality of good and bad within us all. Writing is one way to do this, a chance to include and understand everyone in a unified focus.

HERCULES GATHERS THE GOLDEN APPLES OF THE HESPERIDES

Hercules is instructed to gather these apples, which are guarded by the maiden Hesperides and a hundred-headed dragon. On the way he faces five tests. The first he fails by not recognizing the wise guidance of the gentle messenger Nereus. In the second he disempowers the serpent Anaeus by raising him to the light. In the third he eases Prometheus's suffering in the underworld. In the fourth, falling under the spell of the false teacher Busiris, Hercules is chained to a rock for a whole year. Only then does he see clearly and put Busiris in chains instead. In the fifth test, he comes to the apple tree but loses all thought of it upon witnessing the plight of Atlas bearing the vast weight of the Earth on his shoulders. Hercules' profound sympathy moves him to take the weight from Atlas on to his own shoulders. As he does, the Earth disappears and before him stands Atlas offering a golden apple, and the Hesperides offer him golden apples, too.

This story shows how distraction, other responsibilities and especially false ways of thinking can block the pure golden light of understanding. Selfless kindness for others liberates our minds from deception, so it is easy to see things as they really are.

BROTHERLY LOVE

In Greek and Roman times the constellation of Gemini was a celestial image of the twins Castor and Pollux. Born from the mortal Leda, Castor was the son of the Spartan king Tyndareus and so mortal, while the other brother, Pollux, was the son of Zeus and so immortal. When Castor was killed, Pollux asked Zeus that he be allowed to die. Instead, Zeus proposed that Pollux share his immortality with Castor. Thus, the brothers could remain united, spending alternate days in Olympus, the home of the gods, and in Hades, the underworld. To this day, they represent the unifying capacity of brotherly love.

BROTHERLY LOVE
This early 18th-century star map shows Gemini as the heavenly twins. To honour and remind us of their unselfish love, Zeus placed Castor and Pollux in the skies, to remain united for ever as the constellation of Gemini.

BIRTH CHART ✷ MARILYN MONROE

Marilyn Monroe was born at 0930 PST on 1 June 1926 in Los Angeles, California. Her seductive image is symbolized by Neptune rising creatively in the Leo First House, which is ruled by the Gemini Sun, close to Mercury high in the Tenth and harmoniously trined by Venus in Aries near the Midheaven. With Neptune also making a making a tense, debilitating T-square to her Aquarian Moon with Jupiter in the Seventh House and Saturn in the Fourth, her image helped to

destabilize public perception of relationships. Marilyn Monroe became an object of uneasy desire and frustration for millions – even for other celebrities. Her Gemini and Aquarius combined to make her extremely intelligent but neurotically highly strung. Unable to reconcile the contradictions of being wanted by so many while intrinsically alone, Marilyn died from a drug overdose at the age of 36.

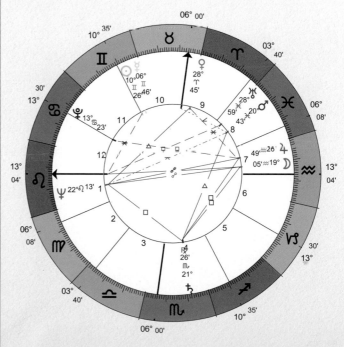

The Sun creates brilliantly and distractedly. Geminis have a restless urge to receive and give information in every way possible; reading, studying, phoning and talking face to face. Enthusiastically and diversely, they enable the numerous projects, ideas and theories they always have on the go. They will engage in anything from the most profound interaction to everyday gossip. Focusing on a central idea is vital. When they overstretch and lose control, others can feel stranded.

The Moon reacts accommodatingly and neurotically. Those with a Moon in Gemini have a curiosity and enthusiasm for mental stimulation that makes their lives exciting and busy. They love to bring others into conversations, as much to pour out personal information as to listen. Reacting too often and too quickly can lead to misunderstandings. Do not allow this. Ask clarifying questions and let people solve their own problems. Then anxiety goes away.

PLANETS IN
GEMINI

THE SUN

THE MOON

MERCURY

VENUS

MARS

Mercury communicates intelligently and unceasingly. The lively minds of those with Mercury in Gemini bubble with ideas that they just cannot wait to develop and express as fully as possible. Anything that enables this is a joy: computers, books, magazines, letters, portable music players. Communication with others is indispensable. Taken to excess, this can tie people up in dilettante distractions. Discriminating awareness will keep the path ahead clear.

Venus loves keenly and flirtatiously. Venus in Gemini symbolizes an intense appetite for mental stimulus. Without it, these people become bored and edgy, at a loss for something to do. With it, they are really alive, excited and enthusiastic. This can make them appear flirtatious. You should not be misled. Usually it is the ideas that are captivating, not whoever they are talking to. When they seek a relationship they will let you know. They will want to talk about that, too.

Mars acts spontaneously and erratically. Those with Mars in Gemini are quick to speak up and communicate what needs to be done, keen to act so that their own and other peoples' suggestions are implemented. However, being busy without clear focus can be counterproductive and work against what has been done before. Minds may be changed, to evade responsibility. By channelling enthusiasm into an ordered plan of action, all that is necessary will be completed well.

Jupiter expands adventurously and unrealistically. When Jupiter is in Gemini, big ideas encourage agendas suggested by the positions of the other outer planets. For example: 1929–30 saw economic upheaval; 1941–2, rapid development in weapons' technology; 1965–6, questioning of social values; 1976–8, economic crisis leading to monetarism; 1988–9, social crisis that lead to the end of the Soviet system; 2000–1, the end of the "dotcom" boom and the 9/11 attacks on New York.

Saturn controls diligently and ineffectively. With Saturn here, innovative ideas are put to the test. Sustainability is the goal. Without it, the best possibilities fall by the wayside. In 1942–4 the Allies' war effort gathered strength, while the Nazis' position weakened. 1971–4 both tested, and saw the failure of, the United States' war in Vietnam and the UK's Heath government. Through 2000–3, decisions on economic and terrorist crises created problems for the future.

JUPITER

SATURN

URANUS

NEPTUNE

PLUTO

Uranus invents revolutionarily and disruptively. Great social and scientific changes disrupt these periods. 1774–82 saw the founding of the USA, shortly to produce its ground-breaking constitution. In 1858–66, the USA was unified through civil war, while Europe made major strides in technology. 1941–9 saw electronic and atomic invention, expansion in social opportunity and more equal relations among nations as they emerged from World War II.

Neptune inspires sensationally and unrealistically. Unusual visions can lead to fantasies that just might come true. Strengthened by the conjunction to Pluto that occurs every 495 years (1891–2), the 1887–1902 transit saw the publication of Oscar Wilde's and George Bernard Shaw's revolutionary social commentaries. At the same time the works of H.G. Wells and Jules Verne founded popular science fiction. These remarkable ideas portended scientific and social change that still fascinates us today.

Pluto transforms earth-shatteringly and unreasonably. In these years ideas are capable of undermining the world's very foundations. 1638–70 saw religious schism and the end of belief in absolute monarchy. England beheaded a king, restored his son as constitutional monarch and, in the same year (1660), founded the Royal Society, setting science on the path to being the "true king". In 1882–1914 every value in Western society was questioned, preparing the way for brutal conflict.

CANCER

Polarity * Negative
Quality * Cardinal
Element * Water
Ruler * Moon

Beneficial * Reassurance
* Nurture * Possibilities
Unbeneficial * Insecurity
* Anxiety * Disharmony

CANCER – THE FOURTH SIGN OF THE ZODIAC

RULED BY THE MOON, Cancer brings a reflective depth that makes Cancerians particularly empathic, understanding with a profound concern that seems to make growth not only possible, but inevitable. Its element, water, also points to the Cancerian's ability to mirror the concerns and emotions of others. Cancer makes an art of the negative: encouraging by reassuring, it constantly creates new possibilities, helping us to live as if at any moment all could be lost. For by moonlight you can never be certain. The subtle light may stir our soul and make it yearn to love, but the dark shadows may hide illusions and dangers.

Cancer illustrates the joys and pitfalls of nurture. The mother surrounds her baby with a crabshell-like armour of protective love and closeness. However, excessive worry and overprotectiveness can have the opposite of the intended effect and cause insecurity, while excessive defensiveness can, like the crab's pincers, appear threatening to others. This risks making matters worse.

A HARD SHELL
This 15th-century illustration shows Cancer the crab, with its pincers and impenetrable shell. The sign has a tendency to slip from nurturing to overprotectiveness and from defensiveness to aggression.

This sign also represents broader aspects of maternal care. Nurture encompasses not simply the physical nursing of a child but also the conditions of the home, the values that sustain it, and the larger society to which it belongs. Cancer rules institutions that support and regulate the care and welfare of the citizen.

The first degree of Cancer is the base of the cardinal axis (with Aries, Libra and Capricorn) that drives the zodiac. It is one of the two solstice extremities of the Sun's annual relationship with the Earth. This sign naturally occupies the Fourth House.

ASSOCIATIONS

Keyword * Carefully	**Parts of body** * Chest and stomach
Favourite phrase * I feel	**Vulnerabilities** * Indigestion, ulcers and chronic diseases
Aspiration * Harmony	
Colour * Ice blue	**Plants** * Rubber and all trees rich in sap
Metal * Silver	
Stone * Pearl	**Herbs** * Flax and privet

THE CRAB

CANCER DECODED

THE ESSENCE OF ASSIMILATION

With the Moon ruling Cancer and Jupiter also strong in the sign, we behave in everything we do as if we are caring for a child, with nothing left to chance. We want our world to feel comfortable and safe, to pour out pearls of profound kindness from our deepest, private selves.

Yet, with Saturn in detriment, we may fear the consequences of giving too much of ourselves. With Mars in detriment too, Cancer's urgency to care is based upon an intrinsic fear of hurt. This can lead to an overprotectiveness that manifests as aggression. Intense inner fear can make us fight brutally, like the crab with its sharp pincers.

Sensing all this intuitively, the Cancerian tendency is not to take on things head on, but to withdraw. We behave like the crab: we prefer to move sideways, to avoid rather than confront. The sense of responsibility that Cancerians feel may be overwhelming. We may be tempted to hide from this responsibility but this is no answer. Left unaddressed, problems can only grow. Only when we attend to them with nurturing care can we feel so safe that comfort and harmony return.

RULED BY THE MOON
The illusory nature of the Moon's light reflects the ambivalence of Cancer. While the world is beautiful and seductive by moonlight, the unwary may be trapped by illusions and hidden dangers.

HERCULES AND THE FAWN

On a hill, beside the temple to which the hero Hercules brought the fruits of his famous labours, stood a slender golden-antlered fawn. In the air were the sounds of two voices: that of Artemis (Diana), goddess of the Moon and divine huntress, claiming ownership of the fawn; and the voice of the god of the temple, instructing Hercules to rescue the fawn from Artemis and bring it to the temple.

For a full year Artemis tricked and deceived Hercules, thwarting his chase. Then one day he found the fawn resting, wearied from the pursuit. He shot it in the foot, took it in his arms close to his heart and carried it into the temple, claiming the fawn was his by right of search and skill. But the god denied him and told him to leave the wounded animal in the temple. When Hercules looked again toward the temple, on the hill beside it stood the fawn, unwounded.

This is a great allegorical lesson about the nature of Cancerian emotional possessiveness and how to transcend it. The hunt for the fawn is our craving for permanent attachment. This craving motivates all our searching and confusion, which may even lead us to wound or harm the very beloved and essential thing to which we seek attachment. Yet the fawn is not hurt and never really goes anywhere. Emotions are the product of our own self-deception, which comes from our desire to be attached. Because we fear losing it, we grasp repeatedly to capture what we want, but in fact already have, failing to realize that it never can be lost.

BIRTH CHART ✴ DIANA, PRINCESS OF WALES

This is the birth chart of Diana, Princess of Wales, who was born at 1945 UT on 1 July 1961 at Sandringham, England. Her Sun was in the Seventh House, harmoniously aspected to Neptune in the very public Tenth House, but ruled by a rebellious Aquarian Moon. This drew

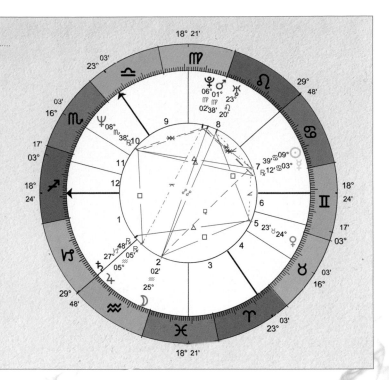

people to her, but in a more dependent way than to, say, the Dalai Lama (see page 156). Many strangers lived a part of their lives through Diana, feeling her happiness and tribulations, rejoicing in her public generosity – and mourning her death as if they really knew her. Her Moon's opposition to her Eighth House Uranus, Mars and Pluto explains the controversy and tragedy of her death.

THE SENSITIVE TOUCH

A useful phrase for Cancerians to bear in mind is "gently does it". Cancerians are sensitive types who at their best care deeply and have a joyfully optimistic outlook on the world. On the other hand, their nature can tip over into hypersensitivity, leading them to feel vulnerable and to become defensive, timid and reclusive. They tend to become deeply involved with others, and this interaction is often the root of any problems. When relating to Cancerians, we should realize that how we speak, not the meaning of the words, is vitally important. The wrong tone can make a seemingly innocuous remark feel aggressive or offensive. Confident reassurance applied with a gentle, understanding touch is the key to righting problems.

Cancerians are prone to insecurity, to sensing imagined threats and attacking preemptively. The key is to avoid overreacting or responding in kind. However much we may feel justified in fighting back, it is better to keep calm and observe whether we are justified in perceiving aggression where none may exist. When Cancerians feel secure, their patience and kindness toward others will be handsomely and delightfully rewarded.

The group of faint stars that make up the constellation Cancer has been associated with crustaceans since the Babylonians of the early second millennium BCE, when its name was Al.lul ("the crayfish"). Being the youngest of the three water signs and the home of the Moon, Cancer epitomizes the intensely protective qualities of birthing and motherhood. But there can be many kinds of mothers, not all of them kind and nurturing: the sign's Babylonian name may be the origin of Lilith, the "feminist" first wife of Adam in Jewish tradition.

LILITH THE SEDUCTRESS
This 1892 painting by John Collier shows Lilith consorting with the snake in the Garden of Eden. In some traditions, this "bad mother" hates children and even feasts upon them.

The Sun creates nurturingly and cautiously. Those with the Sun in Cancer cannot do enough to care for and protect others, especially family and others who are close to them, nursing them, cooking for them or just relaxing with them beside the fire. Providing they feel emotionally secure and in control, they will draw on remarkable hidden depths of healing, but they should always tread carefully. If they feel threatened, they will close up and hide away, or lash out preemptively.

The Moon reacts intuitively and anxiously. Feelings may be so "ahead of the game" that ideas and words can create more problems than they solve. Just being accepted and cared for, and caring for others in return, is enough to feel complete. People with a Cancer Moon flourish if treated considerately in familiar, comfortable surroundings. They will attack to defend themselves if they feel their foundation is threatened and they cannot find somewhere to hide.

PLANETS IN CANCER

THE SUN

THE MOON

MERCURY

VENUS

MARS

Mercury communicates discriminatingly and hesitantly. When Mercury is here, communication is much easier if thoughts and feelings are expressed considerately, with an appreciation of what is needed. The tendency is to hesitate to be open, especially with strangers. Photos of common experiences can help break down barriers. When the barriers are overcome to allow sharing, it will be possible to experience understanding based on emotional insight.

Venus loves maternally and possessively. Those born when Venus was in Cancer are naturally tender and affectionate, but should guard against being taken for granted, especially in unfamiliar situations. They are drawn to pleasant experiences, and are ready, at the back of their minds, to make any necessary adjustments to make things easier. Finding it more comfortable to open up in familiar surroundings, they can become attached and demanding toward people and things that make them feel secure.

Mars acts emotionally and aggressively. The force of Mars here suggests the expression of effusive feelings. This can show itself as bravery that protects people and causes. However, such apparent confidence can be driven by an intense inner anxiety. These fears may be self-fulfilling, because a protective shell can appear confrontational, making others aggressive in return. However, those who really care will understand and find a way through the Cancerian shell, so healing any inner hurt.

Jupiter expands caringly and overwhelmingly.
Those with Jupiter in Cancer cannot do too much for the people and causes to which they are devoted. Their passion for justice and "right" values in society seems to justify extreme action. When Jupiter was in Cancer (1965–7, 1977–9, 1989–90 and 2001–2), the world saw unrealistic social expectations, for example following the fall of the Berlin Wall, and in the War on Terror. The consequences of those times' excesses haunt us today.

Saturn controls carefully and defensively. It insists that structures to ensure self-protection are in place. When Saturn is in Cancer, the sign opposite the one it rules (Capricorn), such rigidity often makes matters worse. It may protect from the hard realities that efficiency demands, but can lead to unnecessary conflicts that turn potential friends into enemies. Such misguided fears led to widespread hostilities during 1914–16, 1944–6, 1973–6 and 2003–5.

JUPITER

SATURN

URANUS

PLUTO

NEPTUNE

Uranus invents idealistically and protectively. Those born when Uranus was in Cancer (1948–56) often yearned in their youth for radical social and political change; this was the West's "hippy generation". As they grew older, these people often became intensely critical about how freedom was expressed. They now question, for example, whether new technology brings more freedom (by enabling greater expression of ideas) or less (by making privacy more difficult).

Neptune inspires responsibly and with self-sacrifice. With Neptune in Cancer emotional sympathies drive belief in matters where issues are not clear. The most recent of these periods (1901–16) saw a confused unravelling of social assumptions in the West, culminating in the cataclysm of the World War I. With Saturn and Pluto transiting Cancer too, Neptunian patriotic and imperial dreams became causes to die for. Yet this was also an era of spiritual awareness, women's suffrage, and social rights and welfare.

Pluto transforms irrevocably and destructively. In Cancer, Pluto radically sweeps away past social structures and assumptions. But overthrowing the old order may not bring happiness. The period 1913–39, for example, was a time of immense social destruction, from the collapse of old monarchical orders amid the violence of World War I to the brutal dictatorships of Stalin, Hitler and Mussolini and the economic collapse of the Great Depression – all of which laid the ground for further conflict.

LEO

Polarity ∗ Positive
Quality ∗ Fixed
Element ∗ Fire
Ruler ∗ Sun

Beneficial ∗ Generosity
∗ Energy ∗ Confidence

Unbeneficial ∗ Egotism
∗ Conceit ∗ Ingratitude

LEO – THE FIFTH SIGN OF THE ZODIAC

LEO IS A KINGDOM RULED BY THE SUN, which radiates light-filled, life-giving energy that initiates and sustains all creation on Earth and throughout the entire family of the solar system. The very essence of kingly generosity, the Sun demands unswerving loyalty and admiration in return. Recognizing this from ancient times, many cultures have respected, honoured and even worshipped the Sun, its seasons and the regal lion that represents its forceful and courageous energy.

Being fixed fire, Leo stimulates and causes action rather than performing it – the lion prefers to sit on its throne while others run around doing things. However, being positive and solar, it does not merely consent to something happening, but actively enthuses over it. This provides Leos with the confidence that makes them feel they can do just about anything, from risky speculation to fun and flirtation, from the joys and challenges of parenthood to original expressions of art, music and dance.

ASSOCIATIONS

Keyword ∗ Proudly	**Parts of body** ∗ Heart and sensory nerves
Favourite phrase ∗ I will	
Aspiration ∗ Gratitude	**Vulnerabilities** ∗ Fevers, heart attacks
Colour ∗ Golden	**Plants** ∗ Citrus and palm trees; seeds of all plants
Metal ∗ Gold	
Stone ∗ Ruby	**Herbs** ∗ Sunflower, marigold and walnut

THE FULFILMENT OF MAN
This 15th-century image of Leo is accompanied by a depiction of a man scything wheat. Associated with the fruition of crops, Leo is linked in Christian iconography with man's fulfilment in the resurrected Christ.

So Leo's radiant beauty, and the energy that encourages us to "have a go", carry all before them and glory in the admiration that they bring. Yet there is a downside. Seeing only from its own point of view, Leo needs and expects to be recognized and admired. The challenge for Leo is to appreciate the whole picture, to recognize and be grateful for the contributions made by others to success. The king who honours his subjects reigns over a secure kingdom where judgments are more than skin deep.

THE LION
LEO DECODED

THE ESSENCE OF COORDINATION

Like the Sun that rules their sign, Leos are confident, radiant and generous. They love to create, romance, let their hair down, have fun and play like (and with) children. Such zest encourages Leos to take risks, even with their own lives. Their courage and enthusiasm light up the lives of those around them. Leos expect others to place them centre stage and honour their wishes, but in return they will benefit from Leo's great generosity.

However, with Saturn in detriment in the sign, time and other practicalities may limit Leo's freedom to enjoy. Realities may expose their flaws and failings, laying bare conceit and self-obsession. Leo's egocentricity may not lie easy alongside demands for consideration toward others.

SHARE AND ENJOY

"We share the pleasure of enjoying this life together" is a concept that no healthy and happy Leo could ever deny. Leos are at their best when interested and enthusiastic and at the centre of things. This encourages their natural generosity, which in turn can prove infectious and bring marvellous benefits to those around them, and indeed the wider world.

When a Leo clearly needs advice, it will go down better if we offer it in a way that suggests that this has always been their plan. Like a king's valued counsellor, we can consider ourselves successful the moment our Leo friend lectures us back with our own ideas. Best of all is when generous Leos thank us for helping them to see things a certain way.

HERCULES SLAYS THE NEMEAN LION

It was said that a fearsome lion so terrorized the Nemeans that they hid in their houses. The lion's hide was impervious to weapons, so Hercules took only his trusty wooden club as he searched on many false trails. Finally, he saw the lion on the path before him and, shouting loudly, rushed toward it. The lion fled but Hercules pursued it to its cave. He blocked the cave's two entrances with wooden beams, trapping both the lion and himself inside. Since weapons were useless, Hercules throttled the lion with his bare hands, then skinned the beast with its own claws. From that time he wore the lion's impenetrable pelt as a form of armour.

From the very beginning, Hercules' attitude shows that power and strength come from courage, and that courage comes from the way we deal with fear. By leaving most of his armoury behind, he demonstrated that confidence and personal strength derive from doing without extrinsic supports. Finally, he killed the lion in its own lair with his bare hands. Likewise in our lives, we alone can get to grips with our fears. In doing so, like Hercules donning the lion's pelt, we become stronger and less vulnerable.

REGENERATIVE POWER

The ancient Greeks identified Leo with the Nemean lion, which the hero Hercules killed as one of his famous 12 labours. In the later centuries of ancient Egypt, Leo was associated with the annual flooding of the Nile, which took place when the Sun was in the sign. In Christian art, a lion symbolizes the resurrection of Christ, the Sun of Righteousness, a solar connection that also derives from the fact that the Sun reaches its full regenerative power in Leo, when harvests come to their full fruition. Leo represents the abundance of summer's height, compared with the barrenness of the depths of winter.

A ROYAL SIGN
In this 15th-century copy of Al-Sufi's *Book of Fixed Stars*, Leo rampages proudly across the sky, the very embodiment of kingly energy. Leos are not noted for serving others; instead their circle benefits from their leadership.

BIRTH CHART ★ J.K. ROWLING

J.K. Rowling was born on 31 July 1965 in Bristol, United Kingdom. We do not know the time, so the chart is drawn without houses and our interpretation is less focused. Her highly creative Harry Potter books and the films made from them have dramatically influenced the imagination of countless children. As the readers grew into adolescence so did the characters in the books, and the challenges they faced became more adult in nature. Rowling created a backdrop and plots that were both fantastic and intensely fascinating. Such

vast creative commitment, combining masses of intricate detail, is driven by a tense T-square aspect between Jupiter in Gemini, a hard-working bundle of planets in Virgo and the emotional discipline of Saturn in Pisces. Mars in Libra trined to Jupiter encourages ideas for exciting battles. Driving it all is a glorious Sun newly entered into Leo.

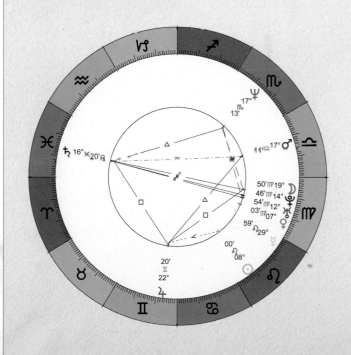

The Sun creates radiantly and self-centredly. The joy of self-expression associated with this sign makes being with Leos a blessing. With Leo around it is much easier to see life as bright and positive, to take risks, play, be generous, create and make amazing things happen. However, Leos do not tend to serve or sacrifice; others benefit chiefly by just being around them and their positive energy. For their part, Leos should remember that they may not always be right.

The Moon reacts innovatively and egocentrically. When people born with the Moon in Leo spot a chance to enjoy themselves, their eyes light up like a child's. They are quick to suggest new ways to have fun. Unlike those with the Moon in other signs, they tend to draw attention to themselves and encourage others to join in. At family celebrations, they are happier when it is left to them to decide what is needed – the proceedings seem to go better that way!

[THE SUN]

[THE MOON]

PLANETS IN
LEO

[MERCURY]

[MARS]

[VENUS]

Mercury communicates proudly and overconfidently. Those born with Mercury in Leo sense a natural calling to seek knowledge and express it confidently. Bright and exciting ideas come quickly to their minds. They love to learn, but often feel that their wisdom is not appreciated. At the same time, it is important for them not to confuse their need for personal recognition and standing with their commitment to a cause or to an area of expertise.

Venus loves joyfully and self-indulgently. Fun is the name of the game for those with Venus in Leo. They love to love, and to be loved even more. That special person in their lives and everything they possess, must be as admirable and admired as they believe or wish themselves to be. However, with so much to be pleased about, it is important (but not easy) for them to know proper limitations. Relying on relationships rather than acquiring more possessions will be the happier path for them to pursue.

Mars acts courageously and dominatingly. Proud leadership with brave self-assertive bursts are the hallmark of Mars in this sign. Such courageous actions give heart to others who join in – providing they are "worthy followers". Such leadership might come across as arrogance, but it need not be. By avoiding overconfidence and the temptation to "rule the roost", those with Mars in Leo can help to bring about great advances in any activity where personal power and courage are the key.

Jupiter expands imperially and excessively. Bringing expansiveness, generosity and an urge for justice, this seems a very good placing, but all too often issues are forced too far: 1931–2 saw the rise of Hitler; 1943–4, war on many fronts; 1955–6, the Soviet invasions of Hungary and Czechoslovakia and the Suez War; 1966–8, rapid acceleration of the alternative culture; 1978–9, the rise of monetarist economics; and, in 1990–91 and 2002–3, war in the Middle East and then in Afghanistan.

Saturn controls reliably and domineeringly. Because it seeks to control and contain, Saturn is not happy in Leo, seemingly intent on thwarting its celebratory freedom. This may be just what is needed to balance past excesses. The years 1916–19, 1946–9 and 1975–8 were marked by sober realities and even harsh conflict, after the premature, simplistic overconfidence shown early in World War I, in the immediate aftermath of World War II and by trade unions during the early 70s.

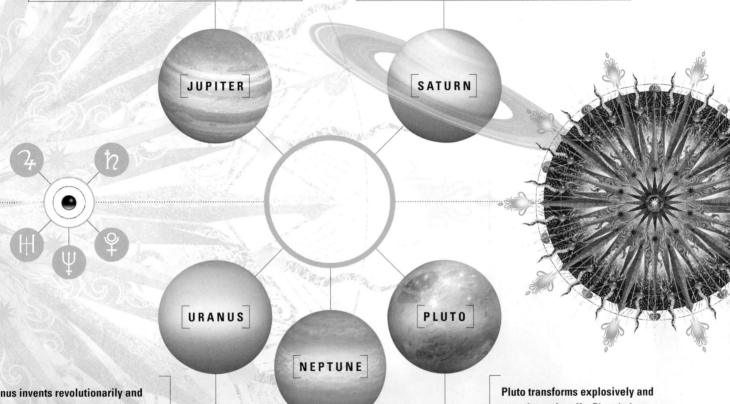

Uranus invents revolutionarily and egocentrically. Remarkable world-changing developments erupt when Uranus is in Leo. The years 1697–1704 saw the rise of the navy on which Britain's imperial might was founded. The period 1787–95 witnessed the French Revolution and Reign of Terror. The unification and rise of Germany took place in 1871–8, as did the Indian Wars in the US and the foundation of the Theosophical Society. And in 1955–62 came the birth of rock 'n' roll.

Neptune inspires hedonistically and self-indulgently. With Neptune in Leo, self-belief can lead to overconfident conceit for good or ill. The English defeat of the Spanish Armada early in the period 1587–1602 inspired a vision of a golden Elizabethan age. The next time Neptune was in Leo (1751–65), Britain's imperial competition with France led to a colonial war. And the next time, the final imperial decline of both Britain and France stemmed from catastrophic war and the unsettled peace that followed it (1914–29).

Pluto transforms explosively and megalomaniacally. Pluto in Leo sweeps away past assumptions about the individual's place in the world, drawing on social upheavals occurring when Pluto is in the previous sign. In 1447–66 the printing press began to give wider access to knowledge; and 1692–1712 saw the beginnings of the Enlightenment. In 1938–58, war and the extreme dehumanization of the Holocaust inspired the founding of the UN and the Universal Declaration of Human Rights.

VIRGO

Polarity ✳ Negative
Quality ✳ Mutable
Element ✳ Earth
Ruler ✳ Mercury

Beneficial ✳ Perfection ✳ Duty ✳ Purity
Unbeneficial ✳ Anxiety ✳ Criticism ✳ Disorganization

VIRGO – THE SIXTH SIGN OF THE ZODIAC

IF WHEAT IS TO REACH MATURITY and ripen for harvest, all conditions must be appropriate at every stage in the growing process. Being negative earth, Virgo seeks to answer the limitations of Gemini, the positive air sign Mercury rules, by only accepting those ideas that are capable of perfect practical implementation. Constant insistence on perfection in this way aspires toward permanent purity. We have to try harder, again and again. For only when everything is pure can we be healthy and secure.

Such an uncompromising, almost didactic assumption explains what lies behind familiar Virgo characteristics. Mutable Virgo's environment soon becomes packed with myriad fascinating items of the finest taste and highest quality. Not necessarily antiques to display, more often they are things in the making: intricate handicrafts, healthy food, manuscripts to edit, projects to research, accounts to analyze and correct. It is a busy world of rigorous, but all too often uncompleted work.

ASSOCIATIONS

Keyword ✳ Precisely
Favourite phrase ✳ I analyze
Aspiration ✳ Divine justice
Colour ✳ Brown
Metal ✳ Mercury
Stone ✳ Sardonyx

Parts of body ✳ Intestines, joints and nervous system
Vulnerabilities ✳ Fevers and heart attack
Plants ✳ Nut-bearing trees; roots of all plants
Herbs ✳ Caraway and myrtle

SIGN OF PERFECTION
This illustration, from a 13th-century Latin translation of a 10th-century Persian astrological text, pinpoints the positions of the stars that make up the constellation of Virgo.

Venus is not well placed here, because Virgo's obsession with duty can overwork and undermine the emergence of its naturally created beauty. Yet, by keeping going, working through the worry, taking joy in every perfect stroke, word, deed and understanding, something uniquely special can emerge.

Virgo is well placed to serve all levels of the world of medicine. Its conscientiousness answers every requirement of cleanliness. Good chemists, Virgos create efficacious portions and, as doctors and specialists, they bring details of case histories together to accurately diagnose cures.

Whatever they do, Virgos can only be happy when aspiring toward perfection. For Virgos, it is only upon this that security and hence justice can rest.

THE VIRGIN
VIRGO DECODED

THE ESSENCE OF DISCRIMINATION

"If a job's worth doing, it is worth doing well" is Virgo's motto for both good and ill. Virgos are hard workers, give attention to detail and never rest until a job is satisfactorily completed. To see, read or hear what a Virgo considers complete, to use a facility that a Virgo has created for you, is to experience quality and comfort. For it is almost certain that your every need has been catered for.

On the other hand, Virgos can work too hard, overfocus on minor details and overlook the big picture. They can build up such neurotic anxiety within themselves and their colleagues that the job is never finished. Negative mutability ruled by Mercury in a negative earth sign can lead to constant

ASTRAEA AMONG THE STARS
Fleeing the evil of the world, the goddess Astraea was set in the stars as the constellation Virgo, while her scales became Libra. Astraea is echoed by the Roman goddess Justitia, who also held scales and was linked to Virgo.

worry, visualizing the many ways things can go wrong. At worst, overwhelmed by such a self-imposed burden, Virgos can reject anything less than absolute perfection and sit despondently in the midst of disorder.

Because Jupiter is in detriment in Virgo, resisting the temptations to expand is the answer to these dangers. Virgos are not obliged to take on more and more and feel responsible about it all. Wise discrimination chooses well and uses the most skilful method to do what is needed. How else can perfection, the basis of all just outcomes, be achieved?

HERCULES SEIZES THE GIRDLE OF HIPPOLYTA

Hippolyta, queen of the female Amazon realm, worshipped at the temple of the Moon, sacrificing to Mars, the god of war. Around her waist was a girdle given her by Venus as a symbol of unity achieved through struggle and strife, of motherhood and the sacred child within us all. She was debating with her maidens whether to give the girdle to Hercules for his sixth labour, when, ahead of time, he burst in and fought with her so blindly that he did not hear her words, nor see her hands holding out the girdle as a gift. He killed the one who loved him most and offered him the greatest gift of all.

This story shows the danger of judging and acting too quickly, when reacting to Virgo. How often is the solution staring us in the face, if we stop, stand back, look and think for a moment? And there is an even deeper lesson than this. The girdle, which Hercules fought for so brutally and unnecessarily, symbolizes the unification of the male and female; the co-creation of a child. More than any other sign of the zodiac, Virgo makes us feel critical and impatient. Yet it is in reacting to Virgo like this that we can lose so much and regret so intensely. Be patient and do what is right – and all you want is yours.

KEEPING UP STANDARDS

When relating to Virgos it is important to remember that all choices are acceptable – providing they are the right choices! It is best not to argue or criticize, but rather to facilitate. If you can, direct headstrong Virgos along less pressured paths, but realize they will see through and resent attempts to bribe. Virgos do not seek easy ways around problems, preferring to maintain their integrity.

So be responsible, share interests and especially standards. When buying presents, it may be best to let your decisive Virgo choose. Find skilful ways to show that nothing is needed in return – as this Virgo gives so much already.

Crucially, if you can ease back and celebrate with your Virgo friend in comfort and excellence, you will know few better places to be.

RULER OF THE HARVEST
Often shown carrying two sheaves of wheat, Virgo is associated with a range of agricultural goddesses including the Greek goddess Demeter. Controller of the seasons, Demeter could bring both life and death to the world.

JUSTICE AND THE HARVEST

In Greek mythology Astraea was the virgin–goddess of justice. Driven away by the lawlessness on Earth, Astraea became the constellation Virgo. She is associated with Nemesis, the goddess whose rightful indignation ensures we "get what is coming to us".

The connection of the constellation of Virgo with wheat and corn dates from Babylonian times, when Mul.apin (686 BCE and 1000 BCE) was known as "the furrow" and the goddess Shala was represented as an ear of grain or corn. The name of Virgo's brightest star, Spica, means "ear of grain" in Latin. From this follows the constellation's association with fertility.

The Greeks and Romans continued the same associations under new names. The goddess of wheat was Demeter–Ceres. Sometimes she was identified as the virgin goddess Justitia, holding in her hand the scales of justice of the next constellation, Libra. In medieval Christian society, Virgo became associated with the Blessed Virgin Mary.

BIRTH CHART ⁎ LOUIS XIV OF FRANCE

Louis XIV was born at 1101 UT on 5 September 1638 at St Ger-en-Ley, France. Ruling from 1642–1715, he made France a stable centre of art and culture. The Moon/Venus conjunction in the Ninth House may explain his renown as the "Sun King", but it is his Tenth House Virgo Sun and ruling Mercury, expressed through a Scorpio ascendant ruled by Mars in Sagittarius, that explains his sumptuous lifestyle, exemplified in the building of the Palace of Versailles. The very epitome of the divine right of kings, Louis patronized an extraordinary flourishing in art, literature, music, architecture and craft.

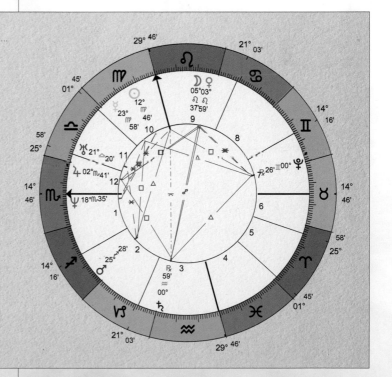

The Sun expresses precisely and hyperactively.
A conscientious need for everything to be properly considered ensures a healthy Virgo's life is industrious. With insight Virgos analyze all they consider to be the necessary details, arranging things systematically. They are ideally suited to editing and administrative organization, but need to beware of overworking. Unnecessarily high standards and too much petty detail can obscure easier solutions.

The Moon reacts fastidiously and dismissively.
When the Moon is in Virgo, the natural inclination is to improve everything to perfection. Only if projects are tangible, or based upon a methodical structure and system of rules, can it be clear whether or not something is right. If it's not, people with a Virgo Moon work at it until it is. As they are uncomfortable unless everything is as it should be, their associates may find them difficult to satisfy, even picky.

PLANETS IN VIRGO

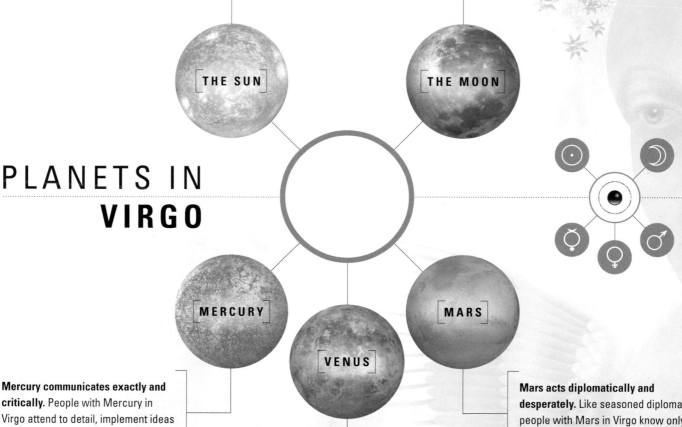

THE SUN

THE MOON

MERCURY

VENUS

MARS

Mercury communicates exactly and critically. People with Mercury in Virgo attend to detail, implement ideas with skilled precision and discover overlooked errors. They are suited for editing, proofing and designing; also for pharmacy, medicine and other careers that involve diagnosis. But heightened care carries a price. Excessive worry debilitates the mind and body, can trap us in details and leave issues unaddressed. Only by finishing will things be made fully right.

Venus loves dutifully and excessively. Their sense of duty means that people born with Venus in Virgo will not rest until all needs are correctly catered for. Intensely aware of quality and rightness, these people are drawn to the highest taste in art, experience and ideas. The planet is in fall, however, so an anxious sense of responsibility can lead them to impose unnecessary demands on themselves or on the people around them. When they smile, relax and walk elegantly hand-in-hand with everything they do, all will be well.

Mars acts diplomatically and desperately. Like seasoned diplomats, people with Mars in Virgo know only too well that lives, theirs included, can depend upon ensuring everything is exactly right. So, they are keen to do what is necessary in a careful methodical way. It is to their credit that they are like this, but they should avoid shouldering such a burden all the time. Others may know more than at first seemed possible and may even have better answers to the problem.

Jupiter expands discursively and endlessly. Jupiter-in-Virgo years are those when people seek the highest truth, wish everyone to live perfect lives and try to explore in ever-greater detail. It may appear that people are more interested in asking questions than hearing answers. Around the world, such times (1955–7, 1967–9, 1979–80, 1991–2, 2003–4) have been full of criticisms, but short on sustainable solutions, and have left more problems than they solved.

Saturn controls correctly and uncompromisingly. These are years (most recently, 1919–21, 1948–51, 1977–80 and 2007–10) when underlying problems, especially those left over from less responsible times, have to be addressed. Those born then tend to grapple with issues and their solutions, being obliged to take life very seriously. They feel frustrated by the lack of realism shown by those who will not take on board what really needs to be done.

JUPITER

SATURN

URANUS

NEPTUNE

PLUTO

Uranus invents radically and unrealistically. This period is dominated by constant adaptations and explorations, through which people try to bring recent dramatic changes into practical focus, seeking to alter society and individual lives for the better. These mutable Uranus-in-Virgo times are naturally inquisitive. There is a tendency to initiate new schemes, but rarely to finish any of them. Consider 1794–1801, 1878–85 and 1961–9 in this light.

Neptune inspires simplistically and fanatically. When Neptune is in Virgo, people have a desperate need for comfort and something tangible to believe in. They seek immediate, effective and practical ways to resolve past uncertainties. This may lead them to accept simplistic and unrealistically concrete answers to problems that go far deeper than they realize. Ignoring, blaming and then forcing people toward such supposed "solutions" led to the fanaticism that dominated 1928–43.

Pluto transforms fundamentally and dismissively. With Pluto in Virgo, the times are concerned with radical improvement that sweeps away the past. All in society is questioned, nothing is sacred, and dishonesty is identified and purified. Yet continual reassessment can degenerate into the dismissal of all that binds society. 1956–71 was such a time. Those born then have had to tackle its aspirations and errors. Their Pluto's house position and aspects show how they trust and cope with trauma.

LIBRA

Polarity * Positive
Quality * Cardinal
Element * Air
Ruler * Venus

Beneficial * Harmonious
* Considerate * Honest

Unbeneficial * Complacent
* Inactive * Unadventurous

LIBRA – THE SEVENTH SIGN OF THE ZODIAC

THE UNIVERSE IS HELD TOGETHER by a profound and perfect balance of forces, a principle encapsulated by Libra. Commencing at the midpoint of the zodiac, Libra's scales symbolize a balanced understanding that puts all things in perspective, so that they can be dealt with appropriately. The sign's element, air, means that it needs to understand every person and situation properly. Being positive and cardinal, it also provides a firm foundation of support and the stability that encourages action.

Venus rules again in Libra, but very differently from how it rules in Taurus. Libra focuses upon both reassurance and responsibility in relationships, aware that our most important relationships become stronger and more stable when we seek to reconcile differences rather than letting problems fester. Active openness and honesty lead to greater love and respect on all sides.

When people come together, Libra provides both security and harmony. Imagine the perfect host, who makes the guests entirely at home and gives them the space and security to relax, share ideas

PERFECT BALANCE
Libra is symbolized in this 12th-century illustration by the scales that enable true understanding and perspective. Calmly seeking ways to restore balance and harmony, Librans do not often give up on their hope in life.

and explore new possibilities and projects together. In such comfortable, safe and conducive surroundings, every wonderful thing we can imagine feels possible.

Since Libra's desire to provide reassurance and stability applies as much to itself as to others, this raises the question of how Librans cope with uncertainty and the inevitable challenges and threats that we all face at some point in our lives. Some may lapse into denial, tempted to do nothing in the hope that a problem will disappear. However, Libra can be firm, gentle and confident, and deal equanimously with instability and challenge. Hence, although they fear falling into the abyss of despair, by facing upsets openly and positively, Librans rarely do.

ASSOCIATIONS

Keyword * Adaptively
Favourite phrase * I balance
Aspiration * Reality
Colour * Rose
Metal * Copper
Stone * Sapphire

Vulnerabilities * Debility
Parts of body * Kidneys
Plants * Flowers of all plants; ash trees
Herbs * Lilac, mint and asparagus

THE SCALES
LIBRA DECODED

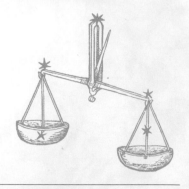

THE ESSENCE OF EQUILIBRIUM

Librans are by nature good companions – friendly and reliable sources of help. They thrive on pleasantness and desire beautiful and comfortable surroundings not only for themselves, but for anyone who wishes to share their lives. When confident about their circumstances Librans will defend their position, stirred on by the need for balance and by a commitment to just outcomes for all.

However, when they lack certainty and feel threatened, Librans can become defensive and suspicious. With Mars in detriment and the Sun in fall, they may lose confidence. This can lead them to act precipitously and feel destabilized, or to avoid action altogether, entering a state of denial or sitting anxiously "on the fence".

THE TWO SIDES OF LIBRA
The desire for accuracy and perspective that underpins the honest and open-minded outlook of Librans is also the source of their vulnerabilities: a fear of leaving familiar terrain and a tendency toward indecision.

HERCULES CAPTURES THE ERYMANTHIAN BOAR

The hero Hercules was instructed to capture a large ravaging boar. However, he was determined to avoid any more killing and so he left his bow behind. On the way, Hercules' centaur friends, Pholos and Chiron, persuaded him to share a cask of wine that was reserved solely for centaurs. The other centaurs were outraged and killed Pholos and Chiron.

Hercules returned to his task and found the boar. It was too fast for him so he set a snare for it, then hid and waited. When the boar was caught, Hercules wrestled it into submission. Hoisting it by its hind legs onto his shoulders, he proceeded down the mountainside, singing in triumph. Everyone he passed laughed at such an ungainly sight.

The Libran tendency toward inaction and distraction, dithering in their comfort zone rather than getting on with the task in hand, is what causes the tragic death of Hercules' friends. Once focused, however, the hero soon finds the most skilful means to master the boar without crude weaponry. With order restored, everyone feels happy and at ease again. When we have the clarity and courage to move beyond the familiar and do what is necessary, balance is soon restored and our problems are easily resolved.

A PLACE OF SAFETY

Although they welcome the challenge of shared risks, which can be measured and contained, Librans do not want to lose control. When fully prepared and equipped, they can show as much courage and resilience as anyone, but they are unnerved by sudden shocks and may react with outrage when treated with disrespect. A Libran's deepest fear is going "off the rails" with nothing to hold on to – their inability to cope in such circumstances means that their friends must be ready to come to their aid.

While reluctant to accept that the grass may be greener outside their comfort zone, Librans will be grateful to anyone who can guide them beyond their familiar place of safety to a world of new experience – especially if they enjoy the journey.

Librans love to plan to bring people together, revel in the joy of meetings and – any initial reluctance overcome – are delighted to enhance the experiences of others. Discussions with Librans on environments, art and fashion will bear fruit. In the company of Libra at its best, we are able to stop still for a moment and find the time, space and support for reflection.

SCALES OF JUSTICE

A pure and kind heart, as the mark of a worthy soul, has been the focus of cosmic justice since at least ancient Egyptian times. Thoth, the scribe of the gods, weighed the heart at death against a feather of Ma'at, the goddess personifying justice and truth (see page 33). If the soul was heavy with sin, it would tip the scales and be destroyed. Ma'at was the fundamental principal of the cosmos; without it, the universe would collapse into chaos. The cusp of Libra is the maturer of the year's two cardinal equinoctial balancing points.

In the Christian tradition, John Milton links Libra with the scales of divine justice. In *Paradise Lost*, God "Hung forth in heaven his golden scales, yet seen / Betwixt Astrea and the Scorpion sign." God weighed all creation against Satan's selfish violence. The scales "quick flew up, and kicked the beam". The balance against him, "the Fiend looked up, and knew / His mounted scale aloft: ... fled/ Murmuring, and with him fled the shades of night."

EQUIPOISE
Librans look to other people for support and respond positively when they receive it. All is possible, when strength and beauty are combined in perfect balance.

Born at 0230 UT on 2 October 1869 at Porbander, India, the frail-looking Mohandas Gandhi (the Mahatma) inspired and drove a movement that ultimately contributed to the defeat of the mighty British Raj. His birth chart reveals why. Gandhi's self-driven determination to struggle non-violently for independence is indicated

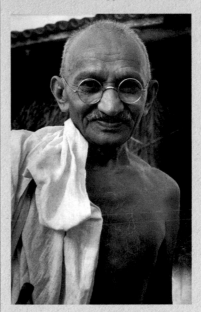

by the Twelfth House Libran Sun, and the Ascendant, ruled by Venus conjunct Mars in Scorpio. They are in a tight fixed T-square to Jupiter and Pluto in the Seventh House and the Moon in Leo in the Tenth. With Mercury in Scorpio, too, Gandhi exploited his unshakeable public charisma by constantly putting himself on the line, taking death-defying risks to undermine his enemy's vulnerabilities.

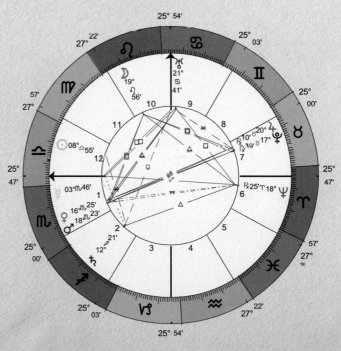

The Sun creates harmoniously and unimaginatively.
Librans are convinced that the best things happen when people and situations are comfortable and harmonious. They endeavour to make peace between people by seeing every perspective, aiming for fair treatment for all sides. With the Sun in fall here, it is important not to accept second- or even third-best for the sake of a "quiet life". Librans must have the courage to maintain their own goals in life, too.

The Moon reacts peacefully and over-accommodatingly.
The reassuring manner of people with the Moon in Libra seeks to ease the impact of sudden events and other peoples' dramas. They are never happier than when keeping life on an even keel. While living in peace is important, they must avoid becoming trapped in someone else's view of what peace means. Just sitting around is mere stagnation. Genuine peace actively creates space for good things to happen.

[THE SUN]

[THE MOON]

PLANETS IN
LIBRA

[MERCURY]

[VENUS]

[MARS]

Mercury communicates properly and carefully. By saying the right thing, people with Mercury in Libra create the impression that they have an intelligent understanding of all that they apply their minds to. They put others at ease, so people listen to their ideas. Preferring not to argue outright, they are careful not to cause upset by saying the wrong thing. This does not mean they change their minds easily, just that they are waiting for the most skilful time to speak.

Venus loves accommodatingly and acceptingly.
With Venus ruling Libra, a cardinal air sign, the ideal scenario is for everyone to experience life as beautiful and to enjoy one another's company. So people with Venus in Libra create conducive social and physical environments, paying heed to mood, décor, art, music and entertainment of all kinds. They must take care that the atmosphere is not simply a distraction that goes to everyone's heads and achieves little or nothing.

Mars acts urgently and defensively.
Those born with Mars in Libra feel the need to address all difficulties and to restore balance, moving away from uncertainty as quickly as possible. Should danger seem to threaten, they will take up the cause of justice. Mars is uncomfortable in detriment here so these people must be careful that their actions do not prove counterproductive. Otherwise, they may upset the proper solution and find themselves fighting for the wrong cause.

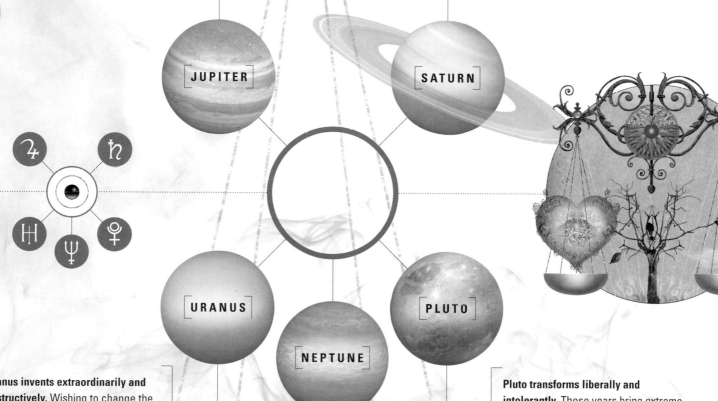

Jupiter expands judiciously and optimistically. When Jupiter is in Libra, we expect the very best and work to bring it about for everyone and everything in our world. It feels long overdue. This tendency to look on the bright side of things can stir expectations of change that in subsequent years may prove to have been over-optimistic. This is borne out by looking at the history of 1945–6, 1957–8, 1968–70, 1980–81, 1991–3 and 2004–5 – and the years immediately after.

Saturn controls reliably and intransigently. The exalted years of Saturn in Libra (1950–53, 1980–83 and 2009–12) realistically consolidate what has gone before. In these periods, overstretched enterprises are restrained within structures or, conversely, projects are released from excessive restraint. What is done may seem harsh or dangerous, but the promise of security is reassuring. Realizing that there must be limits on limitation as well as expansion sets us free.

JUPITER

SATURN

URANUS

NEPTUNE

PLUTO

Uranus invents extraordinarily and destructively. Wishing to change the world for the better leads to new discoveries and social developments that can also make matters worse. 1800–07 was the apex of Napoleon's domination of Europe. 1884–91 saw new developments in communications, transport and countless industrial processes. 1968–75 saw the climax of the Vietnam War, China's Cultural Revolution and widespread economic and social unrest elsewhere.

Neptune inspires romantically and mistakenly. With Neptune in Libra, things may not turn out as expected. Despite a movement toward absolute monarchy in England during 1614–29, Puritan dissent to this idea led to the foundation of New England by the Pilgrim Fathers and, later, the English Civil War. 1778–93 saw popular revolution in France become the Reign of Terror, yet also the birth of Romantic poetry. 1942–57 brought traumatic war that seeded the Cold War, but also the end of European colonialism.

Pluto transforms liberally and intolerantly. These years bring extreme measures and radical rebalancing. In 1478–91 the Tudor dynasty replaced the warring English royal houses, and the Spanish Inquisition was launched. In 1724–37 humane and materialistic philosophy emerged with Voltaire, Rousseau and the births of Emmanuel Kant and Tom Paine. 1971–84 saw an accelerated nuclear arms race, inflation, economic crisis and new attitudes to marriage and sexuality.

SCORPIO

Polarity ∗ Negative
Quality ∗ Fixed
Element ∗ Water
Rulers ∗ Mars and Pluto

Beneficial ∗ Passionate
∗ Perceptive ∗ Fearless

Unbeneficial ∗ Possessive
∗ Resentful ∗ Vindictive

SCORPIO – THE EIGHTH SIGN OF THE ZODIAC

SCORPIO IS CHARACTERIZED by all things that suggest desire, passion and transformation. Mars rules here, joining Scorpio's negative quality and its element of water with clear and effective purpose. With these powerful influences, Scorpios get what they want by concentrating fixed intense action at the point where it will be most effective. In this way, their force becomes irresistible and it is impossible to deny them their desires.

Their knack of getting quickly to the nub of phenomena and sensation makes Scorpios ideal for careers in observation and research. They make good astronomers and surgeons and are effective at many kinds of healing. Their skill in the face of the unusual and the dangerous lends Scorpios a "James Bond" mystique that suggests they have the capacity to confront and master almost any challenge.

Co-ruler Pluto also emphasizes Scorpio's involvement with death and decay in its manifold physical forms. Scorpios may venture into all kinds of dark and forbidding – or forbidden –

FROM DEATH COMES LIFE
A 16th-century Ottoman depiction of Scorpio. This sign teaches the lesson of regeneration: it is through death that life springs up, just as rotting plants provide compost for new ones.

experiences that others would seek to avoid. This capacity to cross frontiers and to make intimate contact with the dark side of life, with the unknown and even the taboo, explains Scorpio's sexual obsessions. In this area Scorpios often have a notoriety that both fascinates and intimidates non-Scorpios. Certainly, their need to have, and refusal to countenance the possibility of not having, is the least attractive and most counterproductive facet of the sign.

From death and decay come the creation and nurturing of new life. And from the unity of sexual ecstasy, new life is created. This is Pluto's, and Scorpio's, vital and reassuring essence. By letting go of the old, we establish the environment for the creation of the new: the phoenix that arises reborn from the ashes.

ASSOCIATIONS

Keyword ∗ Intensely
Favourite phrase ∗ I want
Aspiration ∗ Vision
Colour ∗ Dark red
Metal ∗ Iron
Stone ∗ Opal

Vulnerabilities ∗ Haemorrhoids and ruptures
Parts of body ∗ Sexual and excretory organs
Plants ∗ Leaves of all plants; bushy trees
Herbs ∗ Carnation, broom and tobacco

THE SCORPION
SCORPIO DECODED

THE ESSENCE OF REGENERATION

Scorpios feel at home with danger and often seem able to get away with anything. They have a fearless interest in unusual and unnerving experiences, sometimes even appearing to act as if danger were an irrelevance. They prefer to "cut to the chase", stop all the talking and take effective action or, even better, cause it to be taken. They have an intense – some may say morbid – interest in those intimate and unusual places and possibilities that others avoid. The term "comfort zone" means little to most Scorpios. This curiosity often leads them to make fascinating discoveries.

A STING IN THE TAIL
Taken from a 17th-century deck of Tarot cards, this image shows Scorpio with its stinging tail upraised, ready for anything. The biggest danger Scorpio has to face is that its passions, if thwarted, turn to brooding resentment and vindictiveness.

Others, who may find it hard to say no to Scorpios, often find such intensity inexplicable and alarming. Fearing that they may be led along "forbidden" paths, toward outcomes that they cannot control, they may become anxious just as Scorpios feel comfortable and at home.

HERCULES DESTROYS THE LERNEAN HYDRA

Hercules was instructed to slay the Hydra, a monstrous nine-headed serpent that lived in a lair of perpetual darkness, amid the stench of the stagnant swamps and quicksands of Lerna. Driving it from its lair with fiery arrows, the hero severed one head, only for two to grow instantly in its place. With every attack, the beast became stronger.

In this version of the myth, Hercules remembered the advice of his teacher: "We rise by kneeling." He knelt and used his mighty strength to seize the Hydra and lift it high above his head. The rays of the sun and the blowing of the wind took away the monster's power. As it grew weaker, the nine heads drooped, revealing the one mortal head that Hercules immediately severed and buried, killing the creature for good.

The simple yet incisive imagery expresses the essential nature of negative emotions and attachments, and also how to recognize their true nature and dispose of them. If ignored, our attachment to the dark mire of illusion festers and intensifies. Sniping from a distance (shooting fiery arrows) merely makes things worse. Attacking at arm's length (cutting off a self-duplicating head) only makes negativity stronger. The solution is to have the courage to immerse ourselves in our negative emotions and attachments. In raising and exposing them to the full light of day, we will see just how weak and easy to dispose of they are.

STRENGTH IN UNCERTAINTY

Scorpios tend to stay cool in the face of uncertainty, meeting the unknown without fear. This includes intimate situations. Intimacy leads to passion and desire, which are Scorpio's strength if used kindly – but its curse if they get out of hand.

With Venus and the Moon in detriment and fall, Scorpio's big danger is that its passions will degenerate into intense attachments and jealousy. Then brooding resentment can breed vindictiveness. We let Scorpios down at our peril. But if we show an interest in them and join them in focusing on what needs to done, studied and experienced, all such anxieties will become irrelevant. With Scorpio by our side, we can make remarkable discoveries that lead us to a richer and more profound understanding of life.

BIRTH CHART ✳ PRINCESS GRACE OF MONACO

This movie star and member of one of Europe's oldest royal families was born Grace Kelly at 0531 EST on 12 November 1929 in Philadelphia, Pennsylvania. Few birth charts could suggest more desirability. Her Pisces Moon in the romantic Fifth House trines a group of Scorpio planets rising in the First. To give that edge of grace, Venus is in Libra, the sign it rules, close to the Ascendant. It is small wonder that Grace Kelly was a successful actress and came to the attention of one of Europe's most eligible bachelors, Prince Rainier of Monaco, with whom she had a fairy-tale wedding. The Scorpio–Sun-ruled Leo Midheaven, afflicted by Mercury and Saturn, marks her death in a car crash.

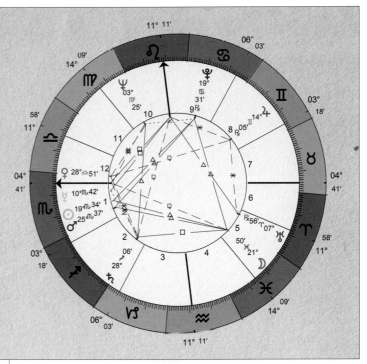

SATAN'S REVENGE

Classical mythology links the constellation Scorpio to the rather dark myth of the hunter Orion. A giant demigod and the son of Poseidon and Euryale (a daughter of King Minos of Crete), Orion was invited by the goddess Artemis (Diana) to go hunting with her. The goddess's brother, Apollo, feared that his chaste sister might succumb to Orion's powerful charms. He told the earth goddess, Gaia, that Orion had bragged of his ability to kill every beast in the world. Angered by this boast, Gaia sent a monstrous scorpion to pursue Orion. As Orion swam to safety, Apollo told Artemis that the swimming figure was a brigand who had come to rape her. She fired an arrow that hit Orion in the head, killing him at once. On discovering the truth of Apollo's deception, Artemis set Orion in the stars, pursued forever by Scorpio, the scorpion.

In Christian tradition, Scorpio represents Satan, the poisonous beast that succeeds in tempting Eve and Adam in the Garden of Eden. In the story, curiosity and an attachment to desire lead humankind to the knowledge of good and evil, destroying its primordial innocence. This act is Satan's revenge for the divine judgment (represented by the preceding sign, Libra) that saw him and his followers cast out of Heaven. The Libra and Scorpio allegories can also be understood as metaphors for internal spiritual progress. Destructive attitudes isolate us from good judgment and lead us to lose something precious, as we cling to passionate needs that will never satisfy us.

THE TEMPTER SNAKE
This medieval depiction of the story of Adam and Eve shows (top right) the snake, associated with Scorpio, that tempts Eve into eating from the Tree of Knowledge, her curiosity resulting in mankind's Fall.

The Sun creates intensely and indulgently. Those born with the Sun in Scorpio are greatly stirred by the idea of being in the thick of things in every way imaginable. They are drawn to discover all intimate secrets, from personal affairs to the mysteries of the entire universe. A constant temptation to over-indulgence, these Scorpio powers are more beneficially and satisfactorily employed to counsel others through periods of emotional or physical pain.

The Moon reacts passionately and intimidatingly. People with the Moon in Scorpio embrace life and engage deeply with others. Whether these others react with excitement or alarm indicates if such involvement will be a help or hindrance. As the Scorpio Moon is in fall, emotional connection and possessiveness can become uncomfortably and vindictively entangled. The way to avoid this is to make intimate contacts, without being selfish.

THE SUN

THE MOON

PLANETS IN
SCORPIO

MERCURY

MARS

VENUS

Mercury communicates shrewdly and suspiciously. Because there is so much to see and know (and second-best is not an option), Mercury placed here means taking life seriously, seeking that essential truth around which real experience and healing revolve. Ever more intense focus in search of deeper insights puts people and objects of study "on the spot". True insights are so vital that it is important to examine all possibilities carefully, taking nothing for granted.

Venus loves passionately and jealously. People with Venus in Scorpio tend to throw themselves into a whole range of experiences, whether that be acting, dancing, music or any form of physical contact – the more "total" the experience, the better. In relationships, they need the most intimate emotional and physical contact. A partner who seeks to abandon them must beware the scorpion's vindictive streak. But by rising above the settling of old scores, pain retreats and new experiences are much more satisfying.

Mars acts incisively and vindictively. Mars, the ruler of Scorpio, seems to carry all before it with efficacious and courageous action. If they have Mars in Scorpio, people are naturally ready for action. Effective and determined warriors, they are a source of strength to friends and of deep anxiety to those who oppose them. Their confident sexuality has an urgent need to be satisfied. The adventurous among us can only be exhilarated by the intense possibilities they have to offer.

Jupiter expands convincingly and obsessively. These Jupiter-in-Scorpio years see people working ever harder to implement improvements promised by recent changes. Such confidence and style will attract excitement and support, providing it is not imposed by empty and ill-considered idealism. Hopes engendered when Jupiter was in Scorpio in recent times (1946–7, 1958–9, 1969–71, 1981–2, 1993–4 and 2005–6) worked out very differently in the years that followed.

Saturn controls responsibly and insensitively. When Saturn is in Scorpio, social attempts are made to curb passions in the service of good order. During these periods, perceived counterproductive behaviour is often challenged. 1923–6 saw Prohibition in the US, the rise of Stalin and the 1926 General Strike in Britain. In 1953–6 the McCarthyite witch hunts occurred in the US and in 1956 the USSR invaded Hungary. In 1982–5, the advent of HIV/AIDs challenged sexual freedom.

JUPITER

SATURN

URANUS

NEPTUNE

PLUTO

Uranus invents challengingly and dangerously. Periods with Uranus in Scorpio demonstrate the risky lengths that societies will go to satisfy their passions. The years 1807–14 saw Europe in crisis and Napoleon's disastrous Russian campaign. The next period, 1890–98, was a time of economic panic followed in Canada by the Klondyke Gold Rush. The years 1974–81 saw a world energy crisis, the advent of monetarism and the birth of Solidarity in Communist Poland.

Neptune inspires deeply and suggestibly. During these periods (most recently 1792–1807 and 1955–70), new beliefs based on intense emotion are stimulated. These can lead to unconventional lifestyles, such as those of some of the early 19th-century Romantics, or of the hippies and other groups in the 1960s. A clash of political and social ideals led to the French revolutionary struggles and then the Napoleonic wars in the former period; and in the latter period, to the Vietnam War and other Cold War conflicts.

Pluto transforms fundamentally and self-indulgently. Pluto's ruling-sign periods in history change the world. During 1490–1503 Columbus "discovered" America (1492) and Vasco da Gama found the route to India via Cape Horn (1498), opening the globe to trade and colonial expansion. More recently, 1983–95 seeded a transformation in sexual attitudes and the development of electronic communications that revolutionized global communications and markets.

SAGITTARIUS

Polarity ∗ Mutable
Quality ∗ Positive
Element ∗ Fire
Ruler ∗ Jupiter

Beneficial ∗ Visionary
∗ Active ∗ Generous

Unbeneficial ∗ Overburdened
∗ Impatient ∗ Undiscriminating

SAGITTARIUS – THE NINTH SIGN OF THE ZODIAC

THE RULING PLANET, JUPITER, is at its most expansively generous in Sagittarius, where it combines with the three archetypal qualities (positive mutable fire) to provide confident flexibility. Sagittarians seem to say yes to every request asked of them and be full of energy in their endeavour to accomplish it. This willingness is driven by a heightened idealistic view of justice: the wish that everything should be right with the world, and as quickly as possible. No one should be disappointed and everyone's needs should be met. Many Sagittarians explore philosophies and religions in their quest to find the answer to the world's ills.

However, Sagittarians should beware being tempted by simple solutions. Black-and-white answers are generally too good to be true. It is neither possible nor necessarily desirable to try to do everything for everyone all the time. Justice is about much more than answering every need. Undiscriminating acceptance leaves too little time to decide between the many mutable possibilities that their positive fire wishes to act upon.

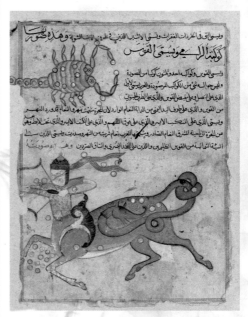

AIMING BEYOND DESIRE

A Persian illustration of Scorpio followed by Sagittarius: passionate need transforming into universal generosity. But energetic fire can be undiscriminating. Sagittarius is more likely to succeed if ambition is targeted, as an archer takes time to aim an arrow.

Yet there is a way that Sagittarius can attain mastery and be effective. The arrow symbol indicates that *focus* is the skilful route to success. Like the archer Sagittarius must hold back and concentrate before firing; determine first which judgment or action will bring about the most change for the good. By focusing upon the ultimate goal, all other aspirations will fall into place and energy can be used most effectively. In ideas, beliefs and actions, this is the Sagittarian path to fulfilment.

ASSOCIATIONS

Keyword ∗ Far-reachingly
Favourite phrase ∗ I see
Aspiration ∗ Victory
Colour ∗ Purple
Metal ∗ Tin

Stone ∗ Turquoise
Parts of body ∗ Liver, hips and thighs
Vulnerabilities ∗ Blood disorders, tumours
Plants ∗ Ash and oak trees
Herbs ∗ Dandelions and moss

THE ARCHER
SAGITTARIUS DECODED

THE ESSENCE OF MOVEMENT

Sagittarians love to get moving: they revel in the sheer joy of motion, whether physical or metaphorical. They find it difficult to refuse a possibility or request, feeling that they will always be able to fit it in somehow. People are drawn to their idealism and gregarious way of bringing others along with them. Their attitude gives hope to others by making the impossible seem possible, even when everyone else is ready to give up in despair. However, they can also be too hedonistic, permissively putting up with behaviour or attitudes that others might regard as unacceptable. Taking on too much can make them feel exhausted and pulled in all directions. Their lives risk becoming a mass of muddled ideas and unfinished business. They may end up making promises they cannot keep and leaving people in the lurch.

HERCULES BANISHES THE STYMPHALIAN BIRDS

The marsh of Stymphalas was terrorized by a flock of monstrous birds with sword-like beaks and iron feathers. Hercules attempted in vain to club the birds or shoot them with arrows. His efforts were counterproductive, as iron began to fall dangerously to the ground. Then the hero recalled the advice he had been given: "The flame that gleams beyond the mind reveals direction sure." At twilight, when the marsh was dense with birds, Hercules beat two cymbals furiously together, making an unearthly clashing sound that was unbearable to hear. The flock rose in terror and disappeared, never to return.

While not touching on Sagittarius's warmth, this labour shows how to resolve the sign's essential problem. For Sagittarians, overwhelming pressures can make life impossible. The solution is to look beyond the trap of immediate demands. What do we really want? By asking the right question we find the simple answer. Sagittarius can find justice by cutting through distraction to higher truth, which resolves all problems.

THE JOY OF MOTION
Sagittarians are drawn to movement: they love to join in with the running herd. However, this attitude can lead them to take on too much, for fear of saying no, and ultimately cause more disappointment to others when they let them down.

A LIFE OF ACTIVITY

Although we may feel that our Sagittarian acquaintances need discipline, the last way to get to their hearts is to try to control them. Some may be wiser than us and have made the best decision already. Even when in the wrong, they will either ignore us, or just go away and avoid making decisions. Sagittarians want people to listen to them, to go along with and help their plans. Helpers are welcome, because the pressures of their commitments can be overwhelming. When they are exhausted, anyone who sees a better way around problems can be a real boon. The important thing for Sagittarians is to feel happy and effective and to keep moving in a direction that everyone feels good about. They love dancing, acting and all kinds of sport. They are never happier than when travelling with the wind in their hair. Anyone who can share in and enable all these actions, while serving the cause of justice, is a real friend of Sagittarius.

DEFEATING DESIRE

The sign has been associated with desire and sexuality since ancient times, perhaps due to its proximity to Scorpio. The image of Sagittarius as a centaur (a beast with the torso of a man and the body of a horse) dates from Babylon, where the sign was linked with a centaur named Pabilsaĝ, who had wings and a scorpion's tail – clearly a reference to the skies near by.

The image of the centaur in general represents the conflict between humankind's base (literally unbridled) appetites and civilized behaviour. In Greek myth, most centaurs were associated with sexual licence and violence, but a few were wise, kindly and civilized, most notably Chiron, who was expert in hunting, warfare, music, poetry and healing. The tutor of several Greek heroes, including Achilles, Chiron became the constellation Sagittarius after his death.

Sagittarius releases and resolves Scorpio's attachment. Its arrow points toward the star Antares, "the heart of the scorpion", representing the theme of piercing and defeating desire – the way to clear away barriers and to succeed.

BIRTH CHART ⭑ JANE AUSTEN

Born at 2345 LMT on 18 December 1775 at Steveston, England, Jane Austen is seen as one of the foremost English authors for the high quality and comic irony of her writing. The foundation and driving force behind both characteristics is the Sun on the Sagittarian Fourth House cusp (Imum Coeli, see page 133). That sign's ruling Jupiter, and nearby Uranus in the Gemini Ninth House, describe perfectly the worldwide fame of Austen's sharply observed and matchlessly ironic novels. The Second House Moon/Venus conjunction in Scorpio, jointly ruled by Mars and Pluto in Capricorn, point to her incisive emotional authority. With it, she describes relationships that are constantly at the point of ending and being gloriously reborn. Both these Scorpio rulers trined to Neptune in Virgo on the Ascendant fit with a mastery of style that continues to captivate readers to this day.

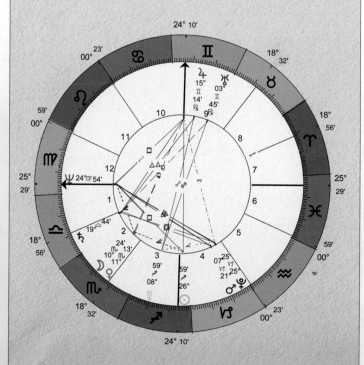

The Sun creates expansively and over-optimistically. A need for action and a fascination with the unknown urge Sagittarians out of their immediate world. Most will go as far as they can to explore foreign lands or new philosophies. Never happier than when figuratively or literally in motion, they love sport and anything that tests the edge of what is possible, but they may say yes too easily and too often. Focusing on the greater good keeps Sagittarians steady.

The Moon reacts generously and permissively. Those born with the Moon in Sagittarius love to encourage others, finding their ideas and experiences stimulating. They take pleasure in never knowing what other people will find out next. They enjoy going places with people, providing they do not take over their lives or cramp their style. They need to check from time to time that they are doing the right things for the right reasons.

PLANETS IN
SAGITTARIUS

[THE SUN]

[THE MOON]

[MERCURY]

[VENUS]

[MARS]

Mercury communicates idealistically and expansively. People with Mercury in Sagittarius love contributing to conversations, especially if the debates are on deep religious or philosophical matters. They believe that everyone has a right to their opinions on how to make the world a better place. Although they may be quick to make up their mind and speak it, they are also prone to changing it. They should listen and consider, as well as suggesting alternatives.

Venus loves open-heartedly and naïvely. Those with Venus in Sagittarius are prone, after little or no persuasion, to throw heart and soul into all sorts of possibilities with people who share their love of adventure. They are fascinated by the life of foreign places. They must discriminate between this healthy, stimulating curiosity and straying into experiences they cannot understand or control. To avoid others taking advantage of them, they have to remember that life is about more than just enjoying the journey.

Mars acts courageously and recklessly. Movement, getting on with life's needs, is the key to feeling alive for those who are born with Mars in Sagittarius. Seeing the way ahead they set off, leaving others to follow in their wake. Their world of busy activity can cause quite a stir, but their courage reassures others. While enjoying this exhilarating flow, they should focus on the goal as well as on the thrill of action. Reckless adventures can have unfortunate outcomes.

Jupiter expands farsightedly and eclectically. When Jupiter is here, understanding broadens with brave new ideas and philosophies. People born in, or living through, such times find it easier to teach and learn. In 1959 the French Fifth Republic was born. From 1983 monetarism transformed the world economy; 1995–6 launched price expansion; by 2006–7 "boom and bust" were said to be "defeated". Unfortunately, as the cycle moved on, the hopes of those years were frustrated.

Saturn controls optimistically and ineffectively. Saturn is all at sea in Jupiter's sign. It can insist on the wrong solution and limit inappropriately, or be indecisive. Either opportunities are missed or permissiveness prevents focused direction. Things can get out of hand. In 1926–9 and 1985–8 the avoidance of hard choices led to the far worse outcomes of economic crash and recession. More than ever in these times caution is needed to make future problems less likely.

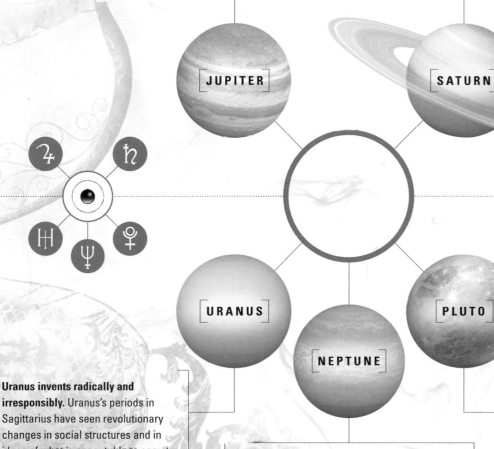

JUPITER

SATURN

URANUS

NEPTUNE

PLUTO

Uranus invents radically and irresponsibly. Uranus's periods in Sagittarius have seen revolutionary changes in social structures and in ideas of what is acceptable to society. During these times we can go anywhere, do anything. The years 1562–70 and afterwards were a great age of buccaneering, with Spanish wealth preyed upon by French, Dutch and English privateers; while 1981–8 saw free-market, monetarist-driven policies in modern nations.

Neptune inspires tolerantly and suggestibly. When Neptune is in Sagittarius, an openness to new experiences creates possibilities beyond the wildest imaginings. From the Renaissance and the first discovery of the "New World" by Europeans (1478–93), to civil and religious wars in Europe (1642–57), the rise and fall of the Napoleonic empire (1805–20) and the climax of the Cold War (1970–84), the issue has always been deciding which belief to trust. Working for the benefit of all, not the few, is the way to avoid (self-) deception.

Pluto transforms enthusiastically and excessively. Pluto in Sagittarius indicates figurative or literal death; and transformation through expansion, whatever the consequences. In 1502–16, the first Spanish explorers arrived in Mexico, and Portugal claimed Brazil. In 1748–52 territorial wars between France and Britain came to a head, and the sextant was invented. The technology of 1995–2008 brought a seemingly limitless expansion in global communications, with profound consequences.

CAPRICORN

Polarity ∗ Negative
Quality ∗ Cardinal
Element ∗ Earth
Ruler ∗ Saturn

Beneficial ∗ Practical
∗ Responsible ∗ Loyal

Unbeneficial ∗ Controlling
∗ Overcautious ∗ Inflexible

CAPRICORN – THE TENTH SIGN OF THE ZODIAC

COMMENCING AT THE (NORTHERN) WINTER solstice, when the Sun is furthest away, Capricorn operates like a chief executive intent on mastering the universe. Its symbol is a goat or goat–fish (a creature with a goat's forequarters and a fish's tail). It is an earth sign and the goat stands for its down-to-earth, sure-footed quality, while its fabulous variant symbolizes both the earth and the ocean depths, pointing to Capricorn's quest for intellectual and spiritual heights counterbalanced by reflection and profound inner searching that is often tinged with melancholy. Capricorn's energy and dynamism derive from this precarious balance between extroversion and introspection. Whichever tendency dominates, Capricorn takes life and responsibility very seriously. Capricorn refuses to rest or compromise in its untiring quest to achieve practical sustainability. Structure is as essential to Capricorn as the body's skeleton or the foundations of a house.

With the Moon in detriment, the sign's serious sense of mission can seem inconsiderate when Capricorns expect more of

THE GOAT
This gold coin, showing Capricorn the goat, was minted in India during the reign of Jahangir (1605–1627). Sure-footed and untiring on the mountain paths, the goat symbolizes this sign's nimbleness, energy and stubborn perseverance.

others than it is easy to give. Jupiter being in fall in this sign can lead to overstructured conservatism and make it difficult to relax control. This may block innovation and opportunity. Feeling the need to abandon the heady idealism of Jupiter-ruled Sagittarius can sour Capricorn's efforts and make them seem infertile and joyless. Trapped in knowing the one "right" way, Capricorns can appear demanding and distant, obstinately sticking to their own approach to doing things.

Or, with the hard work done, is it that Capricorns wisely realize the destructiveness of seeking unnecessary change? Do they live in the loneliness of knowing when there is nothing more to do? If so, in bad times, when our foundations are shaken, Capricorn can be that steadfast, god-like friend with the authority to remind us that all there is to existence is the way things are.

ASSOCIATIONS

Keyword ∗ Usefully	**Vulnerabilities** ∗ Rheumatism
Favourite phrase ∗ I use	**Parts of body** ∗ Knees and bones
Aspiration ∗ Power	**Plants** ∗ Pine and willow; roots of all plants
Colour ∗ Black	
Metal ∗ Lead	**Herbs** ∗ Hyacinth and onion
Stones ∗ Jet and onyx	

THE GOAT
CAPRICORN DECODED

THE ESSENCE OF REGULATION

The surface impression given by Capricorns is often of being soft and politely restrained, bordering on an apparently accepting indifference that is comfortable to be with. However, being ruled by Saturn with Mars exalted, Capricorns can be hard taskmasters, expecting rigorous work from everyone – themselves most of all. In leisure, too, they welcome opportunities to overcome challenges and obstacles, such as cycling long distances or climbing in difficult terrain. Like their sign, the goat, Capricorns cannot be easily manipulated or led. They have minds of their own and are resolutely individualistic. This practical self-reliance can make them uncompromising and impatient, with a tendency to be unsympathetic in the face of what they see as weakness and failure. Excuses and second-best are just not acceptable. However, while Capricorns may seem at times to be intransigent, demanding and distant, anyone seeking security and reliable support will often find them to be their best companions.

HERCULES CAPTURES THE CATTLE OF GERYON

As his tenth labour, Hercules was sent to capture the red cattle of Geryon, which lived on the island of Erytheia in the far West. Protected within a golden chalice, his reward for devotion to the sun god Helios, Hercules mastered the tossing seas and reached Erytheia. He slew Orthrus, Geryon's two-headed guard dog, and the giant oxherd Eurytion. Driving the blood-red cattle before him, he was pursued by Geryon, who breathed fire from all three of his heads. Hercules shot a flaming arrow that fatally pierced the monster's three bodies. Hercules then drove the frequently straying cattle across Europe and over the Alps. On the long way home, he faced many dangers and righted numerous wrongs.

The labour has been interpreted as symbolic of the Sun's passage through Capricorn and certainly contains much solar symbolism, such as the chalice of Helios, while the journey over mountain and sea recalls the symbolism of the Capricorn goat–fish. Persistence and a willingness to undertake hard and long tasks are Capricorn traits. Capricorn, like Hercules, understands that good planning leads to effective action, so that we are not only able to succeed in our anticipated aims, but can also respond to other demands that we meet upon the way.

WORLD-SHAPER

The Sumerian and Babylonian god Ea (also known as Enki) was the creator of the world, and ruled over water as well as human crafts and wisdom. This ancient Mesopotamian seal shows the god with water streaming from his body. Ea's symbols, the fish and the goat, were later combined to make the goat–fish Capricorn.

BUILDING TO LAST

We can rely on Capricorns and on what they build, but we should not expect them to bend to our will. What they want to know is whether something works and will last. They rely upon and judge by results, and are always willing to encourage others to bring their resources to their projects. They are sure in their knowledge of how to do things and are happy to provide all the help and security that others need. While pressing for positive outcomes, Capricorns have no wish to glory in their own success. To be in control is enough and, until that goal is reached, for Capricorns there is always more to do.

THE SIGN OF THE GOAT–FISH

The sign of Capricorn seems to derive from ancient Sumer, where the goat–fish was a symbol of the creator god Ea. Greek and Roman writers refer to the constellation either as a goat or a goat–fish (sea goat), uncertainty arising perhaps from the relative faintness of the constellation. The name Capricorn derives from

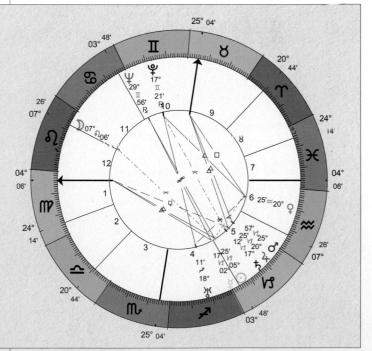

THE HORN OF PLENTY

Capricorn is associated with the cornucopia, the magical goat horn of abundance and fertility. This Thracian gold rhyton (drinking horn) in the form of a goat dates back to the 3rd–4th century BCE.

the Latin for "goat's horn". This alludes to the Greek myth of Amaltheia, a goat–nymph who nursed and hid the baby Zeus from his father Kronos. Zeus made one of Amaltheia's horns into the cornucopia, or horn of plenty, which abounded with whatever its owner desired. This may have seasonal symbolism, with spring's abundance arising from the depths of winter. Earlier Greek myth made Capricorn–Amalthea the nurse of the sun god.

According to a Greco-Egyptian myth the goat–fish represents the nature god Pan. While in the form of a goat, he escaped from a monster into the Nile. The parts of his body that were submerged became the tail of a fish, while the rest of him retained its goat form. In Aztec mythology, what we call Capricorn was linked with Cipactli, a primeval sea monster or crocodile that symbolized the earth floating in the primeval waters and stood for the first day of the Aztec divinatory count of 13 × 20 days.

BIRTH CHART ✶ MARLENE DIETRICH

The singer and actress was born at 2115 CET on 27 December 1901 in Berlin, Germany. Five planets, including her Sun and ruling Saturn, are creatively focused upon the Capricorn Fifth House, harmoniously trined by the perfectionist Virgo Ascendant. This, and her Leo Moon giving generously in the Eleventh, account for why Dietrich's alluring persona and performances enthralled millions during World War II. For a while in those dark years, one of the world's few lights seemed to be her demandingly enchanting presence, which she combined with a voice that Ernest Hemingway claimed "could break your heart".

PLANETS IN CAPRICORN

The Sun creates effectively and unsympathetically.
The natural ambition of Capricorns to achieve important objectives makes them determined and methodical workers who set out to complete what they begin. This sense of responsibility puts them under pressure and they may not suffer fools gladly. They may also become caught up in their own self-importance. But if their goals are focused there is nothing they cannot master and bring to a successful conclusion.

[THE SUN]

The Moon reacts realistically and demandingly.
Responses to the approaches of others may seem reserved, even distant. Relationships become easier with proper boundaries established, and with shared objectives in leisure as well as work. The natural caution and sense of responsibility of those with a Moon in Capricorn can be reassuringly supportive, but they should beware of imposing prior conditions that become barriers to the development of relationships.

[THE MOON]

[MERCURY]

[VENUS]

[MARS]

Mercury communicates carefully and supportively. Those with Mercury in this sign identify and eliminate potential problems. Having carefully considered past experience and accepted authority, they may become entrenched and difficult to challenge, which is daunting to those seeking relationships with them. Lack of flexibility is unsuited to innovation. They come into their own when support and rigorous implementation of systems and structures are needed.

Venus loves cautiously and devotedly. Those with Venus in Capricorn want to progress, but are cautious, controlling their dealings with other people, possessions and the world in general. They may seem to be shy, not wanting to be rushed into commitment; but once committed they feel much more comfortable in established, long-standing relationships. Often appearing to wait cautiously on the sidelines of life, when they do become attached they are truly steadfast toward all the people and objectives they set their hearts upon.

Mars acts forcefully and enthusiastically.
Mars in this sign sets people to work: they cannot wait to roll up their sleeves and get on with the job. With so much realistic, practical energy, those born with Mars in Capricorn find few dare stand in their way and they energize others with their enthusiastic application of the force of necessity. It could be difficult, even dangerous, to oppose the certainty and authority that they seem to have on their side; it may be better to let them carry on in their own way.

Jupiter expands excessively and confrontationally
Jupiter, at cross-purposes in Saturn's sign, can lead to both the imposition of authority and violent challenges against it. In 1984–5 the British government's closure of coal mines led to bitter social unrest, while in India the storming of the Golden Temple led to Indira Gandhi's assassination. In 2008 Jupiter entering Capricorn with Pluto marked the collapse of an unsustainable boom in the global economy and attacks upon bankers.

Saturn controls realistically and restrictively. With Saturn in Capricorn, limits are imposed on what is no longer sustainable, as in 1988–91, which saw the end of Soviet system and Cold War. However, the alternatives may prove even more restrictive. 1929–32 brought reality to financial markets but also the Depression. 1959–62 marked the dismantling of African colonialism, but also the establishment of some dictatorships and the entrenchment of apartheid in South Africa.

JUPITER

SATURN

URANUS

NEPTUNE

PLUTO

Uranus invents radically and intolerantly. New revolutionary understanding upsets structures of social control when Uranus is in Capricorn, as in 1988–96 when electronic trading transformed financial markets. However, the good may be swept away with the bad. In the same period failed Marxist systems ended for millions in Eastern Europe, but the rapid switch to free-market economies left many people in hardship, yearning for old certainties.

Neptune inspires practically and imprudently.
Simplistic devotion to the practical can lead to subtleties that are vital for full understanding being overlooked. Britain in 1656–71 saw a shift to a more secular, rational approach to society and science, but also a rejection of astrology and the need to grasp human motivation fully. In 1820–34 the USA established the Monroe Doctrine against European colonialism in the Americas, but failed to address slavery. In 1984–98 monetarism opened both sides of the Atlantic to greed and waste.

Pluto transforms uncompromisingly and fundamentally. Pluto's cycle reveals the changes we are ready to die for. This is especially traumatic when the planet passes through Capricorn, as we face the need to transform society's structures. Such was the case in 1515–32, the time of the Reformation. 1762–78 saw struggles for democracy and human rights in America and France. The current transit, 2008–24, will challenge the world economy and how we relate to each other and the planet.

AQUARIUS

Polarity ✳ Positive
Quality ✳ Fixed
Element ✳ Air
Rulers ✳ Saturn and Uranus

Beneficial ✳ Humane
✳ Loving ✳ Innovating

Unbeneficial ✳ Intransigent
✳ Self-righteous ✳ Arrogant

AQUARIUS – THE ELEVENTH SIGN OF THE ZODIAC

THE POSITIVE AIR OF AQUARIUS seeks to refresh humanity with eternal wisdom poured down and distributed equally to all. Uranus working through the sign's joint ruler, Saturn, means Aquarius offers revolutionary challenges to the secure conservative structures created in Capricorn. It insists on probing more deeply than Capricorn would find comfortable, believing that more needs to be understood and more questions answered. In any endeavour, Aquarius seeks to consider the views of as many people as possible. Aquarians are often comfortable in occupations involving humanitarian social service, scientific enquiry and political reform, and in other areas that broadly aim to improve the lot of humanity.

But when Saturn is over-emphasized and works through Uranus, Aquarians may let their missionary zeal – their belief that they are the custodians of certain and universal truth – go to their heads. They may come to see their personal preferences as the best and only way, ignoring or denying the validity of other arguments.

THE IDEALIST
A 17th-century image of Aquarius the water-carrier. This sign wants to understand life's imperfections and know how things can improve for the benefit of as many as possible.

They may call for change and revolution as necessary for the "common good", but it will be the common good as they define it. Aquarians are prone to allowing their excitement at novelty, whether in the socio-political or technological realms, to override reflection on its actual benefits. As outsiders, Aquarians may (self-) righteously demand the impossible, while as insiders they will intransigently hold their ground. Potential benefits can be negated as debate degenerates into fighting personal corners.

Yet in the deepest reaches of the Aquarian soul lies a profound love for truth and for all life. Focusing upon this wish to see others happy will rescue debate from petty blind alleys, helping Aquarians to be open to question about their ideas, even to a total change of mind. Ultimately, the Aquarian role is to know the "big picture".

ASSOCIATIONS

Keyword ✳ Knowingly
Favourite phrase ✳ I know
Aspiration ✳ Love
Colour ✳ Turquoise
Metals ✳ Platinum and uranium
Stone ✳ Turquoise

Vulnerabilities ✳ Varicose veins
Parts of body ✳ Ankles and circulation
Plants ✳ Flowers of all plants; most fruit trees
Herbs ✳ Orchid, daffodil and hemp

THE WATER CARRIER

AQUARIUS DECODED

THE ESSENCE OF ASSOCIATION

Aquarians feel a strong urge to be friends with everyone and are open to a wide range of experiences. They see virtue in objectivity and tolerance, tending to join causes that embrace as many people as possible. Feeling that the interests of all should be honoured, especially the vulnerable, Aquarians see through propaganda and manipulation and seek to expose it. Natural revolutionaries, they often adopt positions that oppose the status quo or are otherwise unconventional, seeking to create better openness and understanding by "stirring things up".

LIFE-GIVING WATERS
A medieval portrayal of Aquarius as the carrier of water – the most essential of substances. The role of water-bearer reflects the desire of this sign to be of use to others in some important way. Many Aquarians are drawn to careers in activism or charity work.

HERCULES CLEANSES THE AUGEAN STABLES

Hercules completes with ease the labour linked symbolically with the sign of the water carrier. For 30 years, no one had found a way to clear the vast quantities of noxious cattle dung that had built up in the stables of King Augeas and the surrounding fields, and which was both poisoning and starving the people. All previous attempts having failed, the king was incredulous when Hercules claimed that he could cleanse the stables in a day. Mockingly, Augeas offered the hero a 10th of his cattle if he succeeded, but demanded power over Hercules' life and fortune if he failed. With his semi-divine strength, Hercules easily completed the task by diverting two rivers through the stables. Augeas was not happy, though – he accused Hercules of trickery and threatened to behead him should he ever return.

This task touches on the perceptive power of Aquarius and also its predicament. Understanding the workings of the universe more clearly than others, Aquarians often find that what needs to be done is obvious – so obvious that others may be reluctant to agree, perhaps for fear of seeming foolish that they themselves did not see the solution so clearly. Indeed, the greater an Aquarian's success the more dangerous it is to seek recognition and reward. Evolved Aquarians realize this and take it in their stride, feeling that giving benefit to others is sufficient reward in itself. Like Hercules they simply move on, ready for the next task.

With the Sun in detriment, Aquarians may not focus sufficiently on their own lives, because they put too much energy into helping other people – even if such assistance is not requested and ends up overwhelming those they seek to help. The Aquarian tendency to repeat constantly their key phrase "I know" (either literally or by implication) will certainly tend to irritate. When deluded by misplaced convictions, they may forget basic Aquarian principles and, while claiming to act in the interests of everyone, behave with overbearing arrogance.

ENGAGEMENT AND TRUST

Sharing a common cause is a good way to engage with an Aquarian, maybe through social service (such as charity work) or political activism. Being their opponent will arouse interest and possibly respect. If you want to enjoy successful intimate relationships with Aquarians, do not be put off by their tendency to show equal or even greater concern for others. Aquarians tend to feel that

Born on 12 February 1809 in Shrewsbury, England, with Venus in Aries trined to Saturn/Neptune in Sagittarius, Darwin's research revolutionized scientific assumptions and challenged established religious belief. The publication of *The Origin of Species* (1859) led  to ridicule and character assassination, explained by Mercury, Jupiter and Pluto in Pisces, squared to that Saturn/Neptune. Abraham Lincoln, born the very same day, really was assassinated for his beliefs. In 2009 the two men's status as icons of our time was confirmed by the opening of London's Darwin Centre, and by the inauguration of the USA's first black President.

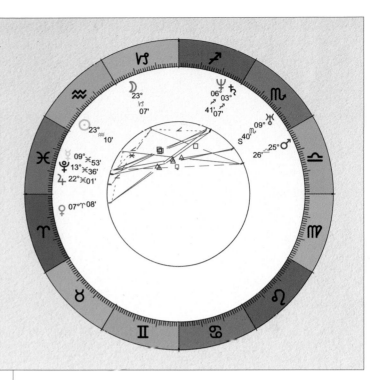

loving one person deeply and loyally does not exclude expressing their humane care and affection for others. They are not being disloyal or unfaithful; rather they are expressing their love for you by the way they care for the world that they are creating with you.

PURIFICATION AND UNDERSTANDING

In the ancient Near East the Sun's passage through Aquarius, the water carrier, coincided with the rainy season, and this may be one origin of the sign's name. Because rain was so essential for farming, the Sumerians gave many individual Aquarian stars names for good luck. The sign has also been linked with the Babylonian deity Ea, the sexless god of waters and streams.

The ancient Egyptians probably adopted the zodiac signs relatively late in their history, via the Greeks. The sign of Aquarius fitted with their ancient god Hapi, who presided over the annual Nile inundation, watering the crops that were harvested by mid-February. Hapi, whose image shows him pouring water onto the Earth from two jars, was associated with purification and renewed fertility: every year the Nile's subsiding waters left a new deposit of rich fertile silt on Egypt's farmland. Today's symbol for Aquarius resembles the Egyptian hieroglyphic for *mu*, meaning water.

The link between Aquarius and purification can also be seen in the name of the month of February, named after Februa, the Roman festival of purification. This included a hilltop ceremony in which priests purified young women with a goatskin thong to ensure fertility and easy childbirth.

The Greeks and Romans also connected Aquarius with Ganymede, cup-bearer of Zeus and the epitome of beauty and innocence. As astrology spread, the heavenly water carrier increasingly became associated with the pouring down of pure understanding for the benefit of all.

BELOVED OF ZEUS

This 16th-century sculpture shows Ganymede being abducted by Zeus in the form of an eagle. Zeus took the boy to Olympus and made him cup-bearer to the gods. Later, he placed Ganymede among the stars as Aquarius.

The Sun creates objectively and arrogantly. Devotion to the "big picture" and group interest, whatever the personal cost, often puts Aquarians at odds with the authorities and conventional opinion. New possibilities draw them magnetically. They challenge what may harm others, especially traditions. However, trying to direct peoples' lives leads to being ignored or labelled a troublemaker. The antidote is to see things through the eyes of others and to speak judiciously.

The Moon reacts tolerantly and permissively. Those with the Moon in this sign accept people as they are, being friendly and helpful without becoming too entangled. Too much emotion can take them into unfamiliar areas that they cannot control. Working in a group to serve society and bring about change can seem more worthwhile, but may just be a way to avoid intimacy. They avoid personal commitments and seek to please everyone, appearing lost if not able to do so.

[THE SUN]

[THE MOON]

PLANETS IN
AQUARIUS

[MERCURY]

[VENUS]

[MARS]

Mercury communicates knowledgeably and domineeringly. Intelligent insights come quickly to those born with Mercury in Aquarius. They are fascinated by the structures of things and organizations, and keen to find innovative ways to improve them. (Anyone not sharing their enthusiasms may resent how they seem to take over.) Committed to knowledge for its own sake, they share all they know, hoping others will use it for the common good.

Venus loves universally and impersonally. Venus in Aquarius means being immediately agreeable and friendly toward everyone, wanting all to enjoy their lives as they wish. Those with Venus in this sign are devoted to the joy of knowing, believing there is no religion higher than truth. Nothing pleases them more than breaking down barriers with courageous, independently-minded friends. It is important to focus enthusiasm for abstract, pleasant-sounding ideals so that others can really benefit from their devotion.

Mars acts enthusiastically and rebelliously. Those with Mars in Aquarius are excited by ideas about radical change. In their headlong ride through life they brush aside excuses, keen to change minds. However, they need to think carefully when challenging the understandings of other people, as their revolutionary anger may not be justified. Creating positive momentum, while leaving room for other views that might improve their plans, will often lead to better solutions.

Jupiter expands hopefully and over-optimistically.
When Jupiter is in Aquarius, new idealistic systems offer great hope for change. We envision, and start to work for, a better world. Such periods include 1961–2 and 2009–10, the hope-filled first years of John F. Kennedy's and Barack Obama's presidencies, and 1997–8, the beginning of Tony Blair's term as British prime minister. 1973–4 saw the end of the Vietnam War and the triumph of Communist rule in Indochina.

Saturn controls responsibly and negatively. In the years that Saturn passes through Aquarius, realism tempers what can be done. Seen positively, the difficulties of such times provide valuable knowledge to ground more sustainable futures. The years 1932–5 saw fascism and economic depression, while 1962–4 saw the assassination of President Kennedy and deeper US involvement in Vietnam. The years 1991–4 brought economic recession.

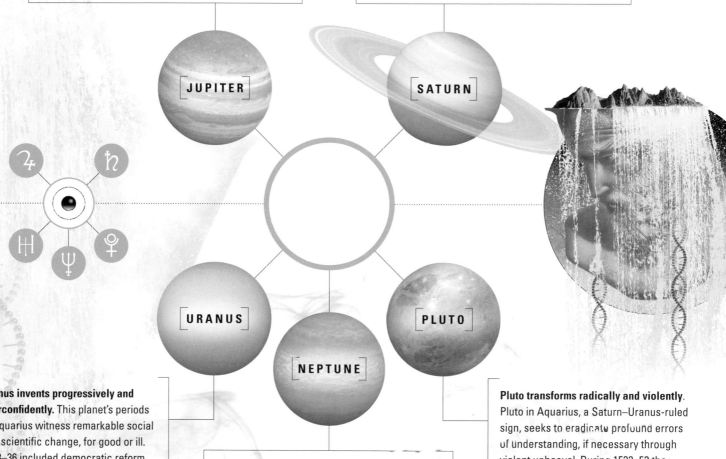

JUPITER

SATURN

URANUS

NEPTUNE

PLUTO

Uranus invents progressively and overconfidently. This planet's periods in Aquarius witness remarkable social and scientific change, for good or ill. 1828–36 included democratic reform in England, revolution in France, the Indian Removal Act in the US, the start of rail travel and the invention of the electric generator and the revolver. 1912–20 saw world war, the end of the European empires and revolution in Russia. In 1995–2003 there was radical change in communications technology.

Neptune inspires idealistically and forcefully.
Neptune's cycle is 164 years and that of Uranus 84 years, so during every other Uranian transit Neptune is also in Aquarius. These transits bring especially strong convictions, reinforcing Uranian changes. In 1834–48 demands for democracy culminated in the 1848 upheavals and Marx's *Communist Manifesto*. 1998–2012 saw the rise of religious fundamentalism, and of claims that there is nothing reductionist science cannot explain – termed "secular fundamentalism" by some.

Pluto transforms radically and violently.
Pluto in Aquarius, a Saturn–Uranus-ruled sign, seeks to eradicate profound errors of understanding, if necessary through violent upheaval. During 1532–53 the English Reformation destroyed the traditional religious structure. In 1777–98, American colonists fought to sever ties with the "Old Country" and bring the United States into being, while on the other side of the Atlantic the French Revolution led to the excesses of the Terror and a pan-European war.

PISCES

PISCES – THE TWELFTH SIGN OF THE ZODIAC

THIS LAST OF THE ZODIAC SIGNS is the most mature and compassionate, because it can be aware of the whole breadth of the universe. The negative mutable water suggests continuous receptive sensitivity, an empathy moved by ruling Jupiter to spread out in all directions, like open hands supporting and seeking to respond to every need. Joint-ruler Neptune is king of the sea which, through the rivers, streams and rains that serve it, makes uninterrupted contact with the myriad places and experiences of the planet and its creatures. So Pisces feels close to the world around it, fascinated by the need to appreciate and care for all. Pisceans are often drawn to careers that heal and serve others; to personal growth in the form of meditation and better understanding of human psychology; to playing and enjoying music and to sharing poetry; to spiritual mysteries and the unworldly – to knowing, in the deepest sense, all that is involved in living.

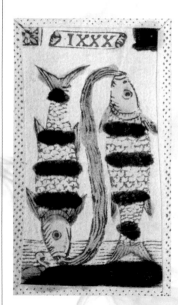

NOTHING IS FIXED
Showing the two fishes that symbolize Pisces swimming in opposite directions yet linked by a cord, this 17th-century image illustrates how feelings can be shared but not fixed, especially not in mutable Pisces.

In psychology the sea is also a symbol of the unconscious, and Pisces is sensitive to subtle needs that those born under other signs might hardly notice. Pisces can seem overwhelmed with responsibility and to be carrying the burdens of the world on its shoulders. It feels demands that others do not seem to care or even know about.

There is no security in gripping on to water. The wisdom of Pisces comes from realizing that to deny our connection with everything, to view life as a battle against the world, is to experience drowning alone. When we let go of attachment to material reality and come to see our essential union with the universe, liberation follows, just as Pisces heralds the arrival of spring, the time of regrowth and resurrection as the year's cycle begins again.

ASSOCIATIONS

Keyword * Sympathetically	**Part of body** * Feet
Favourite phrase * I believe and often suffer	**Vulnerabilities** * Illnesses from impure blood, especially gout
Aspiration * Mastery	**Plants** * Leaves of all plants; trees near water
Colour * Soft sea greens	
Metal * Tin	**Herbs** * Water lily, tulip and fig
Stone * Amethyst	

THE FISHES

PISCES DECODED

THE ESSENCE OF EMPATHY

With Venus exalted in this sensitive sign, Pisceans are presented with a rich kaleidoscope of often overwhelming experiences. They particularly love music and also the sea, especially the shells, creatures and other mysterious things that dwell in it. Seeing everything as one, they seek to respond to all needs as if these were their own, and take naturally to nursing, massage and other healing arts. Intensely aware of the wide range of other people's feelings, Pisceans do not always find it easy to determine the boundaries between themselves and others. They can sometimes be too sympathetic, giving too generously and even unwisely. Their acute sensibility means they have to be careful with even the subtlest of substances that could alter their consciousness. Because Pisceans can be overwhelmed by what most people might hardly notice, they should be extremely cautious with alcohol and drugs, and monitor carefully their reaction to medicines.

HERCULES CAPTURES CERBERUS, GUARDIAN OF HADES

In an esoteric version of this labour, Hercules has to overcome Cerberus, the three-headed dog that barred the entrance to the underworld, in order to rescue Prometheus from its depths. As a punishment for stealing the fire of heaven for humanity, Prometheus was eternally chained to a rock while an eagle pecked out his liver, which again and again grew back for the torture to begin once more. Moved by compassion, Hercules resolved to help him. Hades agreed that Hercules could free Prometheus if he could first conquer Cerberus with his bare hands. Grasping the animal's primary throat in a vice-like grip, Hercules overcame the beast and set Prometheus free.

Hercules' key qualities in this labour demonstrate the qualities of a saviour: compassion, or the giving of the self to others; courage; exactly appropriate action. The hero could not bear to see Prometheus suffer. Without a thought for his own safety, he exposed himself to being trapped in the underworld. Selflessly focused on the job in hand, he perceived which of Cerberus's throats to grasp. So the rescue succeeded. When we are unshakeably dedicated to working for others, we too can withstand trials and see the right thing to do.

BEING AT ONE WITH THE WORLD

As swimmers know, there is no security in gripping on to water. Only by opening out and being at one with the water, by adapting to the buffeting waves of life, can Pisces make progress and avoid being overwhelmed.

DOING THE RIGHT THING

Honesty is the best policy with Pisceans – we should always remember that their intuition will pick up most attempts to deceive. They may seem easily persuaded to serve your needs, but beware of taking them for granted. Pisceans will put up with a lot, allowing themselves to be used far more than they should, but they do have a snapping point. Once this is crossed, emotionally driven resentment can trigger a brutal and vindictive payback. With Mercury in both detriment and fall, words seeking to manipulate or answer their emotional needs are unlikely to have much impact. An honest smile or a genuinely felt look or touch can say much more. Pisceans respond well to kindness. When we do the right thing, without fear and without seeking favour, our Piscean friend will know and we will find them comfortable to be with again.

THE AGE OF PISCES

The Babylonians used the constellation of Pisces in their astronomy. The image of two fish swimming in different directions connected by a common ribbon has been interpreted as a symbol of the Tigris and Euphrates rivers, the lifeblood of ancient Mesopotamian civilization.

In one ancient Greek myth, Aphrodite and her son Eros transformed into (or were saved by) two fishes in order to escape the monster Typhon; the fishes were tied together by cords on their tails to ensure that each always knew where the other was.

From 221 CE when the vernal equinox (20–21 March in today's calendar) astronomically regressed from Aries to Pisces, the sign of the fishes has ruled the present age (there are 12 astrological ages, each of just over 2,160 years, in each 26,000-year "Great Year"). Ever since the early Piscean Age, when Christianity became one of the established religions of the Roman empire, it has dominated world culture – appropriately, as Christ invited his disciples to become "fishers of men". At the dawn of the Piscean period, the sign of the fish, rather than the cross, was the most common symbol used by Christians and its use has been revived among Christians today.

This star was born at 0200 UT on 27 February 1932 in London. Of her many roles, her depiction of the renowned Egyptian queen Cleopatra most expressed the rich range of her birth chart, which made it the part she was, literally, born to play. While Cleopatra's ultimate fate fits with Taylor's sacrificing Sun, Mercury and Mars in Pisces in the Third House, it is the Leo Jupiter, ruling both Sun and Ascendant signs, that shows her imperial beauty. The trine to Jupiter from the Aries Venus/Uranus in the Fourth describes her character's dangerous impulsiveness on screen, as well as her tempestuous real-life relationship with Richard Burton. The squares to that Jupiter from Cancer Pluto in the Eighth and the Moon in Scorpio in the Eleventh, reveal her destiny to play seduction and death hand-in-hand.

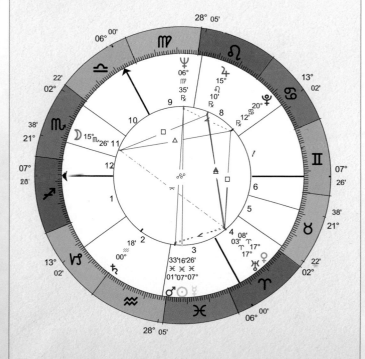

The Sun creates sympathetically and intuitively. Pisceans are naturally understanding and supportive – and expect the world to be the same toward them. Easily stirred emotionally, it seems natural to "be there" for everyone. However, they would be wise to discriminate, as turning a blind eye to manipulation or dishonesty will trap them in situations that wear them down. Resisting undeserving demands will leave strength for when it is really needed.

The Moon reacts empathetically and over-supportively. People born with a Moon in Pisces feel inside the experience of all that happens around them, and can empathize with and reassure others so that no one feels alone. Their naturally intuitive, even psychic, abilities channel a higher level of perception. But as with the Sun in Pisces, it is vital to avoid being worn down. They need to relax (especially in or by water), to rediscover where their responsibilities begin and end.

[THE SUN]

[THE MOON]

PLANETS IN
PISCES

[MERCURY]

[MARS]

[VENUS]

Mercury communicates imaginatively and illogically. With their Mercury in Pisces, people are stirred by words and ideas to exciting possibilities, even flights of fantasy. Poetry opens their hearts. Because they understand intuitively, arguing things out is inconclusive. Heightened perception and emotion-based thinking can cause misunderstanding. Feeling responsible may lead to them making unnecessary apologies. Relying on true feelings should reveal the right answer.

Venus loves totally and unconditionally. Yearning to embrace all that their senses and imagination can experience, those born with Venus in Pisces eagerly seek intimate relationships with people and the world about them. Music, art and stories heighten the connections between them, their loved ones and their world. They should beware of the hurt of separation. Loving like this, they must focus on the nature, not the object of their devotion. Then they have an experience they can never lose.

Mars acts intuitively and ineffectively. With Mars in Pisces deep conviction generates powerfully driven feelings. These can inspire others toward higher understanding and open up possibilities. However, people with Mars in this sign should check that their enthusiasm leaves room for other people's needs and feelings. If they take over, their best intentions may leave them shouldering all the blame, rejected and ignored if things go wrong. To avoid this, they should test the water carefully before plunging in.

Jupiter expands altruistically and unrealistically.
The years with Jupiter in this water sign see powerful sympathies motivating generosity. We want to believe that good things can happen, but such optimism may be unrealistic, even naïve. 1938–9 saw "peace for our time", an attempt to stave off war; in 1962–3 Kennedy created the Peace Corps; 1998–9 saw the expanding "dotcom" business model that collapsed soon after. In 2010–11 economic regeneration was planned.

Saturn controls modestly and unimaginatively. In Saturn-in-Pisces years, kindness motivates the relaxing of structures, but consequences are overlooked. 1905–8 saw the start of Britain's "welfare state" but also military build-up. In 1935–8 the Nazis were allowed to re-arm Germany. In 1964–7 permissiveness erupted, but the grassroots revolution lacked responsibility. The 1993–6 structural reorganization of the world economy triggered a boom but led to global economic collapse.

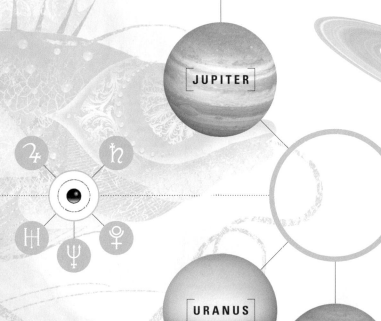

JUPITER

SATURN

URANUS

NEPTUNE

PLUTO

Uranus invents credulously and unrealistically. When Uranus passes through Pisces, amazing answers to past problems can be accepted without question. Simplistic solutions often become beliefs to die for. Thus 1920–28 saw forced collectivization in the Soviet Union, Fascism in Italy and Prohibition in the US. In 2003–11, fundamentalist beliefs threatened security, as well as free expression and action not only between nations, but also in domestic politics.

Neptune inspires profoundly and unshakeably.
With Neptune ruling Pisces, beliefs are felt so deeply that they polarize and separate us, becoming an essential feature of group loyalties. 1520–34 cemented the Protestant–Roman Catholic schism within Europe and 1684–98 saw persecution of Protestants in France and of Catholics in Britain. During the transit of 1848–62, the publication of Darwin's *The Origin of Species* and Karl Marx's *Communist Manifesto* established arguments for a secular society.

Pluto transforms self-sacrificially and cataclysmically. It would be as well for the world to prepare carefully for Pluto's next period in Pisces (2043–67). The last two saw brutal intolerance, with people sacrificed for beliefs. 1552–79 brought the Counter-Reformation, ferocious religious wars, the burning of martyrs and the St Bartholomew's Day massacre of French Protestants. 1797–1823 featured the Napoleonic Wars and the widespread social discontent that followed in a disordered Europe.

WHAT ARE THE 12 HOUSES?

EQUAL AND UNEQUAL SYSTEMS

Astrology envisages the heavens as a great globe with the Earth as its focal point and the ecliptic – the Sun's apparent path around the Earth – at zero degrees of celestial latitude. Each of the 12 signs of the zodiac occupies a 30° longitudinal segment of this celestial globe. Astrologers also divide the heavens into 12 segments known as "houses", but these should not be confused with the signs. Although each house has a favoured zodiac sign as its occupant, the houses and signs are not the same. All or part of any of the 12 signs can occupy any of the houses, as can any of the planets. The deciding factors are the time and date.

Like the terrestrial globe, the celestial globe is divided into 360° of longitude. The degree of celestial longitude that happens to be rising above the eastern horizon at any given moment (for example, at the time of a person's birth) is known as the Ascendant and is taken as the first degree of the First House (the First House "cusp"), which is below the horizon. The houses are numbered anticlockwise, starting from the Ascendant.

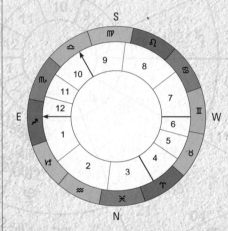

UNEQUAL HOUSES

The houses (see numbers) spin anticlockwise with the Earth, so the heavens appear to spin clockwise. The left arrow points to the Ascendant. During each day, as the Midheaven arrow becomes more (or less) vertical the houses grow larger (or smaller).

TRACING THE ECLIPTIC

The Earth revolves in an anticlockwise direction, making it appear as if the celestial globe is revolving clockwise around the Earth. At dawn, therefore, the Earth is revolving toward the Sun, which appears to rise above the eastern horizon. The Sun continues to "rise" until it reaches its zenith or highest point (the Midheaven of the ecliptic) at around noon, local mean time. The Sun then "falls" through the afternoon and "sets" below the western horizon at dusk, when in fact the Earth is revolving away from the Sun.

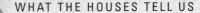

600-YEAR-OLD ASTROLABE

The medieval astrological clock on the City Hall in Prague's Old Town shows three time systems: the sidereal (star) time used to calculate the Ascendant and the Midheaven; the zodiac positions of the Sun, with its daily rising and setting; and the positions of the Moon, with its phases.

Many astrologers divide the day's circle into 12 equal houses from the Ascendant degree. However, others prefer to use an unequal system (see diagram, opposite) that allows for the Earth's tilt on its axis. The time that a 30° ascending zodiac sign takes to pass across the eastern horizon depends on the observer's latitude. Near the equator, each sign takes about two hours, and house divisions are almost equal. At a latitude of 60° north, Libra takes three and a quarter hours, but Aries less than 30 minutes. (In southern latitudes the signs are reversed timewise.)

As the Earth is revolving and tilted, the zenith or Midheaven (Medium Coeli) and the nadir (Imum Coeli, the "Bottom of the Sky") are only at 90° to the Ascendant/Descendant axis for brief moments each day. In the unequal house system the Midheaven

WHAT THE HOUSES TELL US

Each house represents part of our personality, from the everyday to the profound, and corresponds to a key life area: the First House to personality; the Second House to possessions, and so on.

The terms angular, succedent and cadent are allocated to houses counting anticlockwise from the Ascendant, rather as cardinal, fixed and mutable are given to zodiac signs (see pages 58–9). Angular houses occupy the four key points of the birth chart, describing personality, aims in life, relationships and home foundation. Like cardinal signs, these are the activating houses. Succedent houses follow on from and structure what the angular houses have instigated. Cadent houses are not so strong, so these are areas of life where great resources can be available but extra effort is required to be effective.

Any sign can be in any house, but each house is said to have a natural zodiac sign that best fits that house. Hence Aries, the first sign, best suits the First House (personality), while Libra suits the Seventh House (relationships), and so on.

The following pages describe each house, and the significance of each planet when it is present in the house. When interpreting the meaning of planets in our houses we should remember that a planet's zodiac sign will substantially modify any interpretation. Planetary rulership, exaltation, fall and detriment (see page 49) for each house are the same as for its corresponding natural zodiac sign. Much will also depend on the planet ruling the zodiac sign on the cusp of the house.

and Imum Coeli are found on the Tenth House and Fourth House cusps, but the equal house system isolates them from these cusps.

In an unequal system, houses at extreme latitudes become impossibly bunched and an equal house system is needed. In spite of this problem, my research has found similarities between very different cultures at the same latitude around the world. This book therefore uses a house system that allows for latitude, namely the popular Placidus unequal house system, which works well for most of the populated places on the globe.

It may well be that different systems of house division suit different techniques and uses of astrology. Through our varying approaches to astrology we seek to articulate our relationship to the heavens. As we become more experienced, it is good to try different systems and decide which works best for us personally.

THE FIRST HOUSE

PERSONALITY

PROJECTING A SELF-IMAGE

The first of the angular houses, with Aries its natural sign and ruled by Mars, this house encompasses everything about how the self is presented to the world. This includes physical factors, such as bearing, dress, appearance and even, it has been suggested, the shape of the head and the face. The First House also indicates our behaviour: how we approach the world; the impression we make (whether intentional or not); our effectiveness; and our (self-) confidence. This house can show whether we have a taste for action and throwing ourselves at the world; whether we seek to dominate or prefer to take a back seat and not be noticed; whether we enjoy talking, acting, dancing, singing, judging, controlling, listening carefully or deliberately ignoring.

How our personality comes across to others depends implicitly on how we see ourselves. The First House can help us to perceive whether we are self-assured or self-conscious and insecure; or whether we are inclined to be self-obsessed – so concerned with our own way of doing things that we are blind to the effect of our actions.

When our First House is strong we have something special to present to the world. Artists, actors and entertainers of all kinds, salespeople and auctioneers, racing drivers and other sports stars usually have the First House prominent in their birth charts. The key to the successful presentation of the self is awareness: being conscious of the impact we make on the world and on those around us. If we can be relaxed, skilful, confident and aware in our dealings, those who are touched by our lives may become that way, too.

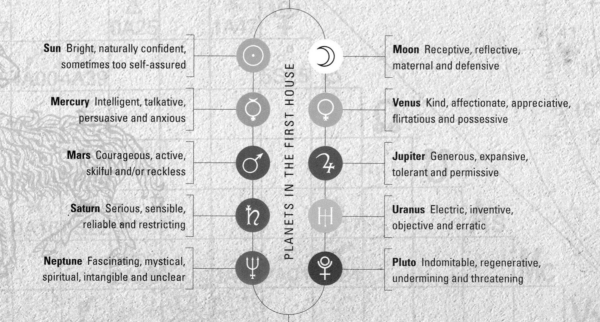

PLANETS IN THE FIRST HOUSE

Sun Bright, naturally confident, sometimes too self-assured

Mercury Intelligent, talkative, persuasive and anxious

Mars Courageous, active, skilful and/or reckless

Saturn Serious, sensible, reliable and restricting

Neptune Fascinating, mystical, spiritual, intangible and unclear

Moon Receptive, reflective, maternal and defensive

Venus Kind, affectionate, appreciative, flirtatious and possessive

Jupiter Generous, expansive, tolerant and permissive

Uranus Electric, inventive, objective and erratic

Pluto Indomitable, regenerative, undermining and threatening

THE SECOND HOUSE
POSSESSIONS

HOLDING ON TO OBJECTS AND FEELINGS

A succedent house with Taurus as its natural zodiac sign, the Second House shows us how we gather and store the fruits of our endeavours. Venus, ruler of Taurus, attaches our discriminating hearts to beautiful art and furnishings as well as to the loveliness of nature's own plants and places.

Second House possessiveness suits the acquisition and retaining of money, and the business activity associated with this. Unsurprisingly, successful entrepreneurs and other business-people often have a strong Second House.

If the Second House shows that we love to fill our world with the best of everything, we should also be aware that we can be overwhelmed when we possess too quickly and forcefully. Our drive to *have* may become so strong that it clutters our lives with far more than is necessary.

This is true also of emotional attachments, which can be even stronger than our feelings for material objects, business success or bank balances. Our need for loved ones can become so intense that we just cannot let go.

Whether our attachment is to special material possessions and wealth, or to individuals, emotional reassurance, freedom of expression, knowledge, social idealism or something else, the desires revealed by the Second House reflect the values that make us what we are.

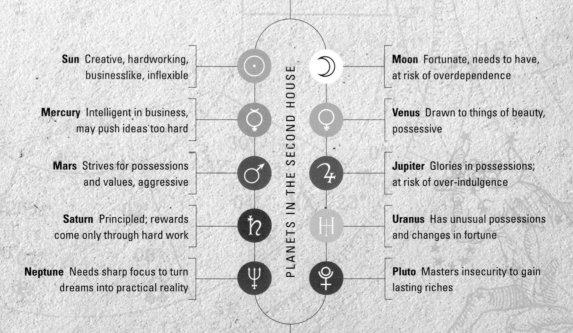

PLANETS IN THE SECOND HOUSE

Sun Creative, hardworking, businesslike, inflexible

Mercury Intelligent in business, may push ideas too hard

Mars Strives for possessions and values, aggressive

Saturn Principled; rewards come only through hard work

Neptune Needs sharp focus to turn dreams into practical reality

Moon Fortunate, needs to have, at risk of overdependence

Venus Drawn to things of beauty, possessive

Jupiter Glories in possessions; at risk of over-indulgence

Uranus Has unusual possessions and changes in fortune

Pluto Masters insecurity to gain lasting riches

THE THIRD HOUSE
SHORT JOURNEYS

HOW WE COMMUNICATE

Cadent and naturally occupied by Mercury-ruled Gemini, this house embraces all means of communication. These include the gathering and dissemination of information and gossip via the spoken and written word, through books, newspapers, the internet and other media. The Third House also describes how we communicate within our immediate social milieu. It shows how children learn and how they are likely to progress (including at school); and also describes the nature of our family beyond our parents (who are discussed in the Fourth House): brothers, sisters, close cousins, uncles and aunts.

The skills and support structures of our community give us the strength and security to grow. If the social environment that we live in and depend on takes care of our immediate concerns, then we will have room to look beyond and focus on what we really want from our lives.

If our Third House is exceptionally strong we may move from one distraction to another, not able to keep what is said or thought in perspective, in extreme cases even becoming schizophrenic. Conversely, too much emphasis on this house can also lead to communities closing in on themselves. For example, schools may become places that simply condition children with unquestioned assumptions based on conventional opinions.

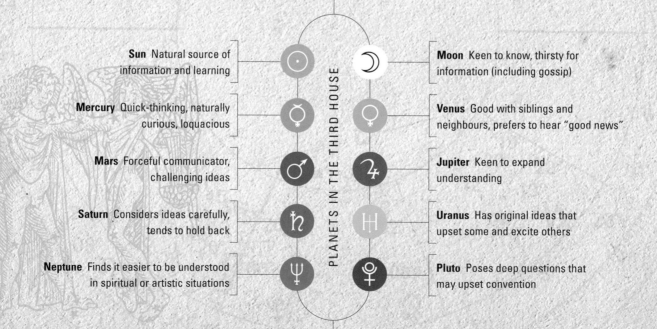

Sun Natural source of information and learning

Mercury Quick-thinking, naturally curious, loquacious

Mars Forceful communicator, challenging ideas

Saturn Considers ideas carefully, tends to hold back

Neptune Finds it easier to be understood in spiritual or artistic situations

PLANETS IN THE THIRD HOUSE

Moon Keen to know, thirsty for information (including gossip)

Venus Good with siblings and neighbours, prefers to hear "good news"

Jupiter Keen to expand understanding

Uranus Has original ideas that upset some and excite others

Pluto Poses deep questions that may upset convention

THE FOURTH HOUSE

HOME AND PARENTS

THE FOUNDATION OF OUR SOCIAL VALUES

This second angular house focuses on the very basis of our lives. With Cancer, ruled by the Moon, as its natural sign, the Fourth House shows us our relationships with our parents, especially the mother who bore us. In this house we also see the kind of home we grew up in – comfortable and stable, or disorganized and constantly changing, or something in-between – as well as the values our parents held dear and inculcated in us. Whether we realize it or not, these experiences formed assumptions that have determined our behaviour throughout life, for good or ill.

As adults, we look to the Fourth House to discover the kind of home that we will create for ourselves, even the type of building in which we choose to live. It can indicate the standards of behaviour that we will expect from all who enter our home, especially if they seek to become part of our extended family; and it can offer insight into how we are as mother or father to our own children. When planets move into our Fourth House, they suggest events that affect the life of our home and family.

If our birth chart is strongly focused on the Fourth House, the idea of "home" is likely to feature in our career. At one level this may mean that we deal in the sale or renovation of other peoples' homes, for example as an estate agent, a builder or a decorator; or, on a more idealistic level, we may feel strongly about the kind of society we wish to live in and create for our children.

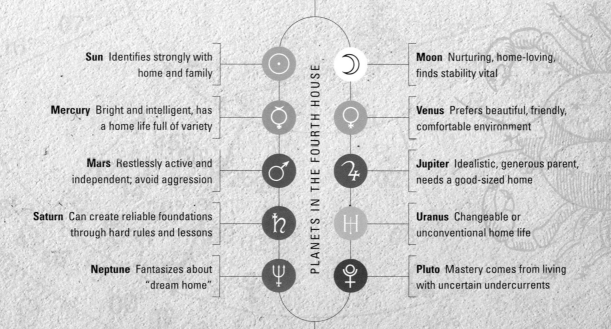

PLANETS IN THE FOURTH HOUSE

Sun Identifies strongly with home and family

Mercury Bright and intelligent, has a home life full of variety

Mars Restlessly active and independent; avoid aggression

Saturn Can create reliable foundations through hard rules and lessons

Neptune Fantasizes about "dream home"

Moon Nurturing, home-loving, finds stability vital

Venus Prefers beautiful, friendly, comfortable environment

Jupiter Idealistic, generous parent, needs a good-sized home

Uranus Changeable or unconventional home life

Pluto Mastery comes from living with uncertain undercurrents

THE FIFTH HOUSE
creativity

DIRECTING OUR CREATIVE ENERGIES

Succedent and naturally occupied by Leo, the Fifth House indicates how we focus our creative energy and experience the pleasures of life. The planets and signs in the Fifth House point toward all kinds of creative enthusiasm. Signs and planets associated with the element air suggest that our creative talents lie in writing or speaking, while water indicates that we are drawn to music, whether playing instruments or singing. Fire in the Fifth House relates to the physically dynamic arts of dance or acting, or to sport, while the presence of earth points to sculpture and painting, or risky "hands-on" projects as a business entrepreneur.

The Fifth House also describes our appetite for pleasure: the games we like to play, the entertainment we seek and how we party. This house reveals our readiness for romance, describes our typical love affairs and lovers, and also suggests whether we can handle the experience of betrayal that romantic adventures so often bring. It also shows if we care for lovers or tend to leave them in the lurch.

The Fifth House indicates our children: what they will be like and how we will treat them, or whether we will have them at all. Raising children is one of the greatest expressions of creativity. As in all our highest artistic endeavours, as parents we create something that is much more than personal self-indulgence.

The Fifth is also the house of speculation in financial markets and gambling. As with romance, we may either be naturally cautious or feel a thrill in taking things to the limit.

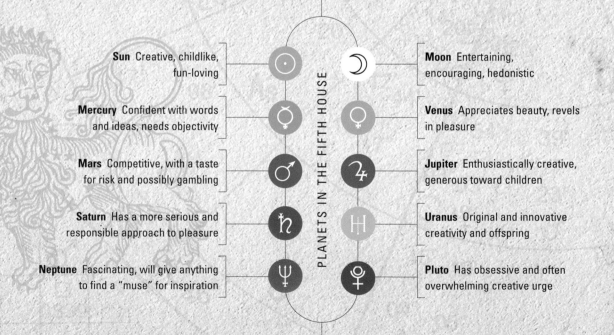

PLANETS IN THE FIFTH HOUSE

Sun Creative, childlike, fun-loving

Mercury Confident with words and ideas, needs objectivity

Mars Competitive, with a taste for risk and possibly gambling

Saturn Has a more serious and responsible approach to pleasure

Neptune Fascinating, will give anything to find a "muse" for inspiration

Moon Entertaining, encouraging, hedonistic

Venus Appreciates beauty, revels in pleasure

Jupiter Enthusiastically creative, generous toward children

Uranus Original and innovative creativity and offspring

Pluto Has obsessive and often overwhelming creative urge

THE SIXTH HOUSE

WORK AND WEALTH

FUNCTIONING EFFECTIVELY

This cadent house, naturally occupied by Mercury-ruled Virgo, reveals how conscientiously and responsibly we consider our work and our own health.

As far as work is concerned, the Sixth House can suggest what employment best suits us (manual, intellectual or organizational); whether we are more effective working in a group or alone; and whether our approach to work is industrious, indifferent or somewhere between. This house also indicates how we are with fellow workers and employers: whether we are contentious and argumentative or, on the other hand, compliant and easily manipulated, taken advantage of by superiors and by fellow employees alike.

If we are employers, our Sixth House describes the nature of those who work for us and our attitude toward them. It deals with many of the issues described above from this perspective.

The Sixth House also provides pointers to our own health, as well as that of any animals we care for. We should use astrology only to complement, not contradict, conventional medical expertise. However, with wise understanding, astrology can offer us clues to possible health difficulties and ways to enhance our well-being.

In this house we also look for information about our capacity to care for others by working in the healing arts and the health industry. This house can even suggest to which area of this vast field we might best apply ourselves.

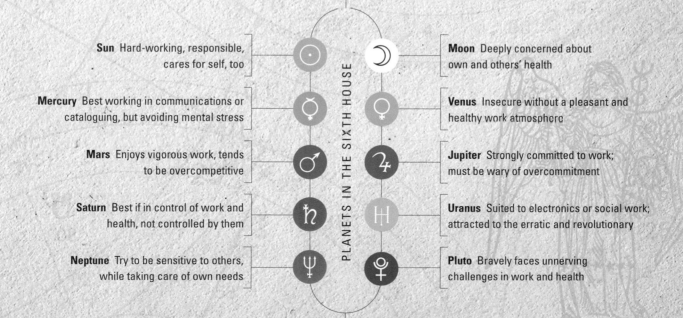

PLANETS IN THE SIXTH HOUSE

Sun Hard-working, responsible, cares for self, too

Mercury Best working in communications or cataloguing, but avoiding mental stress

Mars Enjoys vigorous work, tends to be overcompetitive

Saturn Best if in control of work and health, not controlled by them

Neptune Try to be sensitive to others, while taking care of own needs

Moon Deeply concerned about own and others' health

Venus Insecure without a pleasant and healthy work atmosphere

Jupiter Strongly committed to work; must be wary of overcommitment

Uranus Suited to electronics or social work; attracted to the erratic and revolutionary

Pluto Bravely faces unnerving challenges in work and health

THE SEVENTH HOUSE
RELATIONSHIPS

RELATING TO OTHERS AND THE WORLD

The third angular house, naturally occupied by Venus-ruled Libra, describes how we handle close connections with other people and the world around us.

From studying this house we can learn how to be comfortable with others and make them feel the same with us. We can also learn how to move into unfamiliar territory, embracing new people and experiences in our lives. In developing better understanding of what is outside us, we learn more about ourselves. By working confidently on relationships, however they turn out, we can command respect and enjoy success.

Fruitful intimacy encourages long-term commitments. So it is in the Seventh House that we discover the type of partner that suits us best, and how to build a smooth and resilient togetherness that can withstand difficulty and misunderstanding. In business, this house describes the combining of different talents and resources, and the signing of contracts.

The Seventh House can also highlight areas where we have difficulties, doubts and fears that can put up defensive barriers between ourselves and others. Conversely, this house can indicate whether we are inclined to avoid challenge in relationships, following the path of ease and familiarity – which can also be the path of tedium and of taking others for granted.

The Seventh House cusp (or Descendent) indicates how we respond to the outside world. Planets placed at or close to the cusp act as lenses that modulate how we experience the world.

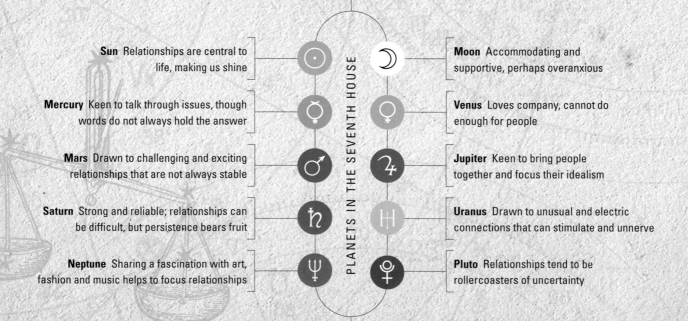

PLANETS IN THE SEVENTH HOUSE

Sun Relationships are central to life, making us shine

Mercury Keen to talk through issues, though words do not always hold the answer

Mars Drawn to challenging and exciting relationships that are not always stable

Saturn Strong and reliable; relationships can be difficult, but persistence bears fruit

Neptune Sharing a fascination with art, fashion and music helps to focus relationships

Moon Accommodating and supportive, perhaps overanxious

Venus Loves company, cannot do enough for people

Jupiter Keen to bring people together and focus their idealism

Uranus Drawn to unusual and electric connections that can stimulate and unnerve

Pluto Relationships tend to be rollercoasters of uncertainty

THE EIGHTH HOUSE

intimacy

SHARING VALUES AND FEELINGS

This succedent house is where the give and take of our interaction with the world is revealed on a more formal footing. With its natural sign being Scorpio, ruled by Mars and Pluto, both the issues we face and the way we deal with them may be uncompromising and demand courage. We may be asked to let go of all personal attachments, even our attachment to life itself, accepting our own mortality. The Eighth House shows how we cope with all the daily "little deaths", the unexpected reverses and changes that life inevitably brings, and which upset our plans and undermine our confidence. Can we see them as opportunities to try again? How do we face the demands of others and the world, especially when expectation is turned upside down?

This house shows our attitude to sharing in its most profound and potentially difficult sense. Here, too, we may gain insight into how we view sexual intimacy.

Many astrologers see the Seventh House as the place where we discover the likelihood of formal legal agreements and disputes, but for others the Eighth House fulfils this role. Perhaps it can be said that the Seventh House reveals our tendency to embark on such agreements and disputes, while the Eighth House, being about shared possessions and emotions, points to how we deal with the process of resolving disputes and defend ourselves against disappointment and the trauma of failure. It is in the Ninth House that we observe our capacity to move beyond these setbacks.

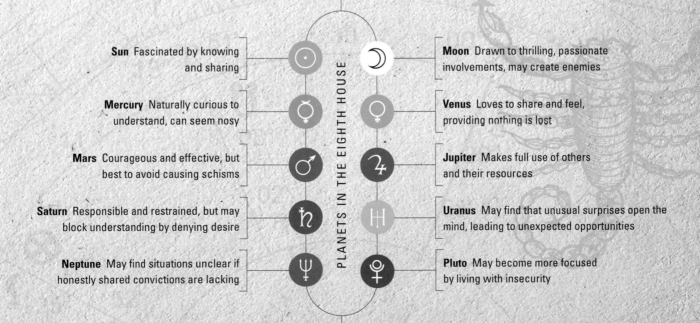

PLANETS IN THE EIGHTH HOUSE

Sun Fascinated by knowing and sharing

Mercury Naturally curious to understand, can seem nosy

Mars Courageous and effective, but best to avoid causing schisms

Saturn Responsible and restrained, but may block understanding by denying desire

Neptune May find situations unclear if honestly shared convictions are lacking

Moon Drawn to thrilling, passionate involvements, may create enemies

Venus Loves to share and feel, providing nothing is lost

Jupiter Makes full use of others and their resources

Uranus May find that unusual surprises open the mind, leading to unexpected opportunities

Pluto May become more focused by living with insecurity

THE NINTH HOUSE

LONG JOURNEYS

FINDING MEANING IN LIFE

Naturally occupied by Sagittarius, which is ruled by mutable Jupiter, the cadent Ninth House could not be more flexible and wide-ranging. This house offers insights into life's long journeys, whether physical, educational or metaphysical. Such journeys all relate to the urge to open up, to explore, to find broader perspective and see things differently: in other words, to find meaning. With planetary strength in this house we will be drawn away from our familiar neighbourhood or "comfort zone", only to return once we have gained knowledge that will serve ourselves and others.

The Ninth House indicates how we relate to distant countries and cultures, and our inclination to journey far from home. We may be disinclined to experience "other-ness" and be susceptible to culture shock, or we may lap up the exotic with eager fascination. For some of us, curiosity may be satisfied by learning about foreign cultures from books, the media and the internet. This house may also reflect a fascination for maps and geography.

The Ninth House can give insight into our educational journey beyond school (Third House). It can indicate how we will experience college or university as educational institutions and whether we will succeed in our studies and social life there. It can help us to discover which subjects would suit us best.

Metaphysical journeys relate to our quest for higher knowledge: our spirituality or philosophy of life. The Ninth House can suggest whether we might be drawn to the priesthood or a similar position as a spiritual teacher or guide.

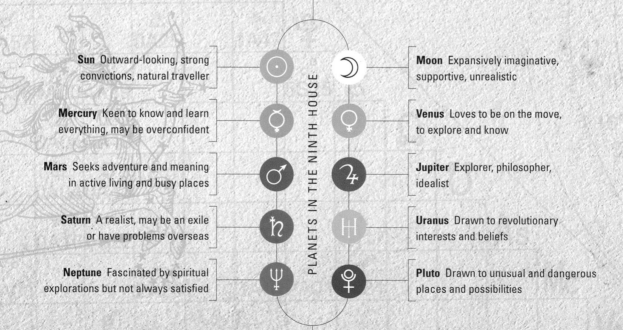

PLANETS IN THE NINTH HOUSE

Sun Outward-looking, strong convictions, natural traveller

Moon Expansively imaginative, supportive, unrealistic

Mercury Keen to know and learn everything, may be overconfident

Venus Loves to be on the move, to explore and know

Mars Seeks adventure and meaning in active living and busy places

Jupiter Explorer, philosopher, idealist

Saturn A realist, may be an exile or have problems overseas

Uranus Drawn to revolutionary interests and beliefs

Neptune Fascinated by spiritual explorations but not always satisfied

Pluto Drawn to unusual and dangerous places and possibilities

THE TENTH HOUSE

PUBLIC IMAGE

SEEKING SOCIAL STATUS

This fourth and final angular house indicates the most public part of ourselves: the face we present to the outside world and the status to which we aspire. The Tenth House is naturally occupied by Saturn-ruled Capricorn. However, our appearance will largely depend on the sign and planets that actually occur in this house. Capricorn is just the intrinsic essence of the Tenth House, showing that solid determination, control and careful organization are vital to our success.

The planets and signs in the Tenth House should be taken into consideration in deciding upon a career, or wondering how to approach the career we already have. Planets near the top of the chart may indicate success: research by the French statistician Michel Gauquelin (1928–1991) showed that Mars and Jupiter were prominent near the Midheaven of successful public figures. Conversely, a lack of such planetary strength in this house may show that neither career nor public recognition are a priority for us.

The cusp of the Tenth House, the Midheaven, is the crown of our personal kingdom and suggests the quintessential image that we wish other people to see, the standards that we uphold to justify our endeavours. Performers or politicians may wonder whether appearing beautiful, careful and conscientious will gain them fans or followers. Others may prefer to lead in a less prominent manner, while many more may be content to live without celebrity or a conspicuous public role. For some, indeed, happiness will lie in obscurity.

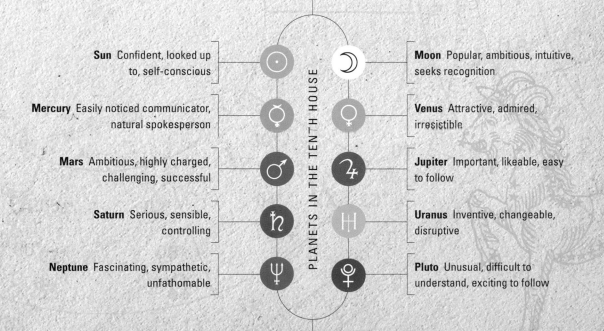

PLANETS IN THE TENTH HOUSE

Sun Confident, looked up to, self-conscious

Mercury Easily noticed communicator, natural spokesperson

Mars Ambitious, highly charged, challenging, successful

Saturn Serious, sensible, controlling

Neptune Fascinating, sympathetic, unfathomable

Moon Popular, ambitious, intuitive, seeks recognition

Venus Attractive, admired, irresistible

Jupiter Important, likeable, easy to follow

Uranus Inventive, changeable, disruptive

Pluto Unusual, difficult to understand, exciting to follow

THE ELEVENTH HOUSE
FRIENDSHIP AND SERVICE

HOW WE SERVE OTHERS

The succedent Eleventh House is naturally occupied by Aquarius, which is ruled by both Saturn and Uranus. Together these key elements create a powerful sense of service. The Eleventh House shows how we may be able to expand beyond individual friendships toward an understanding of the needs of whole communities. This house reveals the extent to which we are naturally inclined to be inclusive, to accommodate all needs and to become friends, in the broadest sense, to all.

So, the Eleventh House reveals the nature of our social lives, what kind of people we tend to associate with and how important a part they play in our lives. This gives an indication of how comfortable we are with broadening our commitment to the whole community, and also highlights what we seek from others and give back in return.

The signs and planets found in the Eleventh House indicate what gifts we may be able to offer to the service of others, whether specialist resources or skills – in administration, plumbing, campaigning, music, writing, performing or whatever – or simply a natural empathy and a helpful physical presence.

If our birth chart is strongly focused in this house it can be a blessing for the world, but not if we lose our identity, becoming caught up in serving other peoples' needs. Of the many practical contributions we can offer, the best are those that help to make people independent. If we all serve one another in this way we all become free, and happiness and friendship can truly spread.

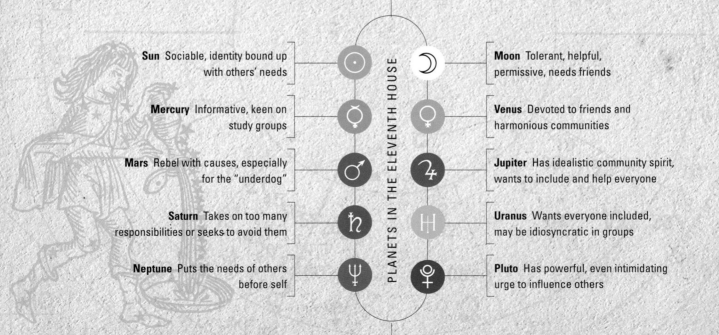

PLANETS IN THE ELEVENTH HOUSE

Sun Sociable, identity bound up with others' needs

Mercury Informative, keen on study groups

Mars Rebel with causes, especially for the "underdog"

Saturn Takes on too many responsibilities or seeks to avoid them

Neptune Puts the needs of others before self

Moon Tolerant, helpful, permissive, needs friends

Venus Devoted to friends and harmonious communities

Jupiter Has idealistic community spirit, wants to include and help everyone

Uranus Wants everyone included, may be idiosyncratic in groups

Pluto Has powerful, even intimidating urge to influence others

THE TWELFTH HOUSE

PRIVATE INNER LIFE

HOW WE SERVE OURSELVES

The cadent Twelfth House is naturally occupied by Pisces, ruled by Jupiter and Neptune, and represents experiences that require inner privacy. The house points toward feelings, knowledge and activities that we are more comfortable handling alone; or which, for better or worse, we do not want others to know about.

At worst, the Twelfth House can show us the extent to which we are at risk of self-undoing – the many ways (including unlawful ones) in which we may act against our own interests. This house may also indicate an illness that we have to face alone. At the other extreme, it may reveal our inclination to perform acts of kindness, selflessness and sacrifice. This urge may arise from caring for another, and be enhanced through practices such as meditation.

A strong birth-chart focus on the Twelfth House may indicate that we will have some connection with facilities and institutions directly linked to these personal experiences and practices, whether positive or not, such as prisons, hospitals, meditation retreats and monasteries. Perhaps we will work with the residents of such places – or be residents ourselves.

Planets strongly placed in the Twelfth House can indicate unstoppable self-reliance. Because we choose to monitor this aspect of our personality from the inside, without reference to others, it can become counterproductive and self-destructive. If we have a strong focus on the Twelfth House, the most difficult thing for us to accept is also the single most generous thing that we can do to help ourselves: allowing others into our inner world.

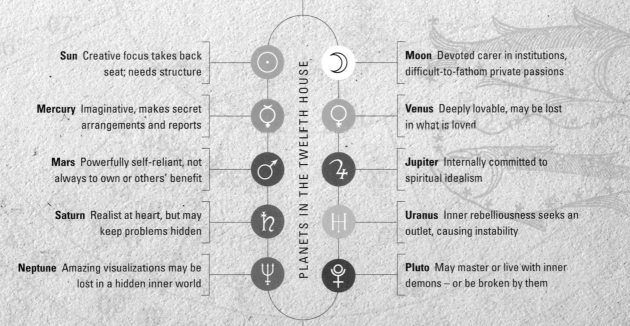

PLANETS IN THE TWELFTH HOUSE

Sun Creative focus takes back seat; needs structure

Mercury Imaginative, makes secret arrangements and reports

Mars Powerfully self-reliant, not always to own or others' benefit

Saturn Realist at heart, but may keep problems hidden

Neptune Amazing visualizations may be lost in a hidden inner world

Moon Devoted carer in institutions, difficult-to-fathom private passions

Venus Deeply lovable, may be lost in what is loved

Jupiter Internally committed to spiritual idealism

Uranus Inner rebelliousness seeks an outlet, causing instability

Pluto May master or live with inner demons – or be broken by them

THE ASPECTS

AS WELL AS OCCUPYING ZODIAC SIGNS and houses, two or more planets can have angular relationships to one another. These are known as the "aspects" that link the various parts of our nature and experience. Aspects are shown as lines connecting planets from different parts of the chart. The position of the lines is determined by a set of rules, based on the number of degrees that separate the planets in the 360° chart circle. An aspect grows in strength as the faster planet moves closer to the exact degree of that aspect, and weakens as it moves away. The range within which a certain aspect applies is known as the "orb". Below the best-known aspects are described in three groups: easy-flowing and stressful ones, and conjunctions.

EASY-FLOWING ASPECTS

The principle easy-flowing aspect is known as a "trine". It is formed when two planets are 120° from one another around the circle. Others are the semi-sextile and sextile (see table, below). Three trines can combine to form an equilateral triangle (grand trine). This indicates intensely strong accumulations – for good or ill – of easy-flowing fire (action), earth (materials), air (ideas) or water (feelings). Two grand trines interlocking make an auspicious six-pointed star.

STRESSFUL ASPECTS

There are two principle stressful aspects: the opposition 180° and the square 90°. Others are the semi-square, sesquisquare and quincunx (see table). A right-angled triangle formed by an opposition and two squares (a T-square) indicates strong tension. Two such triangles together form a square called a "grand cross". There are three crosses representing major life trials in cardinal (activating), fixed (structuring) and mutable (resources) signs; each in turn teaches the wisdom of the Father, Son and Holy Ghost.

CONJUNCTIONS

Planets in close proximity to each other are said to be "conjunct". Some planets can associate comfortably; others may repel each other and give contradictory indications. Charts with many planets bundled close together (a stellium) indicate strong focus or obsession. This can suggest exceptional talent, but also instability or eccentricity.

"GOOD" AND "BAD" ASPECTS

Brief interpretations are given in the tables on pages 148–9. It is wrong to assume that "easy-flowing" aspects in our birth chart are necessarily good and "stressful" ones necessarily bad. Tsunamis and forest fires show easy-flowing energy that is not for the best. Nor are stress and tension intrinsically bad. Stress can be transformed into strength. Eight people with strikingly different viewpoints may well find sustainable solutions. No one is doomed by the aspects in their chart.

TABLE OF ASPECTS

EASY-FLOWING ASPECTS

SYMBOL	ANGLE	NAME	GENERAL SIGNIFICANCE
⚼	30°	Semi-sextile	Combines somewhat easily with
✶	60°	Sextile	Combines pleasantly with
△	120°	Trine	Combines very easily with

STRESSFUL ASPECTS

SYMBOL	ANGLE	NAME	GENERAL SIGNIFICANCE
□	90°	Square	Interacts stressfully with
∠	45°	Semi-square	Interacts somewhat stressfully with
⚺	135°	Sesquisquare	Interacts somewhat stressfully with
⚻	150°	Quincunx	Interacts awkwardly with
☍	180°	Opposition	Confronts and challenges

THE ASPECTS IN ACTION ✳ AN EXPERIMENT

We can experience for ourselves how the aspects work by trying a simple experiment with a group of friends. First, agree on two plans or topics you would like to discuss, one for each of the exercises. Then follow the various seating arrangements described below.

EXERCISE 1 ✳ EASY-FLOWING ASPECTS

This is an exercise in harmony. First follow the solid-line triangle diagram below, seating one person at each point. Each person is trined to the other two, that is, separated by 120°. This arrangement, taking the form of an equilateral triangle, opens people up to each other. Notice how inclusive and supportive discussion feels, with no one confronted face to face. Now add a fourth person where the two dotted lines meet. This position supports the two people at the corresponding solid-line ends. With two more people at the other 60° (sextile) points you would have a strongly harmonious team. To bring 12 into play, use the 30° semi-sextiles (halfway between the 60° points).

After the previous exercise, take a break. Go somewhere alone or where there are new people. Try to clear your mind. Then return to:

EXERCISE 2 ✳ STRESSFUL ASPECTS

Seat four people according to the diagram below, one at each corner of the solid-line square (90°). In this seating arrangement two pairs are face to face (180°), with each pair perpendicular (90°) to the other. Start exploring an entirely new plan or topic. With this seating the relationships are likely to be tenser. The debate will tend to alternate between the opposing pairs who, because they are facing each other head on, are likely to be more challenging or feel challenged; at the same time, the perpendicular pair will struggle to be heard or seem to be interfering. Adding more people at the 45° (semi-square) points exacerbates the situation, giving a sense of people "ganging up". Shown by the green line, the 150° (quincunx) position, being not quite an opposition, is awkward and strained.

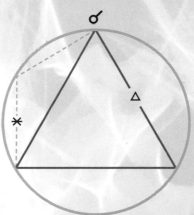

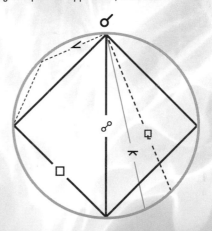

INTERPRETING ASPECTS

THESE THREE TABLES, listing the planetary conjunctions and easy-flowing and stressful aspects, are designed to assist in interpreting a birth chart. However, richer, even radically different interpretations will emerge when we take into account the vital influence of the zodiac signs and houses that the planets occupy. So, the phrases given below must be combined with the planet, sign and house keywords (see pages 154–5), to express the aspect relationship of one planet (in its particular sign and house) to another planet (in its particular sign and house). For example:

Mercury trine Venus = "clever, lovely ideas"

However, if we take into account the signs and houses that might be occupied by Mercury and Venus, the sample result will be much more complex:

Mercury in Virgo in Eleventh House trine Venus in Capricorn in Third House = "thinks precisely to serve the non-parental family cautiously with clever, lovely ideas"

The next part of the book explains step by step how to build a chart interpretation using keywords and phrases (see pages 154–61).

INTERPRETING CONJUNCTIONS

☉ Sun / ☽ Moon	Creations and reactions combine
☉ Sun / ☿ Mercury	Mind needs focus; excitement can burn and confuse
☉ Sun / ♀ Venus	Loving creative pleasure
☉ Sun / ♂ Mars	Energetic creativity – beware impulsiveness
☉ Sun / ♃ Jupiter	Full of hope and generosity – beware over-optimism
☉ Sun / ♄ Saturn	Acts in serious and sensible ways
☉ Sun / ♅ Uranus	Inventive, revolutionary personality
☉ Sun / ♆ Neptune	Spiritual, fascinating, unfathomable – vulnerable
☉ Sun / ♇ Pluto	Unusual, unnerving, explosive, courageous
☽ Moon / ☿ Mercury	Quick, intelligent, sensitive responses
☽ Moon / ♀ Venus	Engaging, supportive, loving, very feminine
☽ Moon / ♂ Mars	Sudden, even combative; count before acting
☽ Moon / ♃ Jupiter	Generously sympathetic, goes out of way for others
☽ Moon / ♄ Saturn	Emotionally restrained, defensive, even distrustful
☽ Moon / ♅ Uranus	Electric and eccentric reactions
☽ Moon / ♆ Neptune	Drawn to fashion, art, even psychic experiences
☽ Moon / ♇ Pluto	Prone to experiencing or creating trauma
☿ Mercury / ♀ Venus	Loves to listen and talk to people
☿ Mercury / ♂ Mars	Quick and combative thinker and speaker
☿ Mercury / ♃ Jupiter	Idealist theories, loquacious
☿ Mercury / ♄ Saturn	Systematic, sensible, but tends to be obstructive
☿ Mercury / ♅ Uranus	Innovative ideas on how we treat others
☿ Mercury / ♆ Neptune	Expresses the unseen – often in art/entertainment
☿ Mercury / ♇ Pluto	Shattering ideas that may not be easy to express
♀ Venus / ♂ Mars	Ambiguity in relationships and gender identity
♀ Venus / ♃ Jupiter	Great generosity, wanting everyone to be happy
♀ Venus / ♄ Saturn	Cautious in love and financial commitments
♀ Venus / ♅ Uranus	Enthusiasm for the thrill of the unusual
♀ Venus / ♆ Neptune	Loves fashion/art, seeks inspiration – avoid "cons"
♀ Venus / ♇ Pluto	Overwhelmed by love or lovers
♂ Mars / ♃ Jupiter	Courageously, if thoughtlessly, leaps into action
♂ Mars / ♄ Saturn	Battles to break down obstacles or create barriers
♂ Mars / ♅ Uranus	Revolutionary actions, possibly troublemaking
♂ Mars / ♆ Neptune	Strongly focused on unusual breakthroughs
♂ Mars / ♇ Pluto	Dangerous actions
♃ Jupiter / ♄ Saturn	Reconciling expansive opportunity with reality
♃ Jupiter / ♅ Uranus	Visionary idealism, seeking radical change
♃ Jupiter / ♆ Neptune	Exploration of new beliefs and religious possibilities
♃ Jupiter / ♇ Pluto	Expansive transformations of consciousness
♄ Saturn / ♅ Uranus	Structural revolution, social upheaval
♄ Saturn / ♆ Neptune	Spiritual realism and/or spiritual materialism
♄ Saturn / ♇ Pluto	Harsh, cold, difficult circumstances
♅ Uranus / ♆ Neptune	Belief in radical change
♅ Uranus / ♇ Pluto	Society in disarray and/or radical change
♆ Neptune / ♇ Pluto	Fundamental change in nature of beliefs/possibilities

INTERPRETING EASY-FLOWING ASPECTS

☉ Sun / ☽ Moon	Self-expression, feelings in harmony
☉ Sun / ☿ Mercury	Good ideas make all seem possible (30° only)
☉ Sun / ♀ Venus	Happiness seems unending (30°/60° only)
☉ Sun / ♂ Mars	The power to do as we wish and carry all before us
☉ Sun / ♃ Jupiter	Feeling encouraged in all we wish to create
☉ Sun / ♄ Saturn	Having right discipline, something to depend on
☉ Sun / ♅ Uranus	Amazingly exciting changes show themselves
☉ Sun / ♆ Neptune	Artistically enchanting, spiritually uplifting
☉ Sun / ♇ Pluto	Can break through barriers, achieve the impossible
☽ Moon / ☿ Mercury	Capable of convincing most people of most ideas
☽ Moon / ♀ Venus	Pleasurable, easy-going, feeling good about people
☽ Moon / ♂ Mars	Encouraging, full of confidence, unstoppable
☽ Moon / ♃ Jupiter	A natural wish to give everyone all they wish for
☽ Moon / ♄ Saturn	Sensible approaches give strength to finish things
☽ Moon / ♅ Uranus	Sheer thrill of change and freedom
☽ Moon / ♆ Neptune	Involved in and inspired by what we do and believe
☽ Moon / ♇ Pluto	Handling danger with confidence
☿ Mercury / ♀ Venus	Clever, lovely ideas
☿ Mercury / ♂ Mars	Confidence to challenge and easily convince
☿ Mercury / ♃ Jupiter	Open to idealism and stories of far-away places
☿ Mercury / ♄ Saturn	Structured understanding, intellectual frameworks
☿ Mercury / ♅ Uranus	Thinking about changing the world for the better
☿ Mercury / ♆ Neptune	Religions and secret wonders seem very possible
☿ Mercury / ♇ Pluto	Turns our ideas about reality upside down
♀ Venus / ♂ Mars	Complementary harmony of male and female
♀ Venus / ♃ Jupiter	Generosity and pleasure seem boundless
♀ Venus / ♄ Saturn	In control of relationships and businesses
♀ Venus / ♅ Uranus	Exciting new people and enterprises
♀ Venus / ♆ Neptune	Beauty and great feelings open to deeper truth
♀ Venus / ♇ Pluto	Feeling good about a relationship or possibility
♂ Mars / ♃ Jupiter	Simply unstoppable, beware of overconfidence
♂ Mars / ♄ Saturn	Realism and courage – the driving force of power
♂ Mars / ♅ Uranus	Everything can and will be changed
♂ Mars / ♆ Neptune	Finding effective, incisive points of contact
♂ Mars / ♇ Pluto	Fearlessly face up to what needs to be done
♃ Jupiter / ♄ Saturn	Systems working effectively together
♃ Jupiter / ♅ Uranus	Flexible idealism aspires toward social justice
♃ Jupiter / ♆ Neptune	Possibilities are truly wondrous and without barriers
♃ Jupiter / ♇ Pluto	Beyond fear; nothing will stop us now
♄ Saturn / ♅ Uranus	Finding ways around barriers – whatever the cost
♄ Saturn / ♆ Neptune	Establishing and developing "undeniable" beliefs
♄ Saturn / ♇ Pluto	Succeeding, or seeming to, when all is against us
♅ Uranus / ♆ Neptune	Beliefs that change everything
♅ Uranus / ♇ Pluto	Radical social change readily accepted
♆ Neptune / ♇ Pluto	Reassessment of beliefs, taking centuries to unfold

INTERPRETING STRESSFUL ASPECTS

☉ Sun / ☽ Moon	Feeling pulled apart at quarter and full Moons
☉ Sun / ☿ Mercury	*Does not form negative aspect*
☉ Sun / ♀ Venus	*Does not form negative aspect*
☉ Sun / ♂ Mars	Life struggles that make or break us
☉ Sun / ♃ Jupiter	Difficult to resist going too far; look to the future
☉ Sun / ♄ Saturn	Building confidence and systems to survive
☉ Sun / ♅ Uranus	Disruptive, troubled; crisis to transform
☉ Sun / ♆ Neptune	Misguided, confused, uncertain; seeking the truth
☉ Sun / ♇ Pluto	Threatened; developing courage in adversity
☽ Moon / ☿ Mercury	Emotional manipulation; serve truth, not guilt
☽ Moon / ♀ Venus	Overdependent on familiar comforts
☽ Moon / ♂ Mars	Emotion-driven aggression or fear, needs mastering
☽ Moon / ♃ Jupiter	Extravagant, over-indulgent; use all of this
☽ Moon / ♄ Saturn	Emotionally fraught, misunderstood; work out rules
☽ Moon / ♅ Uranus	Feeling edgy, restless; do not take things personally
☽ Moon / ♆ Neptune	Manipulation of sympathies acts on unclear beliefs
☽ Moon / ♇ Pluto	Try to see that the only thing to fear is fear itself
☿ Mercury / ♀ Venus	Misplaced affections; learn to trust (45° only)
☿ Mercury / ♂ Mars	Arguments do not end until we either win or let go
☿ Mercury / ♃ Jupiter	Too much to say that's irrelevant; seek higher truth
☿ Mercury / ♄ Saturn	See refusals and procedures as giving strength
☿ Mercury / ♅ Uranus	Disruption; only accept change for the better
☿ Mercury / ♆ Neptune	Lost in doubt; trust yourself – knowing gives control
☿ Mercury / ♇ Pluto	Refuse to fear, then frightening thoughts will fade
♀ Venus / ♂ Mars	Battle or reconcile radical differences
♀ Venus / ♃ Jupiter	Over-indulging; apply discrimination
♀ Venus / ♄ Saturn	Problems can make as well as break relationships
♀ Venus / ♅ Uranus	Don't love change for change's sake; need focus
♀ Venus / ♆ Neptune	Captivated by the fantastic; rest, look, come back
♀ Venus / ♇ Pluto	Let go of attachment
♂ Mars / ♃ Jupiter	Are we fighting and trying too hard?
♂ Mars / ♄ Saturn	Breaking down barriers; what will replace them?
♂ Mars / ♅ Uranus	Revolutionary actions destroy; what do they create?
♂ Mars / ♆ Neptune	Forcing beliefs on others is a futile process
♂ Mars / ♇ Pluto	Doing anything to succeed leaves death the victor
♃ Jupiter / ♄ Saturn	Reality's hard lessons create order out of excess
♃ Jupiter / ♅ Uranus	Aiming for the impossible brings no real benefit
♃ Jupiter / ♆ Neptune	Others may reject our well-intentioned beliefs
♃ Jupiter / ♇ Pluto	*Laissez-faire*, ignoring dangers, has dire outcome
♄ Saturn / ♅ Uranus	Facing the real consequences of change
♄ Saturn / ♆ Neptune	Misunderstanding brings pain; try devotion
♄ Saturn / ♇ Pluto	Serious situations require mature solutions
♅ Uranus / ♆ Neptune	Doing right things for wrong reasons, or vice versa
♅ Uranus / ♇ Pluto	Massive social upheaval; be ahead of the flow
♆ Neptune / ♇ Pluto	Challenge to, and reconstruction of, belief systems

Our ancestors not only observed and measured the cycles of the solar system, they also devised a skilful way of synthesizing the meanings they gave to those cycles: the astrological chart. Still used by the astrologers of today, the chart generates a narrative of the experiences and events of the people and societies on Earth. The step-by-step instructions on the following pages explain how to create a chart and then gradually build up an interpretation. As meaning emerges from the fitting of keywords into first sentences and then paragraphs, so the beauty of the interrelatedness of the solar system will become clear, within and around us all.

PUTTING THE PIECES TOGETHER

THE ASTROLOGICAL BIRTH CHART

MOST PEOPLE KNOW THEIR SUN SIGN, but proper astrologers take account of much more than that. To create a full astrological profile, they will use the time, date and place of a birth or other event to draw up and interpret a full astrology chart. This will display the positions of the planets, signs, houses and aspects.

Astrologers measure this with a frame that is devised by projecting the Sun's ecliptic out to infinity in every direction. This creates a notional three-dimensional ball that is known as the "celestial sphere". Starting from the first point of Aries (see box), this sphere is divided into 12 equal 30° signs of the zodiac, which are named after the constellations near to them. As well as positioning the Sun, Moon and planets from an earthly (geocentric) perspective, astrologers also note which signs are on the horizons as the Earth spins on its axis – the Ascendant in the east and Descendant in the west – as well as which signs are on the higher meridian (Midheaven) and the lower meridian (Imum Coeli). These three-dimensional movements are then simplified on to a flat, two-dimensional chart (see the example opposite).

USING A WEBSITE

Astrology-chart calculations are based on precise astronomical measurements. Calculating and constructing a chart by hand is an advanced skill – an experienced astrologer can take half an hour or more to complete just one. Nonetheless, all serious students of astrology should develop this valuable skill. Seeing how the different components of the chart are calculated and fitted together helps us to understand how the universe works within each of us. Knowing the movements of the planets enhances our

ARIES ✳ THE FIRST POINT OF THE ZODIAC

The zigzag lines indicate the boundaries of the constellations. The ecliptic is the Sun's apparent diurnal path, crossed by the ecliptic meridian (the first point of Aries). From here the 12 signs of the zodiac start. On 9 February 2011, Jupiter and Uranus were either side of this first point. The area of sky shown here is circled on the birth chart, opposite.

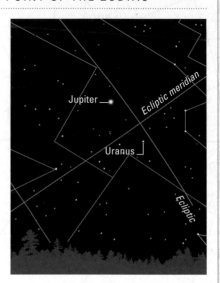

ability to interpret the meaning of the chart. It explains what we all experience; parts of our lives slowing, while others speed up. Sometimes we seem to be fighting with ourselves; at other times everything fits harmoniously together.

Today, amateur astrologers can find a way around the complex technicalities of chart calculation with the help of specialist birth-chart websites that perform the calculations and create the charts for you (see page 169 for more information on this book's dedicated website). All you need to know is your subject's time, date and place of birth. If you do not know the time of birth, you can use either sunrise or noon. However, if you do this the house delineations will be unreliable and should be ignored. An astrological chart can only be as accurate as the information you have provided; always allow for this when interpreting.

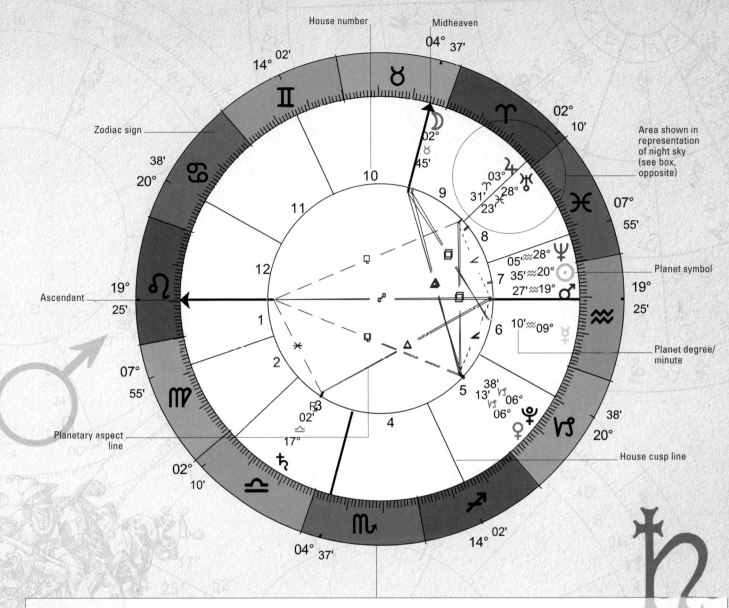

House number

Midheaven
04° 37'

14° 02'

Zodiac sign

38'
20°

Ascendant
19°
25'

07°
55'

Planetary aspect
line

02°
10'

02° 10'

10

11

12

1

2

R 3
02°
17°

4

9

8

7 05'♒28'
35'♒20'
27'♒19'

6 10'♒09'

5 38'
13'♓06'
♓06'

03°
31' ♓28'
23'

Area shown in
representation
of night sky
(see box,
opposite)

02°
10'

07°
55'

Planet symbol

19°
25'

Planet degree/
minute

38'
20'

House cusp line

04° 37'

14° 02'

A SAMPLE BIRTH CHART

The astrological chart displayed above describes the same moment as the fragment of the heavens shown opposite (1900 UT on 9 February 2011, Guildford, UK). The chart has four main areas:

1. The 12 signs of the zodiac make up the outer band, with colours to note their element (red, green, pale blue and dark blue for fire, earth, air and water respectively).

2. Symbols indicate the position of the planets inside the zodiac. Remember that the planets move at varying speeds in an anticlockwise direction. The Moon changes sign every two and a half days, while Pluto can take more than 20 years to change sign. The position of each planet in its sign is indicated in numbers of degrees and minutes.

3. The houses are numbered anticlockwise from the Ascendant, with the cusps marked by the long diagonal lines running between the zodiac band and the central area of the chart.

4. The aspects are the lines that connect the planets across the central area of the chart; blue indicates easy-flowing aspects and red indicates stressful ones.

The pages that follow explain how to explore the meanings of these features and combine them in astrological interpretations that describe our lives.

INTERPRETING THE BIRTH CHART 1

USING KEYWORDS

THE BIRTH CHART OF THE DALAI LAMA is an ideal example to serve as an introduction to the art of astrological interpretation. The facts of his life are well known. Millions have experienced close contact with him in ceremonies all over the world, and he has been portrayed in feature films and interviewed in many documentaries. So, can the rudimentary key astrological concepts be combined to echo what we may feel we already know about the Dalai Lama? Can they help us to go even further in understanding and empathizing with him? The Dalai Lama's chart (see opposite) was created using the web tools described on page 152. The precise time, date and place of his birth were originally provided by his mother: dawn (0407 IST) on 6 July 1935 at Takster, Tibet (36N32 101E12).

This book's sections on planets, signs, houses and aspects each offer fragments of meaning at a variety of levels. By reading these fragments in combination, we start to build up a composite understanding of the whole person. The first level of interpretation is to use the subject's birth chart to combine some basic keywords.

FIRST STEP: PLANET AND SIGN KEYWORDS

These keywords, extracted from the descriptions of the planets and zodiac signs (see pages 28–47 and 60–131), are given in the box of planets and signs keywords (above right). Taking the planets in the order they appear on the list above (Sun, Moon, Mercury and so on), use the listed symbols to find the sign each planet occupies on the chart and then combine each pair of keywords. For example ☉ Sun (creates) in ♋ Cancer (carefully), then ☽ Moon (reacts) in

KEYWORDS * PLANETS AND SIGNS			
PLANET	KEYWORD	SIGN	KEYWORD
☉ Sun	Creates	♈ Aries	Urgently
☽ Moon	Reacts	♉ Taurus	Realistically
☿ Mercury	Thinks	♊ Gemini	Intelligently
♀ Venus	Loves	♋ Cancer	Carefully
♂ Mars	Acts	♌ Leo	Proudly
♃ Jupiter	Expands	♍ Virgo	Precisely
♄ Saturn	Controls	♎ Libra	Adaptively
♅ Uranus	Invents	♏ Scorpio	Intensely
♆ Neptune	Inspires	♐ Sagittarius	Far-reaching
♇ Pluto	Transforms	♑ Capricorn	Usefully
		♒ Aquarius	Knowingly
		♓ Pisces	Sympathetically

♍ Virgo (precisely), and so on. This gives the following list (in planet order, starting with the Sun):

Creates carefully; reacts precisely; thinks intelligently; loves proudly; acts adaptively; expands intensely; controls sympathetically; invents realistically; inspires precisely; and transforms carefully.

SECOND STEP: ADDING HOUSE KEYWORDS

Each of these pairs of keywords applies to a different area of the Dalai Lama's life. To highlight the relevant life area, we add in further keywords relating to the 12 houses (see pages 134–45). These are summarized in the box of houses keywords (opposite). Start from House 1 at the Cancer Ascendant and add in only the first word or words (bold type) at this stage. Work anticlockwise and only include

BIRTH CHART ✶
H.H. THE DALAI LAMA OF TIBET

Use the planet, sign, house and aspect keyword listings on pages 154, 155 and 156 to understand and interpret this and any other birth chart.

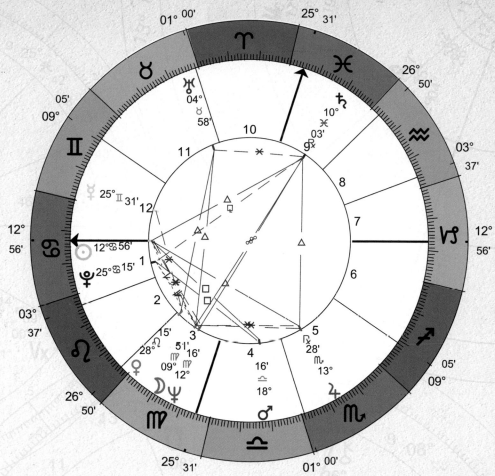

those houses containing planets. This produces the following expanded list:

Personality: creates and transforms carefully; **short journeys**: reacts and inspires precisely and loves proudly; **home and parents**: acts adaptively; **creativity**: expands intensely; **long journeys**: controls sympathetically; **service**: invents realistically; **private inner life**: thinks intelligently

Now improve further by inserting other relevant house keywords (not bold type) and reordering to make proper sentences:
His personality creates and transforms carefully. His communications love proudly and react and inspire precisely. His private inner life thinks intelligently; his home foundation acts adaptively. With intensely expansive creativity, he finds meaning through sympathetic control and inventive, realistic service to the community.

KEYWORDS ✶ HOUSES	
HOUSE	KEYWORDS
First	**Personality**: physical appearance; how we project our self image
Second	**Possessions**: how we value and hold on to objects and feelings
Third	**Short journeys**: non-parental family; how we communicate
Fourth	**Home, parents**: the foundation of our social values
Fifth	**Creativity**: children, fun; how we take risks in romance, and create
Sixth	**Work and health**: how we experience give and take in these areas
Seventh	**Relationships and opposites**: how we relate to others and the world
Eighth	**Shared possessions**: how we share values, feelings and sexuality
Ninth	**Long journeys**: physical, metaphysical; how we find meaning
Tenth	**Public image**: career, ambition, social status
Eleventh	**Service**: friendship, ideals; how we serve the community
Twelfth	**Private inner life**: institutions, self-reliance; how we undermine and support ourselves

THIRD STEP: ADDING ASPECT KEYWORDS

The statement on page 155 does not describe the relationships between the various areas of the Dalai Lama's life. Where are they easy? Where are the stresses and strains? To find this out, we need to add in keywords describing the aspect relationships between a planet in one sign and house, and a planet in another sign and house (see box, below). We also need to reorder the sentences a little (technical information in square brackets will help you to keep track). The interpretation clearly fits the brief biography of the Dalai Lama (right):

His personality creates and transforms carefully [Sun/Pluto in Cancer in the First House] combines very easily with [trines] how he finds meaning through controlling sympathetically [Saturn in Pisces in the Ninth]. Both of these combine very easily with [trine] his intensely expansive creativity [Jupiter in Scorpio in the Fifth]. His communications love proudly, and react and inspire precisely [Venus in Leo and Moon and Neptune in Virgo all in the Third] and combine very easily with [trine] inventive realistic service to the community [Uranus in Taurus in the Eleventh], but they face and challenge [oppose] how he makes long journeys and finds meaning through controlling sympathetically [Saturn in Pisces in the Ninth]. His private inner life thinking intelligently [Mercury in Gemini in the Twelfth] combines pleasantly [sextiles] with his communication of proud love [Venus in Leo in the Third]. His home foundation acts adaptively [Mars in Libra in the Fourth], but interacts stressfully [squares] with the sympathetic personality and useful relationships.

KEYWORDS ✳ ASPECT RELATIONSHIPS

SYMBOL	DEGREE	CONJUNCTION	COMBINES WITH EASE/DIFFICULTY
⚺	30	Semi-sextile	Combines somewhat easily with
∠	45	Semi-square	Interacts somewhat stressfully with
✶	60	Sextile	Combines pleasantly with
□	90	Square	Interacts stressfully with
△	120	Trine	Combines very easily with
⚼	135	Sesquisquare	Interacts somewhat stressfully with
⚻	150	Quincunx	Interacts awkwardly with
☍	180	Opposition	Faces and challenges

Clearly keywords work, but interpretation is about much more than using them automatically. A keyword's function is to trigger an archetype that generates a considerable number of possibilities. These possibilities must always be within the range of that archetype's root meaning. For example, the Sun's root is creative. It may create materially, intellectually or experientially. It may be egocentric. It may even create danger and destruction – but it is always creative. The Moon may enchant or seduce, sympathize or react fearfully, but it will always be about reacting. Mars always acts, however constructively or destructively; Venus will love and express intense attachment. So it is with each planet, sign, house and aspect.

The next stage in interpretation is to combine the possibilities arising from the archetypes, using sensitivity and poetic judgment. The aim is to integrate all our astrological data and archetypal possibilities into a synthesized interpretation that remains true to the mechanical movements and relationships of the Earth and the planets. In this way, astrology integrates art with science.

Before we embark on this deepening task, it will help to arm ourselves with methods that look at the chart as a whole.

INTERPRETING THE BIRTH CHART 2

THE WHOLE CHART AND ITS DYNAMICS

WITHOUT STRUCTURE AND FOCUS the words we speak may teem with meaning but be barely comprehensible. Astrologers must develop the skills of combining and prioritizing. Below are ways to view and synthesize fragments of interpretation. They are summarized in the table of key concepts on page 158.

FIRE, EARTH, AIR, WATER

Look at the Dalai Lama's birth chart. Each planet is associated with one of the elements: fire, earth, air and water (see pages 54–7). Which elements are most strongly represented? The more fire there is, the more active the individual; the more earth, the more practical and materialistic; the more air, the more intellectual and communicative; and the more water, the more sensitive and vulnerable. Consider how the elements will combine. If most planets in the chart are fire and water, the person could be excitingly skilful in action but hot tempered, like the steam of heated water. Fire and air planets lead to exciting ideas but stormy arguments. Earth and water make mud, but also the clay from which beautiful pottery is made. As we can see, the Dalai Lama's planets are mainly earth and water, suggesting that he is sensitive and supportive. Most charts have three or even four elements, combined in different proportions.

TOOLS OF THE TRADE

Used for locating heavenly bodies, this 14th-century astrolabe shows in the detail on its reverse side the achievement of contemporary Islamic scholarship.

CARDINAL, FIXED, MUTABLE

Count the number of planets in cardinal, fixed or mutable signs (see pages 58–9). People with lots of planets in cardinal signs are instigators. Fixed planets offer methods; mutable ones, resources. The Dalai Lama's planets are nearly evenly divided with cardinal slightly stronger, as one would expect for the Tibetan Buddhists' spiritual leader and (exiled) monarch. Combining qualities with elements gives a good initial impression of a person's capacities.

POSITIVE AND NEGATIVE

Count the planets in positive or negative signs (see pages 52–3). Fire and air signs are positive; earth and water, negative. What does this tell us about actions and ideas, compared to feelings and resources? In the Dalai Lama's chart, seven planets are negative, making him very receptive and reflective: like a caring mother.

ANGULAR, SUCCEDENT, CADENT

Count how many planets are in each of these kinds of houses (see pages 133–45). The sign and other factors will modify your judgment. Although his (angular) first house is strong, the Dalai Lama's planets are otherwise mainly cadent. This may explain why he is very influential in some areas (such as promoting Tibetan Buddhism in exile), but less successful in others, notably the restoration of religious freedoms within Tibet itself.

THE QUADRANTS AND HEMISPHERES

The 12 houses can be divided into four quadrants:

First Quadrant: First to Third Houses. Attention here is upon immediate personal needs: how we appear, what we need, our neighbourhood and our close family.

Second Quadrant: Fourth to Sixth Houses. Attention is concentrated upon the home environment and personal experiences with those close to us: mother, children, playmates and work colleagues.

Third Quadrant: Seventh to Ninth Houses. Attention broadens beyond the self to experience the world at large: relationships, shared possessions, far-away places and alien ideas.

Fourth Quadrant: Tenth to Twelfth Houses. Attention focuses on our status and our responsibilities to friends and, ultimately, to our most private selves.

The Dalai Lama's planets are focused mainly in the First Quadrant, making perfect, kind communication his main focus. But there are strong connections from here to the other three quadrants, which show how he presents his communication through service and meditation (Fourth Quadrant, Eleventh and Twelfth Houses), internationally (Third Quadrant, Ninth House) and with creative intensity (Second Quadrant, Fifth House).

The quadrants are also combined to make four hemispheres. When planets are focused in the First and Second Quadrants, concerns are mainly about personal domestic and vocational experience. A concentration of planets in the Second and Third Quadrants indicates that concerns are mainly for others. Such individuals tend to live for other people and are incomplete without them. Planets in the Third and Fourth Quadrants point to concerns that may be adrift from immediate realities: aspirations, ambitions and service to the world.

In the hemisphere of the Fourth and First Quadrants, attention is concentrated upon personal presentation, service and standing. We decide what to give the world and then the world decides about us. The Dalai Lama's planets are focused mainly in this hemisphere.

HOW PLANETS RULE OR ARE EXALTED, IN DETRIMENT OR IN FALL

When interpreting a chart, always take account of the ease or otherwise with which planets "fit" in the signs they occupy. Planets may rule a sign or be exalted there, or they may be in detriment or in fall. The table of key concepts (left) offers clues.

For example: Venus is in detriment in Aries, because the planet is easily overlooked and overwhelmed in such a martial, impulsive context. However, we can go further. Look at the sign at the beginning (cusp) of a house of the Dalai Lama's birth chart. What planet rules that sign? In which house and sign is that planet? For example, the Moon rules the Dalai Lama's Cancer Ascendant. His Moon is in Virgo in the Third House. So his reflective personality is tempered by the communication of purity and perfection – making him a perfect mirror.

TABLE OF KEY CONCEPTS

SIGN	ELEMENT	TRIPLICITY	+/-	RULER	EXALTED	DETRIMENT	FALL
♈ Aries	Fire	Cardinal	+	♂	☉	♀	♄
♉ Taurus	Earth	Fixed	-	♀	☽	♂	
♊ Gemini	Air	Mutable	+	☿		♃	
♋ Cancer	Water	Cardinal	-	☽	♃	♄	♂
♌ Leo	Fire	Fixed	+	☉		♄	
♍ Virgo	Earth	Mutable	-	☿	☿	♃	♀
♎ Libra	Air	Cardinal	+	♀	♄	♂	☉
♏ Scorpio	Water	Fixed	-	♂/♇		♀	☽
♐ Sagittarius	Fire	Mutable	+	♃		☿	
♑ Capricorn	Earth	Cardinal	-	♄	♂	☽	♃
♒ Aquarius	Air	Fixed	+	♄/♅		☉	
♓ Pisces	Water	Mutable	-	♃/♆	♀	☿	☿

INTERPRETING THE BIRTH CHART 3

Goiпg DEEPER

INTERPRETING A CHART is a bit like describing a painting over the telephone. Only one aspect can be described at a time, so it is wise not jump to conclusions based on just one fragment. As our interpretation progresses, we develop a mental picture and increasingly understand the whole, fine-tuning our selections and coming ever closer to the unique reality.

START BY SEEKING GOOD INDICATIONS

The earlier sections of the book describing the planets, signs, planets in signs, houses and aspects give beneficial and unbeneficial ways in which astrological archetypes can be expressed. When first practising astrological interpretation, it is safer and more useful to focus on the beneficial manifestations. Only when we understand interpretation more completely, can we rely on ourselves to make balanced judgments. When you are learning, it is better to look for positive indications.

BRINGING IT ALL TOGETHER

Before attempting to follow the deeper astrological interpretation on pages 160–61, prepare by steeping yourself in the descriptions and associations given in this book for the planets, zodiac signs, houses and aspects.

To help you understand how astrologers put all the pieces together, on pages 160–61 the planet-in-sign meanings will be shown in **bold type**, the planet-in-house meanings will be shown in *italic type* and the planet-in-aspect-to-planet meanings will be shown in **bold, underlined type**.

STAGE ONE: SELECTING AND COMBINING PLANET-IN-SIGN AND PLANET-IN-HOUSE MEANINGS

First, refer back to the zodiac section for **planet-in-sign meanings** for the Dalai Lama's birth chart. Each sign concludes with interpretations of the planets in that particular sign. Ponder the underlying reasoning for each planet-in-sign meaning. Select words from the meanings applying to the Dalai Lama's chart.

Next, consider the *planet-in-house meanings*. Refer back to the basic archetype of each house and its various expressions and levels (see pages 134–45). For each house, a list of keywords for planets in that house is given; select those applying to the Dalai Lama's chart.

Now compare the words you have chosen with the extracts on page 160. These extracts, relevant to the Dalai Lama's chart, combine both planet-in-sign and planet-in-house meanings.

WORLDWIDE ART

This Chinese compass from *c.* 1900 is also an astrological calendar. Calculations in both Chinese and Western astrology are based upon the time, date and place of birth, although their archetypes are very different.

THE DALAI LAMA'S PLANET-IN-SIGN AND PLANET-IN-HOUSE MEANINGS

 SUN IN CANCER ✳ **creates nurturingly** *in personality*
Cannot do enough to care for and protect others; will draw on remarkable hidden healing depths, but should always tread carefully.

 MOON IN VIRGO ✳ **reacts fastidiously** *in communication*
From childhood experiences, natural inclination is to improve to perfection everything. Needs a methodical structure or system of rules … so that things are right, and works at them until they are.

 MERCURY IN GEMINI ✳ **communicates intelligently** *in institutions (monastery – monk)*
Bright, lively minds bubble with ideas that they just cannot wait to develop and express as quickly and fully as possible.

 VENUS IN LEO ✳ **loves joyfully** *in communication*
Loves to love and to be loved … everything we possess must be as admirable and admired as we ourselves are.

 MARS IN LIBRA ✳ **acts urgently** *in home foundation*
Feels the need to restore balance away from uncertainty. Should danger seem to threaten, takes up the cause of "justice and fair play".

JUPITER IN SCORPIO ✳ **expands convincingly** *in creativity*
Works ever harder to bring everyone on board and achieve promised improvements. Others will be excited by his confidence and style.

 SATURN IN PISCES ✳ **controls modestly** *in long journeys (physical and metaphysical)*
While tending to dampen expectations and possibilities, Saturn can also give structural strength if used well here.

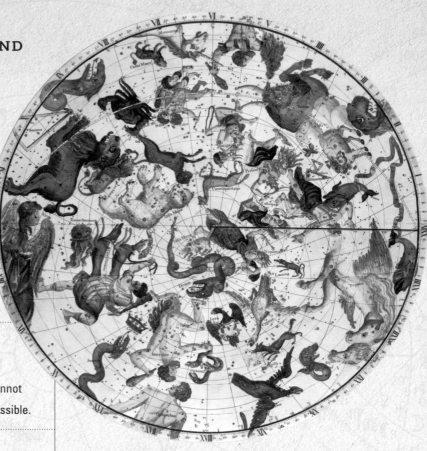

THE ARCHETYPES
Over the centuries the zodiac signs have become associated with mythological creatures and characters, as illustrated in this 18th-century star map. Powerful archetypes, they resonate with aspects of our psyche.

 URANUS IN TAURUS ✳ **invents radically** *in community service*
Uranus's years in Taurus literally change the way the world works. Citizens rebel and their social values are turned upside down.

 NEPTUNE IN VIRGO ✳ **inspires simplistically** *in communication*
Having a desperate need for comfort and something tangible to believe in, seeks immediate, practical ways to resolve past uncertainties that can be implemented effectively.

 PLUTO IN CANCER ✳ **transforms irrevocably** *in personality*
Sweeps away past social assumptions so totally that they are no more than an embarrassing memory of our ancestors' ineptitude and ignorance. There is no going back to that bygone age.

STAGE TWO: COMBINING PLANETS IN SIGN AND HOUSE WITH THE ASPECTS

This stage adds in the **planet-in-aspect-to-planet meanings** to the planets in sign and house. To introduce the method simply, only a selection of the aspects has been chosen. Refer back to the aspect chapter (pages 146–9) to include more if you wish. This will add depth and subtle insight to the interpretation. Each phrase is followed its technical explanation in [square brackets]; sometimes several explanations are combined.

Creates nurturingly [Sun in Cancer] **and transforms irrevocably** [Pluto in Cancer] *in personality* [both in First House] **having right discipline, something to depend on** [Sun combines very easily with Saturn] **and succeeding, or seeming to, when all is against him** [Pluto easy with Saturn], **controlling modestly** *in long journeys – physical and metaphysical* [Saturn in Pisces in Ninth]. **Feeling encouraged in all he wishes to create** [Sun easy with Jupiter] **he expands convincingly** *in creativity and childhood* [Jupiter in Scorpio in Fifth], **but life struggles can make or break him** [Sun stressful to Mars] in *urgent acts* *in home foundation* [Mars in Libra in Fourth].

Reacts fastidiously [Moon in Virgo in Third] **and inspires purely** [Neptune in Virgo in Third] **and loves joyfully** [Venus in Leo in Third] *in communication*, **but emotionally fraught, misunderstood** [Moon faces and challenges Saturn] **misunderstanding brings pain** needs to **try devotion** to solve [Saturn opposes Neptune] and **modest control** *in long journeys – physical and metaphysical* [Saturn in Pisces in Ninth]. All this is made easier by **systems working effectively together** [Jupiter combines very easily with Saturn] **convincingly expanding** *creativity* [Jupiter in Scorpio in Fifth], which reinforces **having right discipline, something to depend on** [Sun in a very easy grand trine to Jupiter and Saturn all in water signs].

Finally, while keeping the basic keyword interpretation in mind, the following paragraph expresses the same meaning in more fluent and non-technical language:

His Holiness the Dalai Lama is a nurturing and uncompromisingly transformative personality with confident yet modest survival instincts that seem to succeed against all odds. He is naturally creative in spite of his life struggles, with a difficult childhood and a stressful home foundation that might have defeated a lesser person. His communication is fastidious, purely inspiring and joyful, but he faces emotional trauma from challenges to his nationality and philosophy. He survives by employing his resources skilfully and communicating in a nurturing manner.

Once familiar with this method, it is possible to give full astrological interpretations that include the longer descriptions and the deeper meanings given in this book. As their confidence develops, students of astrology can move beyond copying and combining words from this and other books to find words of their own. By understanding and honouring the archetypes, they become astrologers.

A GEOCENTRIC VIEW
This model was made around 1713 to show the Earth's diurnal revolution on its axis and the apparent (geocentric) motion of the Sun, Moon, planets and stars around it. These three-dimensional dynamics should always be visualized whenever you are interpreting a conventional flat astrology birth chart.

INTERPRETING THE BIRTH CHART 4

THE CHALLENGE TO TRANSCEND

NOW WE ARE READY TO LOOK AT BOTH SIDES of the coin and consider what astrology can tell us about the less easy experiences in life: when we behave at our worst rather than our best. This is never the result of any astrological "curse". As explained in the introduction to the zodiac (see page 52), "negative" and "positive" are not the same as "bad" and "good". A chart full of "negative" (that is, receptive) planets can describe great supportiveness and discernment. Equally, stressful aspects may indicate pressure in the direction of bad outcomes, but this stress can be overcome. Many Olympic champions face stress and turn it into success. Conversely, "easy" aspects or advantageously positioned planets indicate good outcomes only if advantages are used with purpose and not squandered.

ACCENTUATE THE POSITIVE

So, when interpreting stressful aspects, or difficult planetary placements, always offer the worst-case scenario as just one possibility. Be aware of other, less negative options. An afflicted Twelfth House could indicate time in prison or hospital, or mental illness. On the other hand, it could indicate helping or working with others in those situations. The birth charts of ambulance paramedics often reveal that they are prone to involvement in accidents, but that is not to say that they are liable to suffer personal injury. When the chart of a financially wealthy person reveals them to have a life of poverty, it may not be suggesting that they are suddenly going to lose their fortune, but perhaps that they will find greater happiness and fulfilment – greater spiritual wealth – by channelling their money into a beneficial purpose.

TURNING STRESS INTO SUCCESS
Mercury, Saturn and Neptune in Leo, plus Jupiter and Pluto in Cancer, describe Nelson Mandela's seemingly impossible task of keeping the dream of liberation for his people alive. He endured and achieved success.

The best way to practise the art of chart interpretation is to share the experience with friends. Take 15 to 30 minutes to interpret for someone. Say only what the chart says. If the person is a close friend, try not to be influenced by previous personal knowledge. Ask him or her how your interpretation fits. Listen carefully to what he or she says: often what we see is closer than we could have thought possible. Where things do not apparently fit, try to see why. Adjust the level at which the archetype manifests. Learn from any misunderstandings of the symbolism and adjust for next time: every mistake and disappointment opens doors to greater understanding. There is always much more to learn. Below, by way of example, is the approach to interpretation taken by the author.

1. Start with the Sun sign – nearly everyone knows this from popular horoscope columns. Add in the Moon and the Ascendant (interpret as First House). Say the worst and best way for the three to work together. Most people will be between the two extremes all the time.

2. Take an overall look at the chart, applying the ideas on pages 157–8.

3. Consider where planets are strongly placed and aspected. Using keywords and background explanations, talk about each planet in sign in house, and its aspects with other planets in sign in house.

4. With some of these key aspects talked about, look at the less obvious ones. Do they modify what you thought? Ensure all are covered. Now balance out the contradictions against each other. Discuss the symbolism. Do not struggle to understand, nor hold back. Just let the words emerge naturally.

5. Consider what you have discovered so far. Step back from it. How does it add up? What are the key issues? Throughout, let your subject tell you what he or she thinks. You may be amazed how right the chart is, if you stay open and objective, ready to accept feedback and to learn.

The example below synthesizes *only* the least positive planet, house and aspect ideas for the chart of the Dalai Lama:

Creates cautiously, if feels threatened will close up, hide away – even fight back before attacked [Sun in Cancer]; … loves self-indulgently [Venus in Leo]; … acts defensively; upsets the balance of a proper solution by fighting for the wrong home cause [Mars in Libra in Fourth]; … expands obsessively, too carried away by idealistic risks [Jupiter in Scorpio in Fifth]. Invents radically and destructively in service [Uranus in Taurus in Eleventh]. Reacts dismissively, communicates uncomfortably unless everything is "as it should be"; … picky [Moon in Virgo in Third]. Inspires fanatically, blaming and then forcing neighbours toward supposed "solutions" [Neptune in Virgo in Third]. This leads him to be emotionally fraught, misunderstood [Moon opposed Saturn] and suffering from a lack of understanding [Saturn opposed Neptune], which tends to dampen expectations and possibilities about exile and overseas problems [Saturn in Pisces in Ninth].

Parts of this interpretation may describe some aspects of the Dalai Lama's predicament, but in general we would find it difficult to recognize in this description the man who is respected by millions, nor the life he has led and what he has achieved. It illustrates well the dangers of taking what appears difficult at face value.

We are destined to face our future, but we are not doomed to suffer it. Always remember this (whatever a chart seems to show) and develop the interpretative skills that can help you to find a beneficial way forward. Astrology lays out the territory of our lives, but we have the freedom to choose how we walk through it. Knowing about astrology can make it easier for us to map and monitor progress, and to be clear about the decisions we face. It is the motives behind our actions that largely determine the outcome. Kind motivations usually lead to beneficial outcomes.

Armed with this knowledge you will soon begin to develop your own approach to full birth-chart interpretation (see box above for one approach). Working with both friends and strangers is the key way to learn. It's also helpful to study the charts of widely known people. The birth charts of celebrities found in the zodiac section of this book are fascinating examples of astrology at work, each one accompanied by a very short interpretation to start you thinking. Looking at these mini-interpretations again now, you may find that their language seems less technical and easier to understand than when you first read them.

USING ASTROLOGICAL KNOWLEDGE

IMPORTANT ETHICAL CONSIDERATIONS

It is essential to behave responsibly with the insights about others that you obtain through astrological interpretation. Encourage people to see the astrological information you give them as an opportunity to grow, not a fate that they have to accept. Ensure that intimate knowledge is used for that person's benefit alone and do not divulge information to third parties without permission. (Comparing notes in confidence with colleagues, or discussing public information about famous people may be exceptions to this.) Do not claim to be an expert advisor in areas you do not understand – especially in matters of health and finance. For further information, the Association of Professional Astrologers International (see page 169) has excellent ethical guidelines that you should read and follow.

RELATIONSHIPS

Relationships are as varied as the people in them, and so is the astrology that describes them. The easiest connections between people are not necessarily the best. A Leo may have fun with his "good friend" Aries, but that may not mean that Aries is reliable. An Aquarius and a Gemini may know the answers to many problems, but not to their own ones. We are all influenced by many signs and planets combining in a range of ways. The Fifth House indicates romance, the Seventh sustainable relationships, the Eighth sexuality – but following our planets, aspects and rulerships from this point merely reveals our own needs.

To understand a relationship we need the charts of everyone involved. We use the rules for interpreting single charts to discover the synastry (aspects connection and planetary emphasis) between the charts of the people in the relationship. We can also combine two or more charts into a single composite chart. Now step back and see what all this tells you about the relationship. Ask, "Is this the relationship we want?" and "What do we have to allow for to make it work?" You can develop expertise by reading the many books by experienced relationship astrologers and comparing notes with other astrologers.

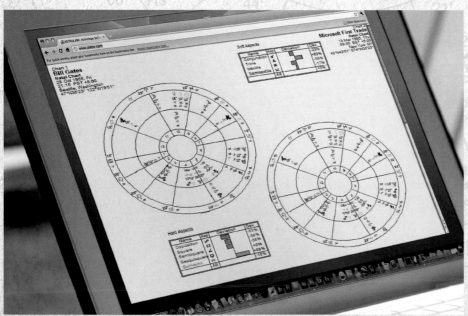

ANSWERING TODAY'S NEEDS
Modern computers can, almost instantly, present all the data that is needed to compare one person astrologically with another or to relate birth charts to past, present and future astro-events.

WORK AND CAREER

Here again the simplistic temptation to allocate specific jobs to specific signs of the zodiac can be very misleading and unhelpful. For example, Virgo's capacity for critical precision is ideal for editing and the restoration of delicate objects, but with the Moon on an Aries Ascendant, trined to Uranus in Sagittarius in the Ninth, a very strong Saturn will be needed to hold attention to the job in hand.

We bring our whole chart into everything we do, and this is especially applicable to our work, upon which we spend a great proportion of our lives. Good astrological careers advice combines the whole chart to indicate the basic work archetype. This work archetype can explain the subject's experience at work, as well as the actual name for the work they do. Personal assistants to business leaders may have charts suited to nursing; the more they are exploited, the stronger the Twelfth House. The Sixth House suggests both the nature and quality of work experience; the Tenth our aspirations and public recognition.

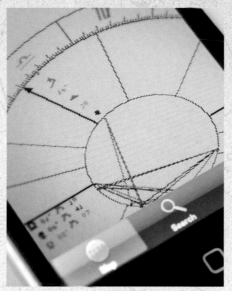

ASTROLOGY ON THE MOVE
Modern mobile phones can access apps and websites that calculate and display any astrology chart, whenever and wherever you need it.

FORECASTING: TRANSITS AND PROGRESSIONS

Comparing planetary positions at a particular time in the past, present or future to their positions at the time of birth can indicate likely past or upcoming experiences. Horoscope columnists compare only the birth Sun sign to the planetary positions on a particular day or week. Then they write a single interpretation for millions of people, born anywhere during that 12th of the calendar year. To have a proper idea, we have to consider at least 10 bodies and their aspects and orientation at the time of birth, and all 12 houses. Then, crucially for proper forecasting, this entire birth-chart information has to be compared to a similar amount of information for each particular moment of time.

Even considering all this detail, it is dangerous for astrologers to make specific predictions. Outcomes depend on the consciousness of the individual. Running inattentively along a cliff edge is more likely to lead to predictable disaster than cautious wide-eyed walking. If we are aware of problems in our relationships, we tend to have more control over outcomes than being blind to the true situation.

Here again, motivation is the key determinant. If we are too hungry for money, recognition and love, grabbing at every chance, we may well destroy other good opportunities. Even if we understand astrology but use it selfishly, knowing what is coming could do more harm than good. Astrology is best used with wisdom, by those who care for the world and have the courage to see everything as it really is. Then we will live the best of lives, expecting and regretting nothing.

With such motivation we can benefit from studying transit and progression techniques, and begin truly to understand the past, present and future, as though they were all one.

LUNAR NODES

The Moon's path around the Earth is oblique to the Sun's ecliptic. So, the solar and lunar paths cross in two places on the zodiac: when the Moon is going from south to north (North Node or Dragon's Head) and from north to south (South Node or Dragon's Tail). These two node points are always exactly opposite each other. Their zodiac positions move slowly backward over a 19-year period. When the Sun and Moon are close to these nodal points, eclipses occur. Astrologers place these nodes on the chart and interpret their sign, house and aspect connections with the planets to assess potential for personal advance into new experiences, on the one hand, and dependence on familiar situations on the other. They are important in the karmic interpretation of the chart.

OTHER ASTROLOGICAL CONSIDERATIONS

AS WELL AS THE EIGHT WELL-KNOWN PLANETS, some astrologers also employ the numerous asteroids, found mainly between the orbits of Mars and Jupiter. Other bodies, called centaurs, orbit the Sun on paths both inside and outside the orbits of the main planets. The best known of these is Chiron. Its astrological meaning follows the mythology of the Greek centaur Chiron, who gained wisdom from enduring the suffering that comes with being wounded.

Recently, astronomers have downgraded Pluto to the status of dwarf planet, mainly because its orbit is irregular and, like that of the centaurs, goes inside that of Neptune. Pluto's downgrading has little effect on astrology. Planets are not sources of energy, sending beams that activate what happens to us on Earth. They are reference points that help us to understand the dynamic status of the whole solar system in terms of the Earth. Dwarf planet or not, Pluto's cycle has marked some pretty earth-shattering cultural changes.

THE AGES OF THE GREAT YEAR

The phenomena of the zodiac signs appearing to be moving slowly backward, when viewed on the same date each year (see page 7), does not mean our relationships with the Sun, Moon and planets are changing. The difference between the Earth's actual and perceived position was identified by Hipparchus, a Greek astrologer living more than 100 years BCE.

By comparing the regressing sidereal zodiac with the fixed tropical one, astrologers describe an historical Great Year approximately 26,000 years long, with 12 "ages", each of just over 2,160 years. Today we are in the last few centuries of the Age of Pisces, with its focus on sacrifice. Before that, until just under two centuries after the death of Christ, was the Age of Aries, the heroic Classical Greco-Roman age; prior to that, the Minoan culture typified the Age of Taurus. Most Indian and some Western astrologers adjust birth charts to allow for the ages. Deep cultural and spiritual reasons for using both perspectives and giving them a complementary role is explained in my book *Astrology and Compassion: The Convenient Truth*.

RESOURCES FOR FURTHER LEARNING

Books on the basic astrology explained in this book and on much more are listed on pages 168–9. On page 169 you will find software that performs far more calculations than those covered here and also gives access to interpretations by expert astrologers. Astrological organizations are also listed; make contact with them. Attending conferences is a wonderful way to encounter the wonders of astrology at first hand.

Vitally, you will also find the link to this book's website, which calculates exact birth charts. Generate and print these, and then use this book to transform the technical details into plain language. Combine and build phrases into a full interpretation.

Through these and other channels you will be able to learn more about the amazing language of astrology, taking your understanding to ever-higher levels.

THE EARTH'S WISDOM
Whatever our technological advances, we will always need astrology – an age-old way of understanding ourselves, our lives and our world.

FURTHER READING
AND RESOURCES

FURTHER READING

Astrology attracts people with fascinating and rigorous minds, so a rich range of books is available to reinforce and extend your knowledge and practice of the subject. As there is space here to mention just a few, only one book per author is listed (with a few exceptions to ensure comprehensive coverage). See each title as a gateway to that author's other invaluable works. Reading the books below will also introduce authors not mentioned here.

INTRODUCTORY BOOKS AND BASIC TOOLS

These three books helped me start to learn astrology and are still available in modern editions:

Hone, Margaret, *The Modern Text-Book of Astrology*, Astrology Classics: Bel Air, 2010

Parker, Derek and Julia, *Parker's Astrology*, Dorling Kindersley: London, 2009

Waite, Herbert T., *A Compendium of Natal Astrology and Universal Ephemeris*, Kessinger: Whitefish, 2010

These are technical reference books needed to perform manual calculations:

Michelsen, Neil F., and Pottenger, Rique, *The Michelsen Book of Tables*, Starcrafts: Epping, 2009

Pottenger, Rique, and Michelsen, Neil F., *The New American Ephemeris for the 20th Century*, Starcrafts Publishing: Epping, 2008

Pottenger, Rique, and Michelsen, Neil F., *The New American Ephemeris for the 21st Century*, Starcrafts: Epping, 2007

Shanks, Thomas, G., *The American Atlas*, ACS: Epping, 1999

Shanks, Thomas, G., *The International Atlas*, ACS: Epping, 1999

KEY-CONCEPT INTERPRETATION

To broaden your interpretive insight:

Brady, Bernadette, *Predictive Astrology*, Red Wheel/Weiser: Newburyport, 1999

Davison, Ronald C., *Astrology*, CRCS: Sebastopol, 1990

Greene, Liz: *Relating: An Astrological Guide to Living with Others*, Thorsons: London, 1995

Hand, Robert, *Planets in Transit*, Whitford Press: Atglen, 2002

Jones, Mark Edmund, *Astrology*, Aurora Press: Santa Fe, 1993

Oken, Alan, *Complete Astrology*, Hays (Nicolas): Lake Worth, 2007

Tompkins, Sue, *The Contemporary Astrologer's Handbook*, Flare Publications: London, 2007

THE HISTORY OF ASTROLOGY

As well as the following, see also various translations of ancient texts by Robert Hand (Arhat) and Benjamin Dykes (Cazimi Press):

Campion, Dr Nicholas, *A History of Western Astrology Volume I: The Ancient and Classical Worlds*, Continuum: London, 2009

Campion, Dr Nicholas, *A History of Western Astrology Volume II: The Medieval and Modern Worlds*, Continuum: London, 2009

Roberts, Courtney, *The Star of the Magi: The Mystery that Heralded the Coming of Christ*, New Page Books: Pompton Plains, 2007

THREE KEY ASTROLOGY SOURCE TEXTS

Abu Ma'shar, (edited and trans. by Charles Burnett), *The Abbreviation of the Introduction to Astrology*, Arhat: Reston, 1994

Lilly, William, (edited by David R. Roell), *Christian Astrology Books 1 & 2*, Astrology Classics: Bel Air, 2005

Ptolemy, Claudius, *Tetrabiblos*, Loeb: Cambridge MA, 1989

SACRED GEOMETRY

Heath, Robin, *Sun, Moon and Stonehenge*, Bluestone Press: Lisburn, 1998

Michell, John, *The New View over Atlantis*, Thames & Hudson: London, 1986

Strachan, Rev Dr Gordon, *Chartres: Sacred Geometry, Sacred Space*, Floris Books: Edinburgh, 2003

PSYCHOLOGICAL, TRANSFORMATIONAL AND COUNSELLING ASTROLOGY

Arroyo, Stephen, *Astrology, Karma & Transformation*, CRCS: Sebastopol, 1984

Clark, Brian, *The Sibling Constellation*, Arkana: London, 1999

Costello, Darby, *The Astrological Moon*, CPA Press: London, 1996

Ebertin, Reinhold, *The Combination of Stellar Influences*, AFA: Tempe, 2004

Gunzburg, Darrelyn, *Life after Grief*, Wessex Astrologer: Bournemouth, 2003

March, Marion D. and McEvers, Joan, *The Only Way to Learn About Relationships (Vol. 5, Synastry Techniques)*, Starcrafts: Epping, 2009

Moore, Thomas, *Planets Within – The Astrological Psychology of Marsilio Ficino*, Lindisfarne Press: Aurora, 1990

Mulligan, Bob, *Between Astrologers and Clients*, Xlibris: Bloomington, 2001

Reinhart, Melanie, *Chiron and the Healing Journey*, Starwalker Press: London, 2010

Rudyar, Dane, *The Astrology of Personality*, Aurora Press: Santa Fe, 1991

Schulman, Martin, *Karmic Astrology* (three vols), Red Wheel/Weiser: Newburyport, 1984

Tyl, Noel, *Synthesis and Counselling in Astrology*, Llewellyn: Woodbury, 2005

MUNDANE ASTROLOGY

Campion, Dr Nicholas, *The Book of World Horoscopes*, Wessex Astrologer: Bournemouth, 2004

Campion, Dr Nicholas, Baigent, Michael & Harvey, Charles, *Mundane Astrology*, Aquarian Press: Wellingborough, 1992

Gillett, Roy, *Economy, Ecology and Kindness*, Kings Hart Books: Witney, 2009

Quigley, Joan, *What Does Joan Say?*, Birch Lane Press: New York City, 1991

Ruperti, Alexander, *Cycles of Becoming*, Earthwalk School of Astrology: Santa Monica, 2005

Tarnas, Richard, *Cosmos and Psyche*, Plume: New York City, 2008

ASTROLOGY IN THE MODERN WORLD

Some contrasting views:

Cornelius, Geoffrey, *The Moment of Astrology*, Wessex Astrologer: Bournemouth, 2002

Elwell, Dennis, *The Cosmic Loom*, Wessex Astrologer: Bournemouth, 2008

Gillett, Roy, *Astrology and Compassion*, Kings Hart Books: Witney, 2007

Harding, Michael, *Hymns to Ancient Gods*, Arkana: London, 1992

FINANCIAL ASTROLOGY

Meridian, Bill, *Planetary Stock Trading III*, Cycles Research: New York City, 2002

Skinner, Christeen, *The Financial Universe*, Alpha Press: London, 2004

Stathis, Georgia, *Business Astrology 101*, StarCycles: Pleasant Hill, 2001

MEDICAL ASTROLOGY

Culpeper, Nicholas, *Complete Herbal*, Arcturus: London, 2009

Nauman, Eileen, *Medical Astrology*, Turtle Books: Grand Rapid, 1996

Ridder-Patrick, Jane, *A Handbook of Medical Astrology*, CrabApple Press: Edinburgh, 2006

Tobyn, Graeme, *Culpeper's Medicine*, Element Books: Salisbury, 1997

RESOURCES

WEBSITES AND SOFTWARE

Your dedicated birth-chart website
This is a very special resource for readers of *The Secret Language of Astrology*. To calculate and print, free of charge, a full birth chart just like those used in this book, log on to: **www.secretlanguageofastrology.com** and complete the online form, entering your subject's name and his or her date, time and place of birth. If you do not know the exact time of birth, use 12 noon and do not interpret the houses and the angles. Also note that the Moon position will only be correct to within 6°. The chart can only be as accurate as the information you have provided; always allow this when interpreting. To help you start on your interpretation, this website also automatically supplies the book's planet-in-sign interpretations that are specific to the chart being generated.

Resources for more advanced astrology
Astrological techniques that compare one person's chart with another's and look into the past and future (see pages 164–5) require more advanced software. Below are some key links.

Astrolabe distributes Solar Fire, the software used in this book and by astrologers worldwide. Astrolabe also offer a wide range of other advanced astrology software. www.alabe.com

Esoteric Technologies, the creators of Solar Fire, continue to develop its features and to distribute it exclusively in Australia. www.esotech.com.au

Astro Data Bank offers access to carefully researched birth data for tens of thousands of famous people. www.astro.com/astro-databank

ORGANIZATIONS AND CONFERENCES

Astrological key concepts make up succinct shorthand that says so much more than ordinary language. So, conversations with other astrologers teem with meaning. Web astrological chat-rooms can be fun and provide amazing insights, but they are not always reliable. National and international conferences are places to open doors of understanding and meet experts and make like-minded friends. All over the world there are excellent schools of astrology that offer diploma and even degree courses. Below are listed some key astrological organizations in the English-speaking world that hold conferences, educate and can point you to teaching institutions and possibly groups that meet in your area. Use them as gateways to many possibilities.

Australia
Federation of Australian Astrologers Inc.
www.faainc.org.au

United Kingdom
Astrological Association of Great Britain
www.astrologicalassociation.com

North America
American Federation of Astrologers
www.astrologers.com

International Society for Astrological Research
www.isarastrology.com

National Council for Geocosmic Research
www.geocosmic.org

CODES OF ETHICS

Understanding a person's astrology can give deep personal insights into his or her nature and life. Whatever your level of astrology, it is important for all concerned that this knowledge is used with the highest ethical standards (see page 164). Before going any further into astrology, you are encouraged to study and adopt the ethical codes devised by the **Association of Professional Astrologers International** (www.professionalastrologers.co.uk) and also by the Federation of Australian Astrologers and the International Society for Astrological Research.

INDEX

ACKNOWLEDGMENTS

AUTHOR ACKNOWLEDGMENTS

The author is deeply grateful to Darby Costello, whose inspiration was important in the origination of this work. The Mars and Gemini sections especially benefit from her early ideas and contributions. Thanks are also due to Dr Nicholas Campion (Senior Lecturer in the School of Archaeology at the University of Wales) for permission to draw extensively from his excellent two-volume *A History of Western Astrology* (full details page 168), when writing the historical introduction to this book. Needless to say, I take full responsibility for my selection and the conclusions are my own! The book's accurate technical foundation is due to the creators and distributors of Solar Fire software (see page 169). The conscientious devotion to this project by the Duncan Baird team (credited on page 4) has transformed my ideas into this beautiful work of art. The determined, intelligent rigour of friends and colleagues has informed and inspired every page. The vision and endurance of my teacher Lama Zopa Rinpoche and patient support of my wife, Carolyn, are the bedrock upon which all that is worthy in this book is based.

PUBLISHER ACKNOWLEDGMENTS

Extracts on page 11 from *A History of Western Astrology Vol I*. Extract on page 19 from *A History of Western Astrology Vol II*. Both by Dr Nicholas Campion, Continuum (London, 2009). Printed by kind permission of Continuum International Publishing Company. Campion © 2009.

The publisher would like to thank Astrolabe and Esoteric Technologies for the use of Solar Fire software to create the astrology charts throughout the book.

PICTURE ACKNOWLEDGMENTS

The publisher would like to thank the following people, museums, and photographic libraries for permission to reproduce their material. Every care has been taken to trace copyright holders. However, if we have omitted anyone we apologize and will, if informed, make corrections to any future edition.

Key:
AA = The Art Archive; AKG = akg-images; BAL = The Bridgeman Art Library; Scala = Scala Archive; WFA = Werner Forman Archive
l = left, r = right, a = above, b = below

Page 2 Philip Perkins www.astrocruise.com; **3** Twing/iStockphoto; **5** Musée Condé, Chantilly/Giraudon/BAL; **6** Visuals Unlimited/Corbis; **7** Alexey Romanov/iStockphoto; **8** Erich Lessing/AKG; **9** nagelestock.com/Alamy; **10** Imagebroker.net/Photolibrary; **11 (a)** Viktar Malyshchyts/iStockphoto; **11 (b)** Gary Christen (Astrolabe Inc); **12** Galleria e Museo Estense, Modena/Alinari/BAL; **13** Robert Harding Picture Library/Alamy; **14** North Wind Picture Archives/Alamy; **15** The Wellcome Institute/Wellcome Images; **16** Scala; **17** Biblioteca Monasterio del Escorial, Madrid/Giraudon/BAL; **19** O'Shea Gallery, London/BAL; **20** Jonathan Blair/Corbis; **21** Culver Pictures/AA; **22** Baris Simsek/iStockphoto; **23** Bruce Coleman Inc./Alamy; **24–5** Design Pics Inc/Photolibrary; **25** Ziutograf/iStockphoto; **26 (a+b)** Baris Simsek/iStockphoto; **27** Philip Perkins www.astrocruise.com; **28 (a)** Baris Simsek/iStockphoto; **28 (b)** Robert Harding World Imagery/Corbis; **29** Dennis Frates/Alamy; **30 (a)** iStockphoto; **30 (b)** Justin Kerr; **31** nagelestock.com/Alamy; **32 (a)** Baris Simsek/iStockphoto; **32 (b)** AlaskaStock/Corbis; **(32–3)** Gary Christen (Astrolabe Inc); **33** British Museum, London/AKG; **34 (a)** Baris Simsek/iStockphoto; **34 (b)** Lisa Thornberg/iStockphoto; **35** Uffizi Gallery, Florence/Scala; **36 (a)** Baris Simsek/iStockphoto; **36 (b)** Alec Pytlowany/Alamy; **37** Biblioteca Estense Universitaria, Modena/BAL; **38 (a)** Baris Simsek/iStockphoto; **38 (b)** Vorderasiatisches Museum, Staatliche Museen zu Berlin, BPK, Bildagentur fur Kunst, Kultur und Geschichte/Scala; **39 (a)** Bibliotheque Nationale, Paris/Archives Charmet/BAL; **(b)** Gary Christen (Astrolabe Inc); **40 (a)** Baris Simsek/iStockphoto; **40 (b)** Musée National de la Renaissance, Ecouen/Giraudon/BAL; **41** Benjamin Albiach Galán/iStockphoto; **42 (a)** Baris Simsek/iStockphoto; **42 (b)** Bibliothèque Nationale, Paris/Giraudon/BAL; **43** Palazzo Vecchio, Florence/Scala; **44 (a)** Baris Simsek/iStockphoto; **44 (b)** The Gallery Collection/Corbis; **45** Shannon Stent/iStockphoto; **46 (a)** Baris Simsek/iStockphoto; **46 (b)** Justin Kerr; **47** Andrea Jones/Alamy; **48** Palazzo Farnese, Caprarola/Alfredo Dagli Orti/AA; **49** Private Collection/BAL; **50** Bodleian Library, Oxford/AA; **51** Robert Fried/Alamy; **52** PlainView/iStockphoto; **53** sx70/iStockphoto; **54** DesignPics Inc/Photolibrary; **55** Darrell Gulin/Corbis; **56** Andrew Cole/Alamy; **57** Panoramic Images/Getty Images; **58** TheCrimsonMonkey/iStockphoto; **59** Rotofrank/iStockphoto; **61** The Wellcome Institute, London/Wellcome Images; **62** Lori Adamski Peek/Getty Images; **63 (a)** Van Gogh Museum, Amsterdam/Superstock/AA; **63 (b)** Private Collection/AKG; **64–5** Alexey Romanov/iStockphoto; **64–5** Baris Simsek/iStockphoto; **67** The Trustees of the Chester Beatty Library, Dublin/BAL; **68** Louvre, Paris/BAL; **69 (a)** Prado, Madrid/BAL; **69 (b)** Biblioteca Reale, Turin/BAL; **70–71** Baris Simsek/iStockphoto; **73** Pierpont Morgan Library, New York/Art Resource/Scala; **74** John Lund/Corbis; **75 (l)** Private Collection/Stapleton Collection/BAL; **75 (r)** AKG; **76–7** Baris Simsek/iStockphoto; **79** Biblioteca Estense, Modena/Gianni Dagli Orti/Art Archive; **80** Katrina Brown/Alamy; **81 (a)** Tim Graham/Getty Images; **81 (b)** Atkinson Art Gallery, Southport/BAL; **82–3** Alexey Romanov/iStockphoto; **82–3** Baris Simsek/iStockphoto; **85** Bodleian Library, Oxford (MS Auct. D. inf. 2.11. folio 7r)/AA; **86** Gerard Degeorge/BAL; **87 (l)** Kharbine-Tapabor/AA; **87 (r)** Mike Marsland/Getty Images; **88–9** Baris Simsek/iStockphoto; **91** Bibliothèque de L'Arsenal, Paris/Archives Charmet/BAL; **92** Private Collection/AKG; **93 (a)** Museo Nazionale Palazzo Altemps, Rome/Gianni Dagli Orti/AA; **93 (b)** Louvre, Paris/Giraudon/BAL; **94–5** Baris Simsek/iStockphoto; **97** Glasgow University Library/BAL; **98** Bibliothèque Nationale, Paris/BAL; **99 (l)** Peter Cook/VIEW/Corbis; **99 (r)** Time & Life Pictures/Getty Images; **100–101** Baris Simsek/iStockphoto; **103** Bibliothèque Nationale, Paris/BAL; **104** Museo Correr, Venice/Alfredo Dagli Orti/AA; **105 (a)** Bettmann/Corbis; **105 (b)** Musée Condé, Chantilly/Giraudon/BAL; **106-107** Baris Simsek/iStockphoto; **109** Museum of Fine Arts, Boston/Helen and Alice Colburn Fund/BAL; **110** Art Wolfe/Getty Images; **111** Private Collection/BAL; **112–13** Baris Simsek/iStockphoto; **115** Private Collection/AA; **116** British Museum, London/WFA; **117 (a)** Archaeological Museum, Sofia/Gianni Dagli Orti/AA; **117 (b)** Moviestore Collection Ltd/Alamy; **118–19** Baris Simsek/iStockphoto; **121** Kharbine-Tapabor/Coll. Perrin/AA; **122** British Museum, London/AA; **123 (a)** Ken Welsh/BAL; **123 (b)** Musée del Bargello, Florence/Scala; **124–5** Baris Simsek/iStockphoto; **127** Museo Correr, Venice/Alfredo Dagli Orti/AA; **128** WIN-Initiative/Getty Images; **129** 20th Century Fox/The Kobal Collection; **130–31** Baris Simsek/iStockphoto; **132–3** Pekka Parviainen/Science Photo Library; **133** Colau/Alamy; **146** sx70/iStockphoto; **147** Josh Westrich/Corbis; **150** Dennis Hallinan/Alamy; **151** Twing/iStockphoto; **156** Jeremy Sutton-Hibbert/Alamy; **157** David Parker/Science Photo Library; **159** Jean-Loup Charmet/Science Photo Library; **160** Stapleton Collection/Corbis; **161** Private Collection/Erich Lessing/AKG; **162** AFP/Getty Images; **164** CJG – Technology/Alamy; **165** Cobalt id; **167** NASA/Science Photo Library/Getty Images.